Entrepreneurial Activity in Malaysia

Paul Jones · Louisa Huxtable-Thomas ·
Syahira Hamidon · Paul Hannon ·
Norgainy Mohd Tawil
Editors

Entrepreneurial Activity in Malaysia

A Country Level Perspective

Editors
Paul Jones
Swansea University
Swansea, UK

Syahira Hamidon
Entrepreneur Development and
Empowerment Division
Ministry of Entrepreneur Development
Putrajaya, Malaysia

Norgainy Mohd Tawil
Bangi, Malaysia

Louisa Huxtable-Thomas
Swansea University
Swansea, UK

Paul Hannon
Swansea University
Swansea, UK

ISBN 978-3-030-77752-4   ISBN 978-3-030-77753-1 (eBook)
https://doi.org/10.1007/978-3-030-77753-1

© The Editor(s) (if applicable) and The Author(s), under exclusive license to Springer Nature Switzerland AG 2021
This work is subject to copyright. All rights are solely and exclusively licensed by the Publisher, whether the whole or part of the material is concerned, specifically the rights of translation, reprinting, reuse of illustrations, recitation, broadcasting, reproduction on microfilms or in any other physical way, and transmission or information storage and retrieval, electronic adaptation, computer software, or by similar or dissimilar methodology now known or hereafter developed.
The use of general descriptive names, registered names, trademarks, service marks, etc. in this publication does not imply, even in the absence of a specific statement, that such names are exempt from the relevant protective laws and regulations and therefore free for general use.
The publisher, the authors and the editors are safe to assume that the advice and information in this book are believed to be true and accurate at the date of publication. Neither the publisher nor the authors or the editors give a warranty, expressed or implied, with respect to the material contained herein or for any errors or omissions that may have been made. The publisher remains neutral with regard to jurisdictional claims in published maps and institutional affiliations.

This Palgrave Macmillan imprint is published by the registered company Springer Nature Switzerland AG
The registered company address is: Gewerbestrasse 11, 6330 Cham, Switzerland

Contents

1 Introduction to Entrepreneurial Activity in Malaysia: A Country-Level Perspective   1
Paul Jones, Louisa Huxtable-Thomas, Paul Hannon, Syahira Hamidon, and Norgainy Mohd Tawil

2 An Overview of Entrepreneurship in Malaysia   11
Syahira Hamidon and Louisa Huxtable-Thomas

3 Proximity, Collaborative Relationship and Entrepreneur's Knowledge Spill-Over Opportunity in a Malaysian Regional Innovation System   37
Gerry Edgar and Zatun Najahah Yusof

4 Knowledge-Intensive Entrepreneurship   59
Farahwahida bt Mohd @ Abu Bakar

5	The Role of Government and Higher Education in Developing Social Entrepreneurship in Malaysia *Norasmah Othman and Radin Siti Aishah Radin A. Rahman*	85
6	Social Entrepreneurship: Policies and Practice in Malaysia *Yasmin Rasyid and Robert Bowen*	117
7	From Producer to Entrepreneur: Entrepreneurial Learning Process of Smallholders in Sabah *Jane Chang, Ainurul Rosli, and Steward Giman Stephen*	135
8	Exploring SME Women Entrepreneurs' Work–Family Conflict in Malaysia *Wendy Ming-Yen Teoh, Chin Wei Chong, Yee Yen Yuen, and Siong Choy Chong*	157
9	Barriers and Facilitators in Applying Industry 4.0 in Small and Medium Enterprises (SMEs) Owned by Graduate Entrepreneurs in Malaysia *Md Asadul Islam, Claire Seaman, Amer Hamzah Jantan, Choo Wei Chong, and Abdul Rashid Abdullah*	185
Index		211

Notes on Contributors

Dr. Abdul Rashid Abdullah is a Senior Lecturer at the School of Business and Economics, Universiti Putra Malaysia (UPM). At the Faculty level, he is the Course Coordinator for International Business Management and is currently the Coordinator for Master Entrepreneurship Program from 2018 to present. Dr. Abdul Rashid Abdullah undertakes research into automotive development, entrepreneurial leadership and tourism management, as well as the development of small and medium industries. In addition, Dr. Abdul Rashid Abdullah has published in journals such as the *International Journal of Integrated Supply Management*, *Journal of International Business and Management*, *International Journal of Advanced Science and Technology*, *Journal of Islamic Accounting and Business Research*, *International Journal of Accounting and Business Management*, *Journal of Management Science and Engineering*, *International Journal of Economics, Commerce and Management*. Dr. Abdul Rashid Abdullah is editor for a book titled New Emergence Issues of Selected Industries in Developing Nations published by UPM Press. He is also the author and co-author for chapters in books published by

UPM Press and International publishers. To date he has been extensively involved in entrepreneurship training and mentoring at national and university levels. He is also actively involved in module writing, case studies and entrepreneurship books.

Dr. Robert Bowen is a Lecturer in International Entrepreneurship at the School of Management at Swansea University, and has previously held academic positions at Aberystwyth University and the University of Nantes, France. He also currently holds a position of Visiting Lecturer at Audencia Business School in Nantes, France. Dr. Bowen undertakes research into rural enterprise, SME internationalisation and place-based marketing, having published in a range of international journals. He is a Senior Fellow of the Higher Education Academy and a member of the Institute of Small Business and Entrepreneurship and Regional Studies Association.

Jane Chang is the CEO of Gritse Community Interest Company, UK. She also teaches at Coventry University London campus and is a Senior Fellow of the Higher Education Academy. Chang is a scholar of cognitive entrepreneurship and entrepreneurship education, with a passion for social innovation. Her work on entrepreneurial mindset and cognition has shifted the mindset of individuals across the world, including in the economically deprived area of London, the interior of Borneo and the scholars of world-class nations, into a space of community learning for value creation mindset. She was a finalist for the Reimagine Education Award in Wharton Business School (the most innovative curriculum design). She has co-founded and run eight entrepreneurial ventures in the area of education and the integrated food industry. A visionary leader who incorporates social innovation and practical entrepreneurship education in everything she does, Chang brings together an impressive eclectic mix of skills and experience as ecosystem builder.

Chin Wei Chong is Associate Professor in the Faculty of Management at Multimedia University, Malaysia. She received her Ph.D. from Multimedia University. Chong is a member of the Editorial Advisory Board of VINE and a reviewer for various KM and management journals. She was awarded by Emerald Literati Excellence Award 2011 as outstanding reviewer and outstanding researcher by MMU. Her publications have appeared in various international refereed journals, conference proceedings and book chapters. Her research interests include soft knowledge management, knowledge sharing, inter-organisational knowledge transfer, people management and volunteerism.

Choo Wei Chong is an Associate Professor in the Department of Management and Marketing at Universiti Putra Malaysia (UPM). He has an undergraduate degree in Statistics and an MSc in Business Statistics from the same university. He holds a Ph.D. in Decision Science from the University of Oxford. His scholarly articles have been published in local and international academic journals such as Journal of Forecasting and Economic Modelling. He has more than 20 years of teaching experience at UPM. Subjects taught include Business Statistics, Quantitative Techniques, Business Research Methods, Principle of Management and Basic Entrepreneurship. His published books include *Business Statistics* (first and second editions) and *Statistics for Management*. His research interests include forecasting, financial times series analysis, GARCH, combining forecasts, volatility forecasting, exponential smoothing, smooth transition exponential smoothing, model selection, neural networks and robust methods.

Siong Choy Chong is Chief Technical Officer of Quality Assurance at Finance Accreditation Agency, Malaysia. Previously, he was a Professor and Deputy Vice Chancellor for Academic Affairs in one of the higher education institutions in Malaysia. Chong has supervised 9 Ph.D. candidates to completion and has published more than 140 articles in journals, conference proceedings and book chapters. He is a recipient of two Emerald Literati Club Awards for Excellence in recognition of being an outstanding reviewer for two Emerald Insight journals and continues to sit on a number of Board of Reviewers. His research interests include entrepreneurship, knowledge management, information technology acceptance and quality assurance in higher education. Chong has also contributed to UNESCO where he led in the development of the Guidelines for the Implementation of Qualifications Frameworks in Asia and the Pacific.

Gerry Edgar, Ph.D. is a Senior Lecturer and Associate Dean at Stirling Management School, University of Stirling. His research interest focuses on the development and effectiveness of collaborative modes of technology transfer; and the impact of information systems and technology on organisational competitiveness. This research is underpinned by a methodological focus on systems methods and scenario development. Prior to joining higher education, Dr. Edgar, an experimental physics, has previously work in high technology industries as a technology analyst and management consultant.

Farahwahida bt Mohd @ Abu Bakar is a Senior Lecturer of Entrepreneurship, Innovation and Management Information System and Chairman of the Entrepreneurial Central Committee at Universiti Kuala Lumpur, Malaysia. She is also a strategic committee of Digital Entrepreneurship under Department of Higher Education, Ministry of Education Malaysia and a Programme Accreditation Assessor Panel in the field of Management Information System and Multimedia from Malaysian Qualification Agency (MQA). She has previously held senior academic posts at Universiti Selangor. Mohd is also involved as an Industry Panel for *"Pembangunan Standard Kemahiran Pekerjaan Kebangsaan (SKPK)"* in the field of Computer Network Engineer (D-051-4/5). She has published more than 60 publications of conference papers, journals, book chapters and modules. Her expertise and passionate in the entrepreneurial and information technology field brought her as a judge in some of ICT project competitions.

Syahira Hamidon is Senior Director of the Ministry of Entrepreneur Development and Cooperatives (MEDAC) in the Administrative and Diplomatic Service, Malaysia. She has worked in the Ministry of International Trade and Industry, Public Service Department, and Ministry of Higher Education. She implemented the National Entrepreneurship Policy 2030, launched in 2019. Her current work involves improving the role of entrepreneurship development and in comparison with other countries. She also prepares inputs for various plans of the country. She does international relations, strategic collaborations with public and private entities, digital economy, social entrepreneurship development and international conferences related to entrepreneurship. She sits on various boards nationally and one International. Hamidon has a Ph.D. in Entrepreneurship from Massey University Auckland, an M.B.A. from UPM, and a B. Commerce from Queen's University Canada. She attended many career development programmes including that of Harvard, Oxford, University of Melbourne, and the US State Department, co-authored books and journal articles, and is a frequent speaker.

Paul Hannon is formerly Professor at Swansea University and Director of the Institute for Entrepreneurial Leadership. He is a graduate entrepreneur who has shaped entrepreneurship and small business development as a CEO, Government Adviser, Academic Director, Professor and Company founder. Paul has worked with governments, global/national agencies, universities and colleges, business and industry partners and professional bodies across Europe and beyond.

Louisa Huxtable-Thomas is Associate Professor in the School of Management, Director of Enterprise and Innovation, and Director of the Institute for Entrepreneurial Leadership (IfEL) at Swansea University, UK. Combining theories and empirical knowledge gleaned from the fields of business, social science, education and psychology, her research interests relate to how people's behaviours, either as leaders, entrepreneurs or policymakers has an influence on societal and economic welfare. Huxtable-Thomas has had a varied career encompassing work in environmental consultancy, policymaking at Regional and Local Government level as well as business support and incubation. Her most recent research focusses on two areas: the theory and practice of entrepreneurial leadership and the use of reflection as appropriate assessment in entrepreneurship and leadership education.

Md. Asadul Islam is a Lecturer at School of Business (AACSB Accredited), Faculty of Business, Design and Arts, Swinburne University of Technology, (Sarawak Campus), Australia. He has gained Ph.D. scroll from Faculty of Economics and Management (AACSB Accredited), Universiti Putra Malaysia (UPM). He has attended in international conferences in Japan, Singapore and Malaysia. He was the Best Presenter at the 4th Singapore International Conference on Social Science &

Humanities (ICSSH) at Nanyang Technological University (NTU), Singapore. He has published research papers relating to human resource management and entrepreneurship. He is currently doing research on entrepreneurship and industry 4.0, green human resource management, millennials and organisational behaviour. He is also a distinguished member at the Academy of Management (AOM) and British Academy of Management (BAM).

Amer Hamzah Jantan is Associate Professor of Organizational Behaviour, Business Communication, Management and Entrepreneurship in the Faculty of Economics and Management at Universiti Putra Malaysia. He teaches undergraduate courses in the above-mentioned areas. He also taught Organizational Behaviour and Business Research Methods at the M.B.A. level. He currently supervises 15 Ph.D. and 1 Master of Science students.

Paul Jones is Professor of Entrepreneurship and Innovation and Head of the Business Department in the School of Management at Swansea University, UK. He is also a Senior Fellow of the Higher Education Academy and a board member of the Institute of Small Business and Entrepreneurship. Previously, he held senior academic posts at Coventry University, Plymouth University and the University of South Wales. He is also editor-in-chief of the *International Journal of Entrepreneurial Behaviour and Research*, Associate Editor of the *International Journal of Management Education* and Series Editor of the series Contemporary Issues in Entrepreneurship Research. In addition, Jones has guest edited 18 special issues in his career. Jones undertakes research into entrepreneurship behaviour and small business management and is widely published in journals such as *Omega, Entrepreneurship and Regional Development, International Small Business Journal* and *Journal of Small Business Management*.

Norgainy Mohd Tawil is an Associate Professor at Faculty of Engineering and Built Environment, UKM with Ph.D. in Property Finance from University of Malaya, 2009. She is now a Certified Trainer of Social Enterprise, Entrepreneurship Empowerment, Design Thinking and Master Trainer of Critical Thinking.

Norasmah Othman is Professor of Entrepreneurship Education and Program Evaluation at the Universiti Kebangsaan Malaysia. She is also an editor of Akademika UKM journal and Malaysian Journal Education. In addition, Othman has also succeeded in publishing seven books in Entrepreneurship entitled: *Entrepreneurship—Catalyst of an Excellent Nation and Life Sustainability; Entrepreneurship and People with Disabilities; Fundamental of Entrepreneurship Education; Entrepreneurship Education at Higher Education Institutions; Teaching Entrepreneurship-Based on Mastery Strategy; Entrepreneurship and Indigenous Peoples, and Entrepreneurship and Youth in Malaysia.* Othman has led numerous research projects under the sponsorship of several ministries in Malaysia, such as Ministry of Education and Ministry of International Trade and Industry. Her research project is focused on her areas of expertise (entrepreneurship education and program evaluation). She's also one of the selected experts chose by Malaysia Ministry of Education in constructing Entrepreneurial Studies syllabus used for 10th and 11th grade students.

Radin Siti Aishah Radin A. Rahman is a Senior Lecturer of Entrepreneurship Education at Centre of Educational Leadership and Policy, Faculty of Education, Universiti Kebangsaan Malaysia and has previously held administrative posts in Assistant Dean (Entrepreneurship and Creativity) and Entrepreneurship Coordinator. She also serves as an editor board member and reviewer for *International Journal of Education and Training (InjET)*, also reviewer for *Malaysian Journal of Education and Centre for the Promotion of Knowledge and Language Learning (MANU)*. Her areas of expertise include social entrepreneurship and *Technical and Vocational Education and Training (TVET)*. She has published a number of articles in scholarly journals and book chapters on entrepreneurship education and social entrepreneurship.

Yasmin Rasyid is the Founder and President of EcoKnights, Malaysia. She is also the Country Sustainability Director with an Australian infrastructure development organisation. Previously, Rasyid was an active social entrepreneur and co-founded Poptani Asia in 2015. She served as the Program Director of Social Entrepreneurship Development at the Malaysian Global Innovation and Creativity Center (MaGIC), a government agency under the Ministry of Entrepreneurship Development (MED) that drives social entrepreneurship development in the country.

Ainurul Rosli is the Reader of Enterprise and Entrepreneurship and Director of Business Engagement in the Brunel Business School at Brunel University, UK. She is the co-chair of Practice and Impact SIG of the Institute of Small Business and Enterprise (ISBE) and a Senior Fellow of the Higher Education Academy. Rosli believes in the importance of university-industry-community interaction and research with impact, which drives forward businesses and societal transformation. As an Entrepreneurship Team Coach and Entrepreneurial Mind-set Practitioner (EMP), she supports individuals who want to run their businesses. Most of her approaches on supporting entrepreneurs emphasise more on team development and learning action network for entrepreneurs. Rosli co-founded several business ventures including a social enterprise, Gritse and Social Innovation Movement (SIM). Her previous professional experience includes various entrepreneurship, strategy and innovation consulting work in London and Malaysia.

Claire Seaman holds the Chair of Enterprise and Family Business at Queen Margaret University in Edinburgh. She has published over 30 journal articles on family businesses in the UK, New Zealand and Latin America and is a regular contributor to family business conferences worldwide. Her recent book, The Modern Family Business, was developed with colleagues and published by Palgrave McMillan. Claire maintains close links with the business community and business organisations such as the Scottish Family Business Association, Family Business United and local economic development agencies. She is a frequent speaker at gatherings of family businesses and professional advisors. This interaction enables her to share insights from evidence based research with practitioners, while ensuring that her research focuses on areas of importance to the family business community, and has led directly to current research that focusses on the European Family Business Associations. Experiences and close interactions with business and business support agencies help keep her professional work rooted into the realties and complex dynamics of families in business who create enterprises that dominate the economic and societal landscape around the world.

Steward Giman Stephen is a Lecturer and Program Leader for Certificate Courses at AMC College, Malaysia. Stephen holds a Ph.D. in Tourism Management with a specialisation in human resources and sustainable practices from University Malaysia Sabah, where he also received a Master's degree in Human Capital Management and a degree in International Marketing. His passion in supporting the tourism industry in Malaysia enabled him to be part of the Borneo Tourism Research Centre, where he was involved with projects focusing on tourism management for resilience and crisis and rural tourism development. He has collaborated with local and international researchers from various disciplines, and an advocator for interdisciplinary research.

Wendy Ming-Yen Teoh is a Senior Lecturer in the Faculty of Business at Multimedia University, Malaysia. Teoh has published her research in several international refereed journals and conference proceedings, including *Total Quality Management & Business Excellence, Equality, Diversity and Inclusion: An International Journal, Internet Research, International Journal of Bank Marketing, Gender in Management: An International Journal*, among others. Her research interests include entrepreneurship, women studies, knowledge management and human resource management. Teoh's perseverance in academic and research activities have enabled her to be appointed as a member of Editorial Boards, academic editor, session chair, advisory panel, postgraduate examiner, speaker and expert panellist. In addition, she was a finalist of the National Outstanding Educator Award organised by Private Education Cooperative of Malaysia in 2019.

Yee Yen Yuen is a Senior Lecturer in the Faculty of Business at Multimedia University, Malaysia. His research interests are knowledge management, information systems, usability studies, cross-cultural studies, disability studies and inclusive society. He has several well referred journal and conference publications on these topics. He also receives several local and international government and private research grants and actively supervise Master's and Ph.D. students in these areas.

Zatun Najahah Yusof is a Lecturer in the Stirling Management School at University of Stirling, UK. She has previously worked in a quasi-government organisation as Training and Development Officer before joining higher education. Her main research interests are entrepreneurship, innovation systems, collaborative relationships and Triple-helix studies in developing countries. She is currently working on number of entrepreneurial education projects in Nigeria, Malaysia and Scotland.

Abbreviations

11MP	Eleventh Malaysia Plan
4IR	Fourth Industrial Revolution
8MP	Eighth Malaysia Plan
AIM	Amanah Ikhtiar Malaysia
ARPANET	Advanced Research Projects Agency Network
ASEAN	Association of Southeast Asian Nations
BCIC	Bumiputera Commercial and Industrial Community
BN	Barisan Nasional
BoG	Bill of Guarantees
CEO	Chief Executive Officers
COR	Conservation of Resources
CSCD	Community Service Centre of the Deaf
CSE	Core self-evaluations
CSO	Civil Society Organisations
ECER	East Coast Economic Region
GDP	Gross Domestic Product
GNI	Gross National Income
GNP	Gross National Product
HEI	Higher Education Institutions
HTTP	Hypertext transport protocol

ICT	Information Communication Technology
IDEA	Impact-Driven Enterprise Accreditation
IoT	Internet of Things
IPMA	Importance performance matrix analysis
KIBS	Knowledge Intensive Business Service
KIE	Knowledge Intensive Entrepreneurship
KL	Kuala Lumpur
KLCC	Kuala Lumpur City Centre
KLIA	Kuala Lumpur International Airport
MaGIC	Malaysian Global Innovation and Creativity Centre
MARA	Majlis Amanah Rakyat
MDEC	Malaysia Digital Economy Corp
MeCD	Ministry of Entrepreneur and Cooperative Development
MED	Ministry of Entrepreneur Development
MHE	Ministry of Higher Education
MSC	Multimedia Super Corridor
MSEB	Malaysian Social Enterprise Blueprint
MSME	Micro, Small and Medium Enterprises
MTR	Mid Term Review
NCER	Northern Corridor Economic Region
NDP	National Development Plan
NEAC	National Economic Advisory Council
NEM	New Economic Model
NEP	New Economic Policy
NGO	Non-government organisations
NIS	National Innovation Systems
NKEA	National Key Economic Areas
NLS	National Level Systems
NMP	National Malaysia Plan
NMP	National Mission Policy
NOC	National Operations Council
NVP	National Vision Policy
OECD	Organisation for Economic Co-operation and Development
OPP1	First Outline Perspective Plan
OPP2	Second Outline Perspective Plan
PH	Pakastan Harapan
PICC	Putrajaya International Convention Centre (PICC)
PKR	Parti KeadIlan Rakyat
PLS	Partial least squares

PM	Prime Minister
PPBM	Parti Pribumi Bersatu Malaysia
R&D	Research & Development
RA	Role Ambiguity
RM	Malaysian ringgit
S&T	Science & Technology
SCORE	Sarawak Corridor Renewable Energy
SDC	Sabah Development Corridor
SDG	Sustainable Development Goals
SE	Social Entrepreneurship
SIFE	Students in Free Enterprise
SME	Small and Medium Sized Enterprise/s
SPV	Shared Prosperity Vision
SS	Spousal Support
TVET	Technical and Vocational Education and Training
UN	United Nations
USA	United States of America
USD	United States Dollar
WISE	Women in Social Enterprise
WSF	World Schedule Flexibility
WWW	World Wide Web

List of Figures

Fig. 8.1 Work-family conflict and job satisfaction of women entrepreneurs (*Source* Authors own) 163

Fig. 8.2 Structural model (*Note* ***$p < 0.001$, **$p < 0.01$, *$p < 0.05$, ns &: not significant. *Source* Developed by the author using data from SmartPLS v.2.0) 169

List of Tables

Table 3.1	Summary views on role of actors in MSC cluster by interviewes respondents	50
Table 3.2	Social dimensions in the MSC cluster	53
Table 4.1	OECD member states	73
Table 5.1	Definitions of social entrepreneurship	89
Table 5.2	Emphasis on social entrepreneurship by Malaysian Government Ministries	96
Table 7.1	Participants background information	143
Table 8.1	Descriptive statistics	165
Table 8.2	Measurement Model	167
Table 8.3	Fornell-Larcker Criterion analysis for checking discriminant validity	168
Table 8.4	Significance testing results of the structural model path coefficients	170
Table 8.5	Mediation analysis results with work-family conflict as the Mediator	171
Table 8.6	Summary of results of hypotheses	173
Table 8.7	Index value and total effects for the IPMA of JS	174

1

Introduction to Entrepreneurial Activity in Malaysia: A Country-Level Perspective

Paul Jones, Louisa Huxtable-Thomas, Paul Hannon, Syahira Hamidon, and Norgainy Mohd Tawil

Introduction

This introduction offers a "state of the nation" evaluation regarding entrepreneurial activity within the Malaysian economy and its impact on the country as it moves towards higher-income status by 2020.

P. Jones (✉) · L. Huxtable-Thomas · P. Hannon
Swansea University, Swansea, UK
e-mail: W.P.Jones@swansea.ac.uk

L. Huxtable-Thomas
e-mail: l.a.huxtable-thomas@swansea.ac.uk

P. Hannon
e-mail: p.d.hannon@swansea.ac.uk

S. Hamidon
Entrepreneur Development and Empowerment Division, Ministry of Entrepreneur Development, Putrajaya, Malaysia
e-mail: syahira@med.gov.my

© The Author(s), under exclusive license to Springer Nature Switzerland AG 2021
P. Jones et al. (eds.), *Entrepreneurial Activity in Malaysia*,
https://doi.org/10.1007/978-3-030-77753-1_1

Malaysia is a unique country, given it is multi-ethnic and multicultural which impacts significantly on its entrepreneurial behaviour (Ismail, 2010). There is increased interest in enhancing entrepreneurial opportunities within Malaysia (Ariff & Bakar, 2002; Mahmood et al., 2020). Entrepreneurial activity within Malaysia is currently underreported within the academic literature (Ariff & Bakar, 2002; Mosbah et al., 2018). Previously, literature has considered the effectiveness of Entrepreneurship Education as taught programmes in a Malaysian context in various business disciplines (Ariff & Abubakar, 2003; Shariff & Saud, 2009; Yu Cheng et al., 2009).

The current literature on Entrepreneurial behaviour in Malaysian literature is typically reported in national level journals (Khan et al, 2017) and typically relate to studies measuring the effectiveness of entrepreneurship education programmes. Moreover, the published studies typically lack complexity and often reflect the introduction of a new curriculum, incentives or systems to encourage or measure entrepreneurial activity and their impact on entrepreneurial attitudes (Zamberi Ahmad, 2013). For example, a typical example relates to the use of entrepreneurial education in single institutional studies (Mustafa et al., 2016). Studies considering female entrepreneurship in Malaysia remain limited in number (Ismail et al., 2012; Teoh & Chong, 2014).

Malaysia is currently a large and growing economy (post Covid) with a focus on SME growth and service delivery policies from a well-financed public sector that supports SME start-up and growth (Islam & Wahab, 2021). Malaysia is a leading exporter of electronics, oil and gas, palm oil and rubber which drives economic growth (OECD, 2019). Other key industries include light manufacturing, pharmaceuticals, medical technology, tin mining and smelting, logging, and timber processing (IMF, 2016). The major trading partners are China, Singapore, the United States, Japan and Thailand, which collectively contributed more than 50% of Malaysia's total merchandise trade since 2010 (OECD, 2019).

N. Mohd Tawil
National University of Malaysia, Bangi, Malaysia

In the OECD's SME Policy index, Malaysia performs more effectively than the region as a whole in its basis for SME support, performing consistently above in all scores than the average for the ASEAN region (OECD, 2018). The Malaysian economy has benefited from the density of knowledge-based businesses and utilisation of the latest technologies in the manufacturing and digital economies (Clarke & Gholamshahi, 2018). Despite these successes, Malaysia has ongoing systemic problems in the SME economy such as higher business failure rates, poor management, regional disparities in wealth which need to be evaluated, reported and appropriate solutions identified (Mustapha & Sorooshian, 2019).

These issues include the emergence of a two-tier society whereby economic wealth is largely located within and around Kuala Lumpur (Tahir et al., 2018). As a result, regional areas of Malaysia suffer from minimal economic growth, high unemployment and a reliance on subsistence/informal entrepreneurship (Zainol & Al Mamun, 2018). Moreover, young people tend to migrate towards the major cities from regional areas, particularly Kuala Lumpur, seeking improved employment opportunities. This results in a talent drain from the regional areas to the major cities. In addition, overall graduate and youth unemployment in Malaysia (individuals aged 15–24), remains high at around 13.2% in 2018. There is also a significant disparity between the number of young males and females in the workplace. Currently, within the regional areas there is over-reliance on agriculture and necessity-based entrepreneurial activity (Tahir et al., 2018).

In response to these societal problems, attempts have been made to encourage effective opportunity focused entrepreneurial activity with the creation of ecosystems (for examples numerous business incubators), seed corn funding and the provision of entrepreneurship education within the University level curriculum to encourage entrepreneurial career choices (Cao & Shi, 2020; Pillai & Ahamat, 2018). Evaluations undertaken to date have been largely uncritical, take minimal account of the Country context and consequently work is required to identify areas of effective practice and opportunities for growth. There is a need for ongoing evaluation to contrast entrepreneurial behaviour across the ASEAN region given the significant economic growth and growing global importance of this region. This text presents the first opportunity to reflect on both the success stories and systemic problems related to effective entrepreneurial behaviour in a Malaysian context. The following sections provide an overview of each chapter.

The chapter by **Syahira Hamidon** and **Louisa Huxtable-Thomas** provides an overview of Malaysia as a country and its current economic policies and status, in order to provide the context and grounding to knowledge for the following chapters. Malaysia has not been the subject of extensive international research and entrepreneurship within this fast-developing country has been overlooked within western academia. This chapter provides the overview of the country's unique geography, demography, history and culture necessary to ground understanding of Malaysia. As well as understanding these informal institutions, later sections on the national economic development plans contextualise the direction that entrepreneurship policy and practice have taken in the period since independence from the United Kingdom. Some focus is given to the formal institutions and organisations created by Government in order to deliver the ambitious vision of successive governments, including specific Ministries and agencies that support the indigenous population, women, children and social entrepreneurship.

Gerry Edgar and **Zatun Najahah Yusof's** chapter focusses on the consequences of poor understanding of the social phenomenon of innovation and the effect immature social infrastructure can have in limiting the benefits of proximity and prevent the entrepreneurial process of knowledge spill-over opportunities. The findings revealed they had low levels of interaction amongst the system communities and weaker relationships with local universities than local government agencies. The chapter contributes novel insights into the theoretical concept of proximity, where a lack of richness of a social infrastructure and low density of informal social networks influences the proximity benefits and limits the opportunity density of entrepreneurs knowledge spill-over. In terms of policy implications, this research highlights the necessity for developing further collaborative relationships with universities, reducing the dependency on local public authorities and investing in a richer social infrastructure or utilises existing mature towns/cities in preference to green field developments.

Farahwahida Mohd's @ Abu Bakar chapter considers the challenges for Malaysia is to be an entrepreneurship nation. This predictably requires a number of knowledge entrepreneurs in various fields related to industries as well as innovation in the field of entrepreneurship. The chapter is based on the approach of a literature theory in economic development, it demonstrates the integration of evolutionary theory and the innovation system approach assigns a principal role to the entrepreneur in the process of economic development. The dissemination, use and creation of knowledge-intensive entrepreneurship is further discussed. The modern-day economy aims to be knowledge-intensive, and knowledge-intensive entrepreneurship can occur in all sectors and countries with the appropriate conditions. This chapter offers an explanation regarding knowledge-intensive entrepreneurship theory, sectors and services in the context of Malaysia including the Malaysia government approach in order to support the small business enterprise in Malaysia.

Norasmah Othman and **Radin Siti Aishah Radin A. Rahman** chapter highlights the efforts of the Malaysian government and the higher education sector to promote social entrepreneurship, through initiatives such as the Malaysian Social Enterprise Blueprint and the Social Enterprise Accreditation Guideline and the role of private organisations in promoting the importance of social entrepreneurship. The chapter discusses the issues of institutional awareness, public perception, and motivation and assesses the level of social entrepreneurship implementation amongst Malaysian students. Malaysia is in the early stages of social entrepreneurship; however, education, government policy, and innovative enterprises have created a culture of social innovation that has generated employment opportunities.

The chapter by **Yasmin Rasyid** and **Robert Bowen** discusses the development of policies and practices within the Malaysian social entrepreneurship ecosystem, with the aim of understanding the role of social entrepreneurship in an emerging economy. This chapter evaluates the most prominent issues of social entrepreneurship in Malaysia, focussing on the actions of policymakers in furthering the reach of social entrepreneurship, as well as analysing working examples across Malaysia. Five case studies of social entrepreneurship across Malaysia are discussed, which underline the growth of the social entrepreneurship ecosystem across the country. Findings identify several challenges for such firms notably awareness of social enterprises, a lack of legal definition and limited resources, particularly financial and human resources.

Jane Chang, **Ainurul Rosli** and **Steward Giman Stephen** chapter acknowledged that independent smallholders increasingly require entrepreneurship if they are to survive. Whilst previous studies in this extensive body of literature focus on entrepreneurial skills, minimal attention has been paid to the learning process leading to the development of these skills. The chapter explores the challenging entrepreneurial learning process, in particular, the transition from production-oriented to multifunctional entrepreneurial activities in the context of palm oil smallholders in Malaysia. The study based on 14 independent palm oil smallholders in the rural part of East Malaysia revealed three significant factors driving entrepreneurial learning: (1) embodying the entrepreneurial identity, (2) crossing the boundaries of palm oil dependency and (3) community collaboration. This chapter provides novel insights for policymakers that deals with rural development as it highlights a different way of capacity building of rural community through entrepreneurial learning.

The chapter by **Wendy Ming-Yen Teoh**, **Chin Wei Chong**, **Yee Yen Yuen**, and **Siong Choy Chong** seeks to develop a model based on the role theory and the conservation of resources (COR) theory to examine the influence of work-level (work schedule flexibility [WSF] and role ambiguity [RA]); family-level (spousal support [SS]) and individual-level (core self-evaluations [CSEs]) factors on work–family conflict and job satisfaction amongst women entrepreneurs. The study employed self-administered survey questionnaires were used to collect data from 304 participants in Klang Valley, Penang, Johor Bahru and Malacca. Using the partial least squares (PLS) analysis approach, SS and CSEs exhibited significant positive relationships with work-family conflict, whilst RA, SS and work–family conflict had positive influence on job satisfaction. It is also found that SS and CSEs on job satisfaction were mediated by work–family conflict. This study contributes to knowledge and practice by providing novel insights to policymakers, ministries and agencies, academics and women entrepreneurs in Malaysia, with the potential of further research in the future.

The final chapter by **Md Asadul Islam, Claire Seamen, Amer Hamzah Jantan, Choo Wei Chong**, and **Abdul Rashid** considers the adoption of Industry 4.0 in SMEs owned by graduate entrepreneurs in Malaysia. The study found that there was a lack of relevant training courses in the University sector considering Industry 4.0. Currently, it was noted that Malaysian entrepreneurs lack understanding of industry 4.0 and are slow in adapting technological changes in their organisation. These findings offer significant insights for the Malaysian government in realising change and providing additional support and training for graduate entrepreneurs.

In summary, these chapters offer novel insights into entrepreneurial behaviour in Malaysia adding to a limited existing literature. The global pandemic has placed additional pressure on the entrepreneurial ecosystem within the country particularly sectors such as the tourism industry and the service sector. The recovery post-pandemic will be dependent on how the economy can effectively reset itself and recover lost markets. This book has sought to provide fresh insights into the development of the Malaysian economy as an entrepreneurial nation. The further development of a knowledge economy is discussed as is the importance of innovation as a core competency of a developing economy. The growing importance of the social enterprise to the Malaysian economy is discussed as is the need for its further development. Several social enterprise case studies are discussed and best practice identified.

It is apparent that research into entrepreneurial behaviour within Malaysia remains nascent in comparison to other developing countries. For example, in an African context there is a significant body of emergent literature evaluating entrepreneurial behaviour which has appeared in journals, journal special issues (Jones et al., 2008a, 2008b, 2008c) and academic books (Dobson et al., 2020). A similar body of literature needs to emerge in Malaysia and there is a need for further research exploring the development of entrepreneurial ecosystems specific to the region, the effective provision of entrepreneurial education and growth of social enterprise. Emergent forms of entrepreneurial behaviour including technology and creative industries focused entrepreneurship should also be evaluated. The need to further encourage female entrepreneurship throughout Malaysian society is also of critical importance. Furthermore, the authors of this text would encourage entrepreneurial scholars to contrast practice in a Malaysian context with other developing and developed economies in future research studies. There is also a need for the academic community to support the further development of scholarship in South East Asia through special issues, journal publication support and edited books.

References

Ariff, M., & Abubakar, S. Y. (2003). Strengthening entrepreneurship in Malaysia, Malaysian Institute of Economic Research, Kuala Lumpur, pp. 1–22.

Ariff, M., & Bakar. S. Y. A. (2002). Strengthening entrepreneurship in Malaysia, Malaysian Economic Outlook: 1st Quarter 2002 update, Proceedings of the *7th Corporate Economic Briefing*, 2002, Malaysian Institute of Economic Research, Malaysia, pp. 1–22.

Cao, Z., & Shi, X. (2020). A systematic literature review of entrepreneurial ecosystems in advanced and emerging economies. *Small Business Economics*. https://doi.org/10.1007/s11187-020-00326-y.

Clarke T., & Gholamshahi S. (2018). Developing human capital for knowledge based economies. In T. Clarke & K. Lee (Eds.), *Innovation in the Asia Pacific*. Springer. https://doi.org/10.1007/978-981-10-5895-0_12.

Dobson, S., Jones, P., Agyapong, D., & Maas, G. (2020). *Enterprising Africa transformation through entrepreneurship*. Routledge.

IMF. (2016). Malaysia-2016 Article IV Consultation-Press Release; Staff Report; and Statement by the Executive.

Islam, A., & Wahab, S. A. (2021). The intervention of strategic innovation practices in between regulations and sustainable business growth: A holistic perspective for Malaysian SMEs. *World Journal of Entrepreneurship, Management and Sustainable Development* (ahead-of-print). https://doi.org/10.1108/WJEMSD-04-2020-0035.

Ismail, H. C., Shamsudin, F. M., & Chowdhury, M. S. (2012). An exploratory study of motivational factors on women entrepreneurship venturing in Malaysia. *Business and Economic Research, 2*(1), 1–13.

Ismail, N. W. (2010). The effect of language on trade: The Malaysian case. *International Journal of Business and Society, 11*(1), 51–58.

Jones, P., Maas, G., Dobson, S., Newbery, R., Agyapong, D., & Matlay, H. (2018a). Entrepreneurship in Africa, part 3: Conclusions on African entrepreneurship. *Journal of Small Business and Enterprise Development, 25*(5), 706–709.

Jones, P., Maas, G., Dobson, S., Newbery, R., Agyapong, D., & Matlay, H. (2018b). Entrepreneurship in Africa, part 2: Entrepreneurial education and eco-systems. *Journal of Small Business and Enterprise Development, 25*(4), 550–553.

Jones, P., Maas, G., Dobson, S., Newbery, R., Agyapong, D., & Matlay, H. (201c). Entrepreneurship in Africa, part 1: Entrepreneurial dynamics in Africa. *Journal of Small Business and Enterprise Development, 25*(3), 346–348.

Khan, N. U., Rasli, A. R., Hassan, M. A., Noordin, N. F. M., & Aamir, M. (2017). Assessment of imbalance among environmental and economic performance within Malaysian manufacturing industry: A sustainable approach. *International Journal of Energy Economics and Policy, 7*(4), 149–155.

Mahmood, T. M. A. T., Mamun, A. A., & Ibrahim, M. D. (2020). Attitude towards entrepreneurship: A study among Asnaf Millennials in Malaysia. *Asia Pacific Journal of Innovation and Entrepreneurship, 14*(1), 2–14.

Mosbah, A., Debili, R., & Merazgac, H. (2018). First-generation immigrant entrepreneurship in Malaysia: What do we know so far? *Kasetsart Journal of Social Sciences, 39*(2), 351–357.

Mustafa, M. J., Hernandez, E., Mahon, C., & Chee, L. K. (2016). Entrepreneurial intentions of university students in an emerging economy: The influence of university support and proactive personality on students' entrepreneurial intention. *Journal of Entrepreneurship in Emerging Economies, 8*(2), 162–179.

Mustapha, N. M., & Sorooshian, S. (2019). SME performance measurement: A technical review of Malaysia. *International Journal of Innovative Technology and Exploring Engineering, 8*(8), 1808–1812.

OECD. (2018). SME policy index: ASEAN 2018: Boosting competitiveness and inclusive growth. https://asean.org/wpcontent/uploads/2018/08/Report-ASEAN-SME-Policy-Index-2018.pdf. Accessed 21 May 2020.

OECD. (2019). OECD Economic Surveys, July 2019 overview. http://www.oecd.org/economy/surveys/Malaysia-2019-OECD-economic-survey-overview.pdf.

Pillai, T. R., & Ahamat, A. (2018). Social-cultural capital in youth entrepreneurship ecosystem: Southeast Asia. *Journal of Enterprising Communities: People and Places in the Global Economy, 12*(2), 232–255.

Shariff, M. N., & Saud, M. (2009). An attitude approach to the prediction of entrepreneurship on students at institution of higher learning in Malaysia. *International Journal of Business and Management, 4*(4), 129–135.

Tahir H. M., Razak N. A., & Rentah, F. (2018). The contributions of Small and Medium Enterprises (SME's) on Malaysian economic growth: A sectoral analysis. In: A. Lokman, T. Yamanaka, P. Lévy, K. Chen, & S. Koyama (Eds.), Proceedings of the *7th International Conference on Kansei Engineering and Emotion Research*. Advances in Intelligent Systems and Computing (Vol. 739). Springer.

Teoh, M. Y., & Chong, C. (2014). Towards strengthening the development of women entrepreneurship in Malaysia. *Gender in Management, 29*(7), 432–453.

Yu Cheng, M., Sei Chan, W., & Mahmood, A. (2009). The effectiveness of entrepreneurship education in Malaysia. *Education + Training, 51*(7), 555–566.

Zainol, N. R., & Al Mamun, A. (2018). Entrepreneurial competency, competitive advantage and performance of informal women micro-entrepreneurs in Kelantan, Malaysia. *Journal of Enterprising Communities: People and Places in the Global Economy, 12*(3), 299–321.

Zamberi Ahmad, S. (2013). The need for inclusion of entrepreneurship education in Malaysia lower and higher learning institutions. *Education + Training, 55*(2), 191–203.

2

An Overview of Entrepreneurship in Malaysia

Syahira Hamidon and Louisa Huxtable-Thomas

Malaysia: Geography and Structure

Malaysia is a country of 330,803 km² located in Southeast Asia, sitting in the triangle between the Indian Ocean, the North Pacific and directly north of Australia. The country is made up of Peninsula Malaysia (130,590 km²), also known as West Malaysia, and East Malaysia which comprises of two states, Sarawak (124,450 km²) and Sabah (73,620 km²). The South China Sea separates mainland Malaysia from the East Malaysian states, which, together with Brunei and Indonesian Kalimantan, are found on the island of Borneo (CIRCA, 2015).

S. Hamidon
Entrepreneur Development and Empowerment Division, Ministry of Entrepreneur Development, Putrajaya, Malaysia
e-mail: syahira@med.gov.my

L. Huxtable-Thomas (✉)
Swansea University, Swansea, UK
e-mail: l.a.huxtable-thomas@swansea.ac.uk

Malaysia's immediate neighbours are Thailand to the north, Singapore to the south and Indonesia to the west. There is also Brunei sandwiched between the two East Malaysian States. Being close to the equator, Malaysia experiences an equatorial climate characterized by high temperature and humidity all year round. The normal temperature is between 26 and 32 °C. Malaysia has only two seasons, dry or wet. The wet season occurs between September and December on the west coast of Peninsula Malaysia and between October and February on the east coast. Heavy rainstorms accompanied by violent winds as well as thunder and lightning, known as monsoon storms, are also common. Approximately 60% of the country is covered by tropical rainforest (Tang, 2019).

Malaysia is a Federation with a Parliament at the national level. The 13 states (11 on the mainland,[1] two in east Malaysia) are administered by individual state governments. In addition to the 13 states, there are three federal territories, Kuala Lumpur, Putrajaya and Labuan all of which are directly administered by the Federal Government. The entire state of Malaysia had an estimated population of 32.6 million people in 2019. Malaysia has few highly developed urban areas with dense population, while large swathes of the country are sparsely populated giving an average population density of 95 per square kilometre. By comparison the estimated population density of the United Kingdom UK) is two and a half times as much.[2]

History of the Nation State

The contemporary Federation of Malaysia did not exist until 1963. Prior to that, what is now modern-day Malaysia passed from empire to empire, having been Hindu, Buddhist, Islamic and Christian colonists over an 1800-year recorded history (Alatas et al., 1998). Being on an important trading route and port, it came to the attention of successive world powers and in turn, Portuguese, Dutch, British and Chinese invasions

---

[1] Peninsula Malaysia consists of 11 states, namely, Perlis, Kedah, Penang, Perak, Kelantan, Terengganu, Pahang, Selangor, Negeri Sembilan, Melaka and Johor. West Malaysia consists of Sabah and Sarawak, each a state in its own right.
[2] Population figures come from Statista.com. Date last accessed: 27 March 2020.

made their mark on Malaysian society. In the seventeenth and eighteenth Centuries, when much of the colonization and conflict occurred, Malaysia consisted of several kingdoms or states (Sultanates), all in West Malaysia (Andaya & Andaya, 2001). The most famous Sultanate was Malacca, which fell to the Portuguese in 1511. Then, Tanah Melayu came under the Dutch in 1641, followed by the British in 1874 with the Pangkor Treaty.

British Colonization and Its Legacy

The greater interest of the British in the Malay nation started with the founding of Singapore in 1819 by British man, Sir Thomas Raffles (Turnbull, 1989b). Singapore, a small island at the southern part of the Malay Peninsula and a strategic seaport, thrived as a new international trading centre, confirming British dominance of commercial interest in the region. The Treaty of London was signed in 1824 to avoid Anglo-Dutch conflict in the Straits of Malacca. Under this treaty, the Malay world was distinctly divided into respective Dutch and British spheres of influence, with the former in control of the Indonesian archipelago after acquiring Bengkulen from the British and the latter taking over Malacca from the Dutch to add to their possessions of Penang and Singapore. This treaty is also seen as the basis for contemporary boundary delineation between Malaysia and Indonesia (Alatas, 1989).

When the Treaty of London was signed, the British showed no interest in interfering with the local politics nor to expand its territorial possessions beyond Penang, Singapore and Malacca. Even today, east Malaysia sees a proportional lack of development that is attributed to the concentration of colonial influence in the west (Jomo & Hui, 2003). This policy changed 50 years later due to pressure resulting from the growth of capitalist enterprise mainly in Singapore, as well as the expansion of commercial agriculture, the growing demand for tin in the international market and the influx of Chinese immigrants into the Malay Peninsula (Turnbull, 1989a). Due to these factors, the British Government found the excuse to expand its political control to Malay States, in order to protect its trade interests.

The feuds among Chinese secret societies (mainly over tin rights), the Malay disputes over succession and the proliferation of piracy activities also opened up opportunities for the British to further intervene in Malaysia beyond trade. The Pangkor Treaty was signed in 1874 signifying the formal relationship between the British and the Malay States where British influence was further extended to the hinterlands of the Malay Peninsula as well as to Sabah and Sarawak. The total colonization of Malaysia was effected in 1914 when the State of Johor fell under British rule (Andaya & Andaya, 2001).

Unlike its predecessors, the Portuguese and the Dutch, British colonization made significant impacts on Malaysia's political, economic and social structure. Firstly, it strengthened the formal hierarchy of political power in Malay society with the ruler at the top and peasants at the bottom of the social hierarchy (Drabble, 2000). In this regard, the British colonial government recognized the needs to accommodate the interest of the Malay ruling class in order to get approval and cooperation essential for the success of British rule in Malaysia. In addition to the Malay rulers, established aristocratic families were given special privileges as their influence and cooperation were needed to maintain the stability of British economic control over the Malay region (Alatas, 1997). Consequently, it resulted in a gap between the topmost level of the Malay ruling class and the rest of Malay society.

Secondly, British colonization created a dual economy in Malaysia where large and modern corporations owned by foreigners existed side by side with small businesses owned by the Chinese and traditional agriculture and fishing activities owned by the Malays (Drabble, 2000). The Malays were seen by the British as best suited in a traditional occupation such as rice growing. This resulted in the British colonial government making no effort to encourage the Malays to be involved in modern activities where the presence of the Chinese was prominently evident.

Thirdly, British colonization contributed to the emergence of Malaysia's pluralistic society following the massive influx of immigrant labour from China and India (Searle, 1999). Although the Chinese and Indians had visited the Malay region long before the arrival of the British, the influx of their migration only begin in the second quarter of the nineteenth century. Between 1911 and 1931, the British colonial government encouraged unrestricted immigration from China and India to meet the increased demand of workers as a result of the boom in the tin and rubber industry, as well as the growth of Penang and Singapore as trade centres in the region (Andaya & Andaya, 2001).

Finally, British colonization has been blamed as one of the factors for the decline of Malay entrepreneurship in Malaysia (Ahmed et al., 2005). It is argued that long before the advent of the British and the other immigrant races, notably the Chinese, the Malays had enjoyed a period of economic independence and were involved in commercial activities with domestic traders as well as with foreign traders from India and Arab countries (Drabble, 2000). The involvement of Malay entrepreneurs was notable during the era of the Malacca Sultanate (A.D. 1400–1500) as they were actively involved in trading and business activities (Ahmed et al., 2005). As a result of this, it is not surprising that many Malays regard the Malacca Sultanate as the symbol of Malay sophistication in trade and businesses (Jesudason, 1990). These entrepreneurial traditions, however, failed to develop further as a result of British colonial subjugation.

Scholars have attributed several factors that could explain why Malay entrepreneurship declined as a consequence of British colonization (Drabble, 2000). Under the British colonial government "divide-and-rule", Malaysia's society was segregated according to ethnic identities, social status and economic status. This was done to enable the British to control the three major ethnic groups of the country, namely, the Malays, Chinese and Indians. The Malays were encouraged to settle in rural areas with agricultural activities as their major occupation, whereas the Indians were mainly settled in rubber plantation working as labourers (Drabble, 2000). By contrast, the Chinese were given favourable treatment by the British who saw them as a more sophisticated and organized society that could facilitate British businesses and administration, thus they were mainly placed in urban areas with business activities as their major occupation (Gullick, 1981). The British made no effort to encourage the Malays to move into the urban areas where the majority of business took place and consequently, they were left behind in terms of commercial experiences and business know-how (Mahathir, 1970).

The British mercantile and colonial policies were also seen as effectively discouraging the Malays from being involved in entrepreneurial activities (Peletz, 1998). British policies made it illegal for the Malays to convert their rice-growing land into more profitable rubber plantations and penalized them for not working their paddy fields. These regulations effectively stunted Malay abilities to move out from their traditional subsistence economic activity and excluded them from the new opportunities provided by the tin mining and rubber industries being taken advantage of by settlers, as well as other European-backed commercial enterprises (Andaya & Andaya, 2001).

Scholars also argue that British education policy was inadequate in preparing the Malays for modern economic activities (Gullick, 1981; Shome, 2002). This is because British colonial education policy was fundamentally shaped by the identification of race with specific economic functions. To safeguard their economic interest, the British allocated different roles for Malaysia's ethnic groups: the Europeans to govern and administer, the immigrant Chinese and Indians to labour in the export industries and commercial sectors, and the Malays to farm the lands (Andaya & Andaya, 2001). The aim of the British education policy was merely to provide a basic vernacular education for the Malay children to be better farmers and superior fishermen, with limited opportunities of English-medium education only for the Malay elites (Shome, 2002).

In brief, there is clear evidence that the British colonization of Malaysia made a significant impact on Malaysia's political, economic and social structure. It reinforced the formal hierarchy of Malay political power via the Rulers and elites, contributed to the emergence of Malaysia's pluralistic society by bringing in Chinese and Indian labour to support British plantations and mines, but caused a decline in entrepreneurial tradition among the Malays during the Malacca Sultanate, through British colonial policies restricting Malay activities in business while favouring the Chinese (Andaya & Andaya, 2001).

British Colonial rule ended with a Japanese invasion and domination by the Japanese between 1941 to 1945, then back to the British from 1946 to 1957. When Malaya gained independence from the British in 1957, it was renamed the Federation of Malaya, with its former name Tanah Melayu (Land of the Malays) being retained in the Malay language.

Contemporary Malaysia Since Independence

Since independence in 1957, Malaysia has had a written Constitution with a parliamentary democracy and main institutions familiar in western governments of the Executive, the Legislative and the Judiciary, supported by the Civil Service, the Police and the Military. Its constitution provides for a constitutional monarchy with the monarch, officially called the "Yang di Pertuan Agong" (can be regarded as the King of Malaysia), serving a normal fixed term of five years after being elected by the nine Sultans, at a special Conference of Rulers convened specifically for that purpose. The selection is rotated among the nine Sultans in the country according to a list that grew out of the first rotation that began in 1957. The Yang Di Pertuan Agong is recognized not only as the sovereign head of the nation but also as the titular head of the military and head of the Islamic religion, the official religion of Malaysia. The political and executive power lies with the parliamentary Cabinet headed by the Prime Minister (PM).

Malaysia has had 14 general elections since its independence[3] and eight individuals have acted as Prime Minister.[4] For 61 years, the Barisan Nasional (BN) alliance of parties had been in power, toppled only by the new Pakatan Harapan (PH) coalition government in May 2018; a coalition which comprises of four parties, Parti Pribumi Bersatu Malaysia (PPBM), Parti Keadilan Rakyat (PKR), Democratic Action Party (DAP)

---

[3] (1959, 1964, 1969, 1974, 1978, 1982, 1986, 1990, 1995, 1999, 2004, 2008, 2013, 2018).
[4] The first being Tunku Abdul Rahman (starting from 1957, but between a 1955 election in Malaya before independence, as the British wanted to get Malayans then familiar to elections before granting freedom from being a colony, he was called Chief Minister of Malaya), the second, Tun Abdul Razak (starting 1970), the third, Tun Hussein Onn (starting 1976), the fourth Tun Mahathir Mohamad (starting 1981),the fifth Tun Abdullah Badawi (starting 2003), the sixth Dato Seri Najib Razak (starting 2009) and the eighth Tun Mahathir Mohamad (starting 2018, an unexpected comeback at 93 years old, having been Malaysia's fourth prime minister). In March 2020 the current Prime Minister (at the time of writing), Tan Sri Dato' Haji Muhiaddin bin Md Yassin, was appointed, just as the COVID-19 pandemic crisis started to take hold in Malaysia.

and Parti Amanah. Academics in the field are seeking to determine what led to the change, citing factors as diverse as social media marketing, coalition formation and partisan bias (Kassim, 2018; Rahim, 2018; Ufen, 2019). That is the subject for other scholars to investigate—but provides useful context for this chapter in that, after some significant growth in the economy and eminence in the ASEAN region in several areas, the country is undergoing a period of political upheaval that mirrors that seen in Europe and the USA.

Malaysia achieved independence from the British in 1957. After independence, Malaysia made impressive progress in social and economic development. However, the benefits of this progress were not evenly distributed among the different ethnic groups in Malaysian society. The Malays were still very poor and were mainly concentrated in rural areas depending on agricultural and fishery activities as their major sources of income (Mahathir, 1998). The income disparities between the Malays and the other ethnic groups, especially the Chinese, were very wide. The Malays were also under represented in the modern sector of the economy, particularly in commerce and industry. In addition, where their presence was felt, they were highly concentrated in the lower levels of the occupation hierarchy, mainly in the unskilled and semi-skilled categories (MTR 2MP, 1973). In addition, although participation of the Malays in the entrepreneurial sector had improved following independence, the stark reality of their under-representation in this rapidly growing sector remained.

The subservient nature of the Malay economic position, despite the country's independence, has created dissatisfaction among the Malays and sowed the seeds of distrust and discontentment in their relationship with the non-Malays, especially the Chinese (Gomez, 1999). Not long after Malaysia's general election in 1969, a racial clash erupted between the Malays and the Chinese, killing at least 196 people with over 400 injured (Mahmud, 1981). This riot served as an eye-opener for many regarding the fragility of Malaysia's pluralistic society. Recognizing the severity of the problems and the urgent need to address them, the government, through the National Operations Council (NOC), introduced the far reaching reforms of the New Economic Policy.

In between the first Malayan general election in 1955, as preparation for independence in 1957, to the introduction of a new economic policy in 1971, Malayan economic planning was in five year plans beginning with the First Malayan Plan in 1955–1959, a Second Malayan Plan in 1960–1964, and then retitled as the First Malaysian Plan in 1965–1969. These plans were about providing basic infrastructures, like roads, electricity and water, basic amenities like building new schools, hospitals, clinics, and community halls, continuing an agricultural and plantation economy, dominated by the British, the beginnings of simple manufacturing by the Chinese in addition to established British and European companies having factories with well-known brands and products of that era, mainly food and consumer, building public offices all over the country for a new nation, and welfare services.

Building a Malay economy was done by an agency called Majlis Amanah Rakyat (MARA), which was set up in 1966 to develop both education and business for Malays indigenes through various training courses and educational programs. MARA from the early days have been successful in the education side, the Malay human resource development of professionals and managers for mainly the private sector. It was done not only through Institut Teknologi MARA (ITM), the network of colleges offering professional courses, in every state, which later became UiTM, a university, the biggest in the country, but by sending students oversea to study for both first degree and Masters level. On entrepreneurship and as business owners, the achievement is not so spectacular. The root cause appears to be the dominance of foreign and Chinese businesses, their hold on the economy through their supply chains, networks and associations. The Malays were mainly rural, while the Chinese urban up to 1970.

The Chinese, because of their decades of being close to the British in the business sector as employees, emerged as entrepreneurs on their own with no government assistance. They built shops that became the nucleus of towns throughout the country and built a network of supply chains interacting between the factories, wholesalers, retailers and consumers. Malay businesses had to source supplies from them. During the period until the early 1970s, the resentment of the Malays kept increasing, a feeling of being shut out from the economy and the towns, that independence had not brought the expected comforts and rise in standards of living. They felt second-class in their own land (Andaya & Andaya, 2001).

The New Economic Policy

The New Economic Policy (NEP) started in 1971, as an ambitious national blueprint for Malaysia's socio-economic development. It was incorporated in the country's First Outline Perspective Plan (OPP1) covering a period of 20 years from 1971 to 1990 (Malaysia, 1973). The government realized that poverty and racial economic imbalances were the root causes of the unhappiness that had precipitated the 1969 riots (Hamidon, 2014). To address this issue and to promote unity among different races among Malaysian population, the government introduced the national ideology or Rukunegara in 1970, which called for a rejuvenated Malaysian society with a common value system that would transcend existing ethnic, cultural and socio-economic differences.

Guided by the principles of Rukunegara, the NEP was formulated with the objective of achieving national unity through the two-pronged strategy of:

i. Eradicating poverty by raising income levels and increasing employment opportunities for all Malaysians, irrespective of race;
ii. Accelerating the process of restructuring Malaysia society to correct economic imbalances, so as to reduce and eventually eliminate the identification of race with economic function.

In order to achieve the objectives of the second prong, the three important aspects to accelerate the process of restructuring Malaysian society under NEP were:

i. Restructuring of racial composition in employment
    As Malay representation in the fast-growing modern sectors of the economy was limited, the government felt that economic growth

by itself would not be able to uplift the economic position of the Malays to any significant level (Malaysia, 1973). Government intervention to alter the imbalances found in the racial composition of the country's labour force was considered crucial for the success of NEP. The government also saw the need to reduce racial inequalities found in the job hierarchy by expanding the Malay share of professional, managerial and technical personnel.

ii. Restructuring of Wealth Ownership

The government argued that ownership and control of assets or wealth were crucial to correcting the existing income imbalances among major races in Malaysia (Malaysia, 1973). Although restructuring of employment patterns would be able to reduce some inequality in average wages and salaries, it would not have been sufficient to significantly affect the total income differences of the population. This was because wages and salaries only accounted for 50% of total personal income and the other half came from ownership and control of wealth. The government also argued that as the economy developed and the country's financial structure became more sophisticated, the key element to reduce the imbalances would be through ownership of capital in the corporate and non-corporate sectors of the economy (Malaysia, 1973). Despite the country's independence, foreign interests dominated the ownership and control of the Malaysian economy. In this respect, they accounted for 60.7% of the total share capital of limited companies in Peninsula Malaysia. In contrast, Malay interests only constituted about 2% of the total with the Chinese owning 22.5% and the Indians 1%, respectively (Malaysia, 1973). To fight against the imbalances, NEP targeted by 1990, the Malays and other Bumiputeras (being Malaysians of indigenous origin) should own and control at least 30% of the equity capital in the corporate or business sector, with the foreigners and other Malaysians owning 30 and 40% respectively.

iii. Creation of a Malay Commercial and Industrial Community

The third important element in the NEP strategy to achieve economic equality in a pluralistic society of Malaysia was the creation of a viable and thriving Malay Commercial and Industrial Community better known as the Bumiputera Commercial and Industrial

Community (BCIC). Under this strategy, Malay entrepreneurs were to be nurtured. The NEP targets were that within one generation or about 20 years, the Malays would own, manage and control at least 30% of the country's commercial and industrial sectors at all levels of economic activities (Malaysia, 1973).

The NEP has been successful in attaining its first objective of eradicating poverty and reducing inter-ethnic income disparity. However, it has been less successful in attaining its second objective of reducing economic imbalances and providing a conducive environment for the development of Malay entrepreneurship. This can be attributed to a number of limitations and shortfalls in the implementation of the policy as well as the inability of the poor to take full advantage of the opportunities created by the NEP. While the number of businesses owned and managed by the Malays have increased during the period of NEP, there is still a question of their viability and competitiveness in the open market. Malay entrepreneurs are also seen as too dependent on government assistance due to their lack of capital, business experiences and skills, innovativeness and perseverance (Hamidon, 2014). The culture of entrepreneurship and risk-taking has yet to be fully implanted in the Malay business community. There is also an urgent need for them to be actively involved in the management and decision-making process of their business ventures, not just in terms of ownership. Despite the mixed success of the NEP, it has prompted the government to incorporate the twin-pronged objectives of the policy in the country's subsequent development policies.

The National Development Plan (NDP)

The National Development Plan (NDP) was introduced in 1991, covering the 10-year period from 1991 to 2000 (Malaysia, 1991). It was incorporated in Malaysia's Second Outline Perspective Plan (OPP2) which provided the platform for the actual implementation of the policy. While the NDP continued to maintain the two basic strategies of the NEP, it also introduced several new dimensions. These include shifting the focus of poverty eradication strategy in addressing deep-rooted poverty by emphasizing employment opportunities, to the rapid development of an active BCIC as a more effective strategy to increase Malay participation in the modern economic sector, and relying more on the private sector to achieve the restructuring objectives. The NDP recognizes that equity ownership alone would not be sufficient to effectively promote Bumiputera participation in the economy if the newly acquired wealth is not retained and enlarged, and if the Bumiputeras are not given enough experience in business operations.

At the end of the NDP period (1990–2000), the policy after NEP, the incidence of poverty among Malaysians was further reduced from 16.5% in 1990 to 7.5% in 1999, with the incidence of deep poverty reduced from 3.9 to 1.4% during the same period. Significant progress has also been achieved in terms of employment restructuring, the proportion of Bumiputera in the professional and technical employment categories increased from 60.5% in 1990 to 63.8% in 2000 (OPP3, 2001).

Likewise, as a result of various measures undertaken by the government to promote the development of BCIC, the number of Bumiputera enterprises in both the corporate and non-corporate sectors increased quite substantially during the NDP period. Nevertheless, they remained small and proportionately fewer than non-Bumiputera businesses. Bumiputera businesses were also lagging behind in terms of technology utilization, business experience and managerial skills (OPP3, 2001).

The National Vision Policy (NVP)

Although significant progress had been achieved in poverty eradication and employment restructuring under the NDP, the performance of Bumiputera equity ownership in the corporate sector and the promotion of a viable, resilient and competitive BCIC still needed further attention. The National Vision Policy (NVP) was then introduced in 2001 with the aim of establishing a progressive and Prosperous "Bangsa Malaysia" or Malaysian Race where different ethnic groups live in harmony and are engaged in full and fair participation in the economy. This is considered key to national unity (Malaysia, 2001). The policy combines the main strategies of the NEP with that of the NDP to achieve balanced development of the ethnic groups in the economy.

In addition, the NVP introduced new policy directions with four main aims:

1. Developing Malaysia into a knowledge-based society;
2. Eliminating poverty in remote areas and among aborigines including Bumiputera minorities in Sabah and Sarawak, as well as increasing the income and raising the quality of life of those in the lowest 30% income category;
3. Achieving effective Bumiputera participation and equity ownership of at least 30% by 2010;
4. Increasing Bumiputera participation in the leading sectors of the economy.

Initially, the NVP was formulated as a 10-year plan (2001–2010) of which the first five years were incorporated under the Eighth Malaysia Plan (8MP). However, with the change of the PM in October 2003, the rest of the NVP was reformulated as the National Mission Policy (NMP) under the Ninth Malaysia Plan (NMP).

Towards the end of NMP many new Bumiputera entrepreneurs had been successfully nurtured through various government initiatives, particularly by the Ministry of Entrepreneur and Cooperative Development (MeCD). However, their sustainability and competitiveness were still in doubt. This is because Bumiputera entrepreneurs were still seen as being too dependent on government contracts and assistance. Their capability to move from the low-end to high-end economic value was also limited. This could be attributed to their lack of knowledge, capital and business experience. The fact that the business value chain in Malaysia was predominantly dominated by the Chinese could also make it difficult for the Bumiputera to upgrade their businesses (Hamidon, 2014).

The New Economic Model

The New Economic Model (NEM) was formulated in 2010 by the country's National Economic Advisory Council (NEAC), established under the premiership of the sixth Prime Minister of Malaysia. The core principles of NEM were high income, inclusiveness and sustainability. Its aims were for Malaysia to be a developed nation by the year 2020, a population enjoying a high quality of life with a high level of income resulting from economic growth that is both inclusive and sustainable (NEAC, 2010).

Despite the country's success to transform from a poor agricultural-based country to a middle-income, industrial-based one, Malaysia is still facing the internal challenge of breaking away from the phenomenon known as "middle income trap" (Woo 2009). Malaysia's (Gross National Product) GNP per capita in 2010 was about USD7,600 annually or RM2,000 a month, way below the standard of a high-income country. Accordingly, the NEM targeted for the country to achieve a GNP per capita of USD15,000–20,000 in the year 2020. The NEM further envisioned for the economy of Malaysia to be market-led, well-governed, regionally integrated, entrepreneurial and innovative. One of the elements considered crucial to attain these objectives was for the country to have a conducive environment for entrepreneurship development. Accordingly, the government has stepped up its efforts under the Tenth (2010–2015) and the Eleventh (2016–2020) Malaysia Plans, to encourage and support the growth of Malaysia's business community and innovative start-ups (Malaysia, 2010).

Towards the end of the half-term of the Eleventh Malaysia Plan (11MP), a significant change of government took place, as a result of the country's 14th General Elections held on 9 May 2018. For the first time, after 61 years, the 2018 election caused a change of government from Barisan Nasional (National Front) coalition to another coalition named Pakatan Harapan (Coalition of Hope), formed in 2015. With the new government in place, a new policy direction was introduced to replace NEM, namely the Shared Prosperity Vision 2030 or better known as the SPV2030.

Malaysia Today

Government

Malaysia's federal government is composed of 28 Ministers (the Cabinet), 27 Deputy Ministers and 24 Ministries. Following the British framework and system, Malaysia has a bi-cameral parliamentary system consisting of the House of Representatives (Dewan Rakyat) and the Senate (Dewan Negara). Members of the Dewan Rakyat, 222 of them representing their respective parliamentary constituencies, are elected by the people through general elections held essentially every five years. The Dewan Negara has 70 Senators, 26 of its members nominated by the states, with the other 44 members appointed by the Yang Di Pertuan Agong on the advice of the Cabinet (ILBS, 2008).

In comparison with the Dewan Negara, the Dewan Rakyat is more powerful and influential in many respects, including the size of its membership, the authority in relation to Money Bills such as taxation and expenditure of public money, the stronger linkage to the people as MPs who are elected by the people, thereby becoming their representatives, and the right for one of the members to become a PM when having the confidence of the majority of the House.

However, a Senator can be made a Minister on being chosen by the PM. It can be only one member from the Senate as currently, or limited to a few, if the PM sees none from the House of Representatives is qualified enough for specific Ministries or functions in the PM Department. Debates in the Senate take place only after the sitting of the House of Representatives, and it attracts less attention as it is treated less seriously despite being a formal process of making bills passed by the Lower House into laws. Even if the Senate rejects a bill from the House of Representatives, there can only be a delay of one year, before it can be sent to the King for assent into law.

People and Population

As at end of 2018, the total population of Malaysia is estimated at 32.4 million, broken into 90.2% citizens and the rest non-citizens; about 80% of the population is in Peninsular Malaysia (the rest in Sabah and Sarawak, with the former having more than the latter); and about 80% in Peninsular Malaysia are on the western side of the peninsular, led by Selangor with 6.5 million people.

Malaysia's population is made up of many ethnic groups, but with three races account for 85% of the population, being Malays about 51%, Chinese about 23% and the Indians below 7%. The population of East Malaysia, of about 6.5 million, is more diverse. Within Sabah, there are about 31 different indigenous groups which include the larger communities like the Kadazan and the Bajau. In Sarawak, there are about 26 indigenous groups including the Iban, the Bidayuh and the Penan (MEA, 2019).

The Malays together with the other indigenous groups of Malaysia are recognized by Malaysia's constitution as the "sons of the soil" or Bumiputera (Federal Constitution, 2008). This classification is for the purpose of deciding eligibility for certain privileges, aids and opportunities for socio-economic re-engineering of the population. It started under the New Economic Policy in 1971. By 2020, the social and economic inequalities viewed as effecting the Malay and indigenous people were still in place, especially compared to the Chinese who are dominant in business. The preferences were designed to enable closing the economic and social gap between races. What observers might view as discrimination against minorities by the Malay majority, is seen in Malaysia as an outstanding issue to correct the inherited inequalities left by the British and the various colonial powers before them. The ongoing tension between the indigenous and minority populations has been the subject of study by Gomez (2008), Jesudason (1997) and Rashid and Ho (2003).

Malaysia has diversity too in religion, and freedom in religion and its practices is a feature of the nation. Whilst Islam is the official religion of Malaysia, other religions are allowed to be practised in harmony with Islam under Malaysia's constitution. The country has about 61%

Muslims, 20% Buddhists, 10% Christians and 6% Hindus (Federal Constitution, 2008). Up until 1978, education in Malaysia was undertaken in English, creating a bilingual population capable of communicating in a global language. Today, Malay and English are compulsory in all schools, while education can also be obtained in vernacular schools in Mandarin or Tamil (depending on the school).

New Policy Directions and Initiatives

Through various government policy initiatives and programmes, Malaysia has achieved significant progress and successes since its independence from the British six decades ago. A poor agricultural-based Malaysia has transformed into a fast-growing middle-income industrial country with its own global and multinational firms including Petronas, Maybank and Genting (Gomez, 2009). During the period 2016–2017, the economy of the country recorded an average growth rate of 5.1% per annum, with its Gross Domestic Product (GDP) recording a modest growth of 4.2%, despite the challenging external environment and weak commodity prices.[5]

The economic growth has benefitted and enhanced the well-being of the country's population in terms of higher income, greater employment opportunities, improved access to education, a better quality of healthcare, more affordable housing and safer living environment. The poverty rate of the country has been prominently reduced from 20.7% in 1984 to less than 0.4% in 2016 (Malaysia, 2018). Access to infrastructure facilities as well as transportation networks and connectivity has also been improved, which support economic expansion. In terms of competitive advantage, Malaysia is no longer dependent on traditional factors of production namely labour, land and natural resources but is transitioning towards a knowledge-based economy. This transition has enabled the country to enhance its competitiveness in generating higher value to the economy.

---

[5] World Bank Data. Data.worldbank.org/country/Malaysia. Last accessed 27 March 2020.

Nevertheless, certain issues and challenges still persist. These include a growing ageing population, socio-economic disparities between income groups, between different ethnic groups, between states and regions, as well as between urban and rural areas. In addition, the country is faced with problems of high unemployment and underemployment among youth due to the mismatch between demand and supply. Malaysia's labour market also faces low labour productivity growth which is due to the rising number of workers and the low use of technology, as labour-intensive industries such as agriculture, manufacturing and construction rely heavily on cheap foreign labour. On this aspect, a majority of Malaysian businesses are still concentrated in the lower end of the production value chain with low adoption and application of high technology (MEDAC, 2019).

Moreover, employee salaries in Malaysia are not commensurate with labour productivity, being on average at USD340 which is much lower as compared to developed countries such as Germany, Singapore, United States of America and the United Kingdom where the average salary was USD510 for every UDD1.000 of output (Bank Negara Malaysia, 2017). Likewise, Malaysia's Compensation of Employees (CE) to GDP of 35.7% in 2018 is still considered low if compared to countries like Germany at 51.5%, the United Kingdom at 49.4%, Australia at 47.2% and Singapore at 39.7% (MEA, 2019). The distribution of low corporate profits to employees as indicated by the CE together with the rising cost of living have made economic growth less felt by the people. The most affected group is the bottom 40% of the population or the B40 due to insufficient income to cover the cost of living as a majority of them are involved in low-paying jobs and micro businesses. For instance, analysis shows that a majority of Malaysians will run out of money in a week's time if their source of income is lost; 75% would have difficulty to provide RM1,000 during emergencies, and only 3 million out of 14.5 million employees have retirement money. In order to overcome all these challenges, the Government of Malaysia has come out with a new policy direction of the country for the next ten years (2020–2030), namely, the Shared Prosperity Vision 2030.

Shared Prosperity Vision 2030 (SPV 2030)

The basic idea of Shared Prosperity Vision (SPV) was introduced by the current Prime Minister of Malaysia, Tun Mahathir Mohamad, during the tabling of the Mid-Term Review of the Eleventh Malaysia Plan (MTR 11MP) on 18 October 2018. Subsequently, its framework was laid down on 9th May 2019 at the Putrajaya International Convention Centre (PICC) during the "One Year of Pakatan Harapan Anniversary" celebration as the government. A formal plan was then officially launched in October 2019 as a new approach to ensuring Malaysia continues to grow sustainably through an equitable and inclusive economic distribution of wealth or prosperity. Emphasis will be placed on narrowing the economic gap and income disparities among ethnicities, regions and supply chains while improving the purchasing power of the people. Special attention will be given to nine target groups namely, bottom 40% of society (B40) group/poor and economically vulnerable, community in economic transition, indigenous community, Bumiputera in Sabah and Sarawak, persons with disabilities, youth, women, children and senior citizens, to ensure that the country's wealth can be enjoyed by all. The three main objectives of the Shared Prosperity Vision are:

1. **Development for All**
   Restructuring the economy of Malaysia to be more progressive, knowledge-based and high-valued with full community participation at all levels;
2. **Addressing Wealth and Income Disparities**
   Addressing economic disparities across income groups, ethnicities, regions and supply chains to protect and empower the people in ensuring that no one is left behind; and
3. **United, Prosperous and Dignified Nation**
   Building Malaysia as a united, prosperous and dignified nation, and subsequently becoming an economic centre of Asia. The final aim of the Shared Prosperity Vision is to provide a decent standard of living to all Malaysians by the year 2030. In order to achieve its primary aim and objectives, SPV has outlined 15 guiding principles, seven strategic thrusts and eight enablers. In formulating its policies

and strategies, the SPV2030 will emphasize on an outcome-based approach with clear and measurable goals and targets. Thus, the indicators to measure national development will not be solely based on GDP, rather they will also encompass distribution of national wealth, increase in purchasing power and enhance wellbeing to benefit the people.

National Entrepreneurship Policy 2030

One of the objectives of the Shared Prosperity Vision is to restructure the Malaysian economy with the involvement of all segments of society in contributing to the country's socio-economic growth based on knowledge and high societal values. In this context, entrepreneurship is an important and strategic component to drive Malaysia towards a united, prosperous and dignified nation. Within the National Entrepreneurship Policy 2030, entrepreneurship is also regarded as a promising social approach for the country to escape the middle-income trap (Woo, 2009) with the intention of helping Malaysia to become an economic centre in Asia by the year 2030.

Recognizing the crucial role of entrepreneurship in the socio-economic development of the country, the Pakatan Harapan (PH) government re-established the Ministry of Entrepreneur Development (MED) on 2 July 2018. Since then, the Ministry has proactively been preparing a holistic and conducive entrepreneurship ecosystem to support the country's socio-economic agenda. Within a year of its re-establishment, MED has introduced a National Entrepreneurship Policy covering a 10-year period (2020–2030), Known as NEP2030. This policy will act as a strategic document to drive a culture of entrepreneurship in the country, with the ultimate objective of creating a holistic and conducive entrepreneurial ecosystem for Malaysia to be a thriving Entrepreneurial Nation by the year 2030.

Targets, Objectives and Strategies of NEP 2030

NEP 2030 is formulated to develop an entrepreneurial ecosystem in Malaysia that will enhance the country's competitiveness in a time where the country is facing a highly competitive global economic field and challenges emerging from the Fourth Industrial Revolution (4IR) as well as creating an entrepreneurial culture in Malaysian society. According to the National Economic Census (2016), there are 920,624 business establishments in Malaysia. This includes:

- 13,559 large enterprises (1.5%);
- 20,612 medium enterprises (2.2%);
- 192,783 small enterprises (20.9%); and
- 693,670 micro-enterprises (75.4%).

The above statistics indicate that 98.5% (908,065) of businesses established in Malaysia are Micro, Small and Medium Enterprises (MSMEs). It is therefore, imperative that Malaysia focusses its efforts on further catalysing its MSMEs growth momentum as well as invest and adopt the risk-sharing approach in identifying and developing new economic drivers.

In addition, there are 14,247 cooperatives in Malaysia with total memberships of 6.05 million individuals, turnover worth RM40.32 billion and total assets amounting to RM142.86 billion (SKM, 2018). Thus, it is incumbent for the government to capitalize on the strength and sizeable number of cooperatives and its members into a progressive, innovative and competitive driver in the economy by encouraging cooperatives to venture into high-growth sectors. Emphasis should also be given on strategies to enhance contributions from the cooperative movement as an enabler and catalyst for empowering the B40s and generate new employment opportunities. In line with the Government's shared prosperity concept, the NEP 2030 sets out five objectives, namely:

1. To create holistic and conducive entrepreneurship ecosystem for sustainable, balanced and inclusive socio-economic development in Malaysia;
2. To develop a Malaysian community that is imbued with an entrepreneurial mindset and culture;
3. To increase quality, viable, resilient and competitive entrepreneurs with a global mindset;
4. To boost capabilities of Micro, Small and Medium enterprises (MSMEs) as well as cooperatives; and
5. To make entrepreneurship a career of choice.

NEP 2030 targets for Malaysia to rise higher in the rankings of global entrepreneurship, competitiveness, ease of doing business and innovation indices. Specifically, the target for 2030 is to be in the top 25 ranks of the Global Entrepreneurship Index (currently 58 out of 137 countries); top 15 of the Global Competitive Index (Currently 27 of 141 countries); top 10 in the World Bank Doing Business Report (Currently 12 of 190 countries); and top 20 of the Global Innovation Index (currently 35 of 129 countries).

In addition to the position in global indices, NEP 2030 aims to increase MSMEs contribution to GDP to 50.0% (currently 37.4%), generation of employment to 80% (currently 66.2%), contribution to total export value to 30.0% (currently 17.5%) and for the turnover of cooperatives to grow to RM100 billion (currently RM40.3 billion). To ensure the achievement of the set targets and to meet the aspiration of establishing Malaysia as a leading entrepreneurial nation in 2030, NEP 2030 has highlighted six strategic thrusts and 19 strategies.

The Malaysian government is aware the success of NEP 2030 would require effective collaboration and sustainable coordination efforts, combined with commitment and support from all stakeholders especially its people. It is hoped that through the implementation of the 19 strategies under the six strategic thrusts of this policy, Malaysia would be able to quantum leap as a competitive, prosperous and dignified entrepreneurial nation in 2030.

Summary

Race or ethnicity, religion, westernization, liberalism and free choice have been, and continue to be, competing forces or influencers in the development of Malaysia. To date, Malaysia is seen as a moderate, open, forward-looking, progressive, modern nation, accepting westernization and various global trends. This is evidenced by foreign investments, the extent of trade and its acceptance of millions of foreign workers, as well as being the regional headquarters for multinational and global brands including Shell, Braun. In conclusion, Malaysia has a significant number of assets and is well-placed to take advantage of its open worldview, geographic location and natural resources as an entrepreneurial nation. What has not yet been established is the academic understanding of the entrepreneurial realm.

References

Ahmed, Z. U., Mahajar, A. J., & Alon, I. (2005). Malay entrepreneurship: historical, governmental and cultural antecedents. *International Journal of Entrepreneurship and Innovation Management, 5*(3/4), 168–186.

Alatas, H. (1989). *Management of success: The moulding of modern Singapore.* Institute of Southeast Asian Studies.

Alatas, S. F. (1997). *Democracy and authoritarianism in Indonesia and Malaysia: The rise of the post-colonial state.* Macmillan.

Alatas, S. H., Khoo, K. K., & Kwa, C. G. (1998). *Malays/Muslims and the history of Singapore.* Centre for Research on Islamic and Malay Affairs.

Andaya, B. W., & Andaya, L. Y. (2001). *A history of Malaysia* (2nd ed.). University of Hawai'i Press.

Bank Negara Malaysia. (2017). Annual Report. https://www.bnm.gov.my/doc uments/20124/829200/cp01.pdf.

Cambridge International Reference on Current Affairs (CIRCA) (Eds). (2015). *Atlas: A pocket guide to the world today* (6th ed.). Mainland South East Asia. Dorling Kindersley.

Drabble, J. H. (2000). *An economic history of Malaysia, c.1800–1990: The transition to modern economic growth.* Macmillan.

Gomez, E. T. (1999). *Chinese business in Malaysia: Accumulation, accommodation and ascendance.* Curzon Press.
Gomez, E. T. (2008). Inter-ethnic relations, business and identity: The Chinese in Britain and Malaysia (2011). In N. Tarling & T. Gomez (Eds.), *The state, development and identity in multi-ethnic societies* (pp. 45–70). Routledge.
Gomez, E. T. (2009). The rise and fall of capital: Corporate Malaysia in historical perspective. *Journal of Contemporary Asia, 39*(3), 345–381.
Government of Malaysia. (2008). *Federal Constitution.* Kuala Lumpur.
Gullick, J. (1981). *Malaysia: Economic expansion and national unity.* Ernest Benn.
Hamidon, S. (2014). *The development of Malay entrepreneurship in Malaysia.* Institut Terjemahan & Buku Malaysia.
International Law Book Services (ILBS). (2008). *Malaysia Kita: Panduan dan Rujukan Untuk Peperiksaan Am Kerajaan.* International Law Book Services.
Jesudason, J. V. (1990). *Ethnicity and the economy: The state, Chinese business and multinationals in Malaysia.* Oxford University Press.
Jesudason, J. V. (1997). Chinese business and ethnic equilibrium in Malaysia. *Development and Change, 28*(1), 119–141.
Jomo, K. S., & Hui, W. C. (2003). The political economy of Malaysian federalism: Economic development, public policy and conflict containment. *Journal of International Development: The Journal of the Development Studies Association, 15*(4), 441–456.
Kassim, Y. R. (2018). *Malaysia's 2018 general election: Alternative scenarios?* Nanyang Technical University.
Mahathir, M. (1970). *The Malay Dilemma.* Marshall Cavendish Editions.
Mahathir, M. (1998). *The way forward.* Weidenfeld & Nicolson.
Mahmud A. A. (1981). *Malay entrepreneurship: Problems in development. A comparative empirical analysis.* Unit Penyelidikan Sosioekonomi, Jabatan Perdana Menteri.
Malaysia. (1973). *Mid-term review of the Second Malaysia Plan (MTR 2MP) 1971–1975.* The Government Press.
Malaysia. (1991). *The Second Outline Perspective Plan (OPP2) 1991–2000.* The Government Press.
Malaysia. (2001). *The Third Outline Perspective Plan (OPP3) 2001–2010.* Percetakan Nasional Berhad.
Malaysia. (2010). *Tenth Malaysia Plan 2011–2015.* The Economic Planning Unit, Prime Minister's Department.
Malaysia. (2018). *Mid-term review of the Eleventh Malaysia Plan (MTR 11MP) 2016–2020.* The Economic Planning Unit, Prime Minister's Department.

Malaysia Co-operative Societies Commission (SKM). (2018). *Cooperatives Sector Economic Report 2018*. Malaysia: SKM.

Ministry of Economic Affairs (MEA). (2019). *Wawasan Kemakmuran Bersama 2030*. Attin Press Sdn Bhd.

Ministry of Entrepreneur Development & Cooperatives (MEDAC). (2019). *Dasar Keusahawanan Nasional 2030*. MEDAC.

NEAC. (March, 2010). *New economic model for Malaysia: Part 1*. National Economic Advisory Council.

Peletz, M. G. (1998). The "great transformation" among Negeri Sembilan Malays, with particular reference to Chinese and Minangkabau. In R. W. Hefner (Ed.), *Market cultures: Society and morality in the new Asian capitalism* (pp. 173–200). Westview Press.

Rahim, S. (2018, August 4). *Social media and political marketing: A case study of Malaysia during the 2018 general election*. 5th International Conference on Social and Political Sciences (IcoSaPS 2018). Atlantis Press.

Rashid, M. Z. A., & Ho, J. A. (2003). Perceptions of business ethics in a multicultural community: The case of Malaysia. *Journal of Business Ethics, 43*(1–2), 75–87.

Searle, P. (1999). *The riddle of Malaysian capitalism*. Allen & Unwin.

Shome, A. (2002). *Malay political leadership*. Routledge Curzon.

Tang, K. H. D. (2019). Climate change in Malaysia: Trends, contributors, impacts, mitigation and adaptations. *Science of the Total Environment, 650*, 1858–1871.

Turnbull, C. M. (1989a). *A history of Malaysia, Singapore and Brunei*. Allen & Unwin.

Turnbull, C. M. (1989b). *A history of Singapore, 1819–1988*. Oxford University Press.

Ufen, A. (2019). Opposition in transition: Pre-electoral coalitions and the 2018 electoral breakthrough in Malaysia. *Democratization, 27*(2), 1–18.

Woo, W. T. (2009). Getting Malaysia out of the middle-income trap. *SSRN*. https://ssrn.com/abstract=1534454 or https://doi.org/10.2139/ssrn.1534454.

3

Proximity, Collaborative Relationship and Entrepreneur's Knowledge Spill-Over Opportunity in a Malaysian Regional Innovation System

Gerry Edgar and Zatun Najahah Yusof

Introduction

Innovation, diversity and function were considered as crucial conditions in an innovation system to produce Porter's competitiveness determinants (Porter, 1990). The diversity of system elements in innovation were considered less diverse if its functions (in micro and macro level) were less workable (Intrakumnerd et al., 2002; Patel & Pavitt, 1994). This research explores the conditions of a Malaysian regional system focusing on an information and communication technology (ICT) and biotechnology cluster of Multimedia Super Corridor (MSC) region by looking at the consequences of social functions conditions with the role of actors and its relationship. The impact of poor social infrastructure was found to be one of the major determinants in the MSC development in relations with the opportunity for entrepreneur's knowledge spill-over; and

---

G. Edgar · Z. N. Yusof (✉)
Stirling Management School, University of Stirling, Stirling, UK
e-mail: z.n.mohdyusof@stir.ac.uk

© The Author(s), under exclusive license to Springer Nature Switzerland AG 2021
P. Jones et al. (eds.), *Entrepreneurial Activity in Malaysia*,
https://doi.org/10.1007/978-3-030-77753-1_3

this was discussed in the chapter. This study concludes on the challenges for knowledge spill-over and the benefits of proximity cannot be fully utilised if the social functions was not ready for the system actors in regional and cluster development. Thus, influencing the effectiveness of the innovation process and technology transformation for Malaysia.

Proximity and Innovation System

The success of innovation is not only judged by its products and/or the services offered but also the effectiveness of the crucial components that support the innovation system itself such as the role of actors (institutions, governments, industries), supporting policies; learning and relationship patterns, common shared culture and geographic concentration (Etzkowitz, 2008; Oprime et al., 2011; Porter, 1990; Saxenian, 1985, 1994; Staber & Sautter, 2011). By recognising the importance of effective components of an innovation system, innovation can be said to be well managed even though there are many challenges (nature of the business and institution organisations, the business environment, and the approach of technological innovation) that are inherent in the process (Dodgson, 2000). However, understanding the competitiveness and technological development in the wider environment that forms the immediate innovation systems (i.e. national, regional, sectorial and/or technological system of innovation) could assist policy advisers and users in lowering the cost of said challenges.

According to Edquist (1997), increased interest in studying the concepts of systems of innovation started in the early 1990s with work by Freeman (1987), Lundvall (1992) and Nelson (1993) on national systems of innovation (NIS), followed by Carlsson (1995) on technological systems; and later Cooke (1996) from the perspective of regional systems. This evolution of the boundaries of the "innovation system" has refined understanding of the concept through investigations of various industry scopes, case studies and functions. Despite each system having a different emphasis, an appreciation of the various system mechanisms is essential to understanding and investigating the dynamics of innovation activities in context. This ability to manage the complexity of operationalising the concept of innovation processes reduces risks when attempting to design an innovation system able to create, incubate, develop, diffuse and utilise knowledge for innovation and competitiveness (Carlsson et al., 2002; Lundvall, 1992). Innovation systems represent a rich combination of innovation activities in the local innovative milieu; supporting policies, interactions and network linkages (Cooke, 2001) of participating system actors, such as institutions (universities), firms (industries) and government.

The geographical perspective (Carlsson et al., 2002) of specific physical boundaries at the nation or country level are classed as national level systems (NIS). The NIS concentrates on national local factors, interaction of system actors and how the nation learns in their unique practices and culture (Bryant et al., 1996; Freeman, 1987; Lundvall, 1992; Nelson & Rosenberg, 1993; Patel & Pavitt, 1994). Further to this, Porter (1990) discussed the importance of national determinants and characteristics influence on competitive industries and individual firms. For example, "home demand conditions" such as the size, pattern of growth and supporting policies can reinforce each other to form unique development paths for informed local firms.

The regional aspect was later added to the NIS literature as a subnational boundary system (Edquist, 1997) to investigate the complexity of innovation systems that are geographically or regionally (spatially) distinct. The analysis of regional innovation system highlighted the role of geographic proximity of firms with local system institutions such as universities, suppliers and government agencies that influence the competitiveness of individual organisations (Cooke, 1996). Related studies by Saxenian (1994) investigated the "regional industrial systems" of Silicon Valley and Route 128, with Marshall's (1930) concept of "industrial districts". The regional concept highlights the benefits of proximity for successful economic agglomeration (cluster) and high impact on specialism of local learning, interaction, networking and collaboration throughout the local milieu (Cooke & Morgan, 1994); which create its own unique identity over time. For instance, the closeness of individual firms and/or organisations with knowledge and research institutions i.e. universities provide opportunities in collaborative innovation arrangements (such as joint-research projects, utilisation of facilities and equipment, consultancies, and trainings) facilitates a rich transfer of knowledge. This is noted for enhancing the absorptive capacity (Cohen & Levinthal, 1990) of individual organisations (firms, universities or institutions) on knowledge and learning for innovation through its networking practices, opportunities for knowledge density spill-over, and enhances the closeness or trust-based relationships.

A key component of a regional innovation system is the role of the regional government and its policies, especially those known to accelerate innovation activities in companies, such as financial aid (Cooke et al., 1997). This is based on the importance of a deeper understanding and vested interest in the regional situation from local regional policy developers and advisors. Local knowledge facilitates a greater awareness of the connective mechanisms, local factors and competences to enable informed planning and implementation of supporting policies for the regional development. The local government or public sector interventions are necessary to influence regional growth and lower the risk of system and market failure (Cooke, 2001; Cooke & Morgan, 1994; Saxenian, 1994). Therefore, the issues of closeness of proximity benefit the degree of trust and relationship formation (formal and informal interaction) among firms (industries) and institutions (universities, agencies, and/or public sectors) that can influence the opportunities for knowledge spill-over.

A different, but related, sectorial approach on perspectives of innovation systems contrasts those of the geographically bound systems (national and regional system). The "sectorial system of innovation" focuses on innovation in specific sectors (industry) or technology. Carlsson's (1995) early studies on Swedish technological systems, such as pharmaceutical, electronics and computers formed the term "technological system" and highlighted its distinct features (Carlsson & Stankiewicz, 1995) based on the characteristics of specific technology including the organisations (firms and institutions), learning and interaction within the system's components and network of relationships (Carlsson et al., 2002). These relationships evolve over time to enhance innovative capabilities that are not necessarily within the boundaries of a nation or region (Malerba, 2004). Hence, the sectorial or technological system combines the geographical and sector or technology elements and functions of specific system actors, economic areas, networks and interaction. This is an assumption that sectorial systems of innovation overlap NIS (Malerba, 2002) and are very similar to Porter's (1990) concept of clustering for competitiveness.

Development of cluster studies can be and must be related to the understanding of innovation systems; in particular the regional approach (Vaz et al., 2014). The innovation system involves the characteristic of system actors (firms and institutions) and influenced by the behaviour and capabilities of learning, networks and interaction within or beyond local milieu boundaries for innovation (Cooke, 2001). This also comes with the benefits of proximity or closeness between actors in their mutual environment which encourages and supports healthy learning and the relationship ultimately promotes entrepreneurial activities.

Collaborative Relationship and Knowledge Spill-Over

Close relationships form more readily between actors i.e. university, industry and government agencies when closeness of proximity represents an important enabler of social interaction and working collaboratively (Clark, 1983) in order to achieve a common goal or working with a special agenda such as profit maximisation, technology breakthrough and self-recognition; which is mostly mentioned in the literature of regional cluster studies (DTI, 2004). The active inter-organisational relationships among actors in the industrial cluster (Oprime et al., 2011; Saxenian, 1985, 1994) could stimulate the development of a cluster or region as knowledge resources become vigorous for organisations to be competitive (Porter, 1998). According to Etzkowitz (2008) the role of the actors such as universities, firms in the industry and government interconnecting with each other could support the regional development process from the "*knowledge, consensus and innovation spaces*" which forms his Triple Helix concept of innovation relationships. This issue highlights the importance of social capital in the development of healthy relationships and interactions among actors that are essential for an effective and workable innovation system as well as entrepreneurial development and processes.

Furthermore, Saxenian (1985) highlighted that social interaction among Stanford University's scientists and local entrepreneurs sparked the spin-offs and creation of local technology champions that formed the basis of the success of Silicon Valley. However, there was chaos on the provision of local social infrastructure such as the shortages of residential properties, transportation networks and the environment in the 70s when the production from the microelectronics industry was at its highest; before the big manufacturers relocated to other cheaper areas. Later, they left the North Silicon Valley as the high research and control centre, while the South and West became the growing microelectronic manufacturing centre. This showed that the social dimension influences organic cluster developments and it also matters for engineered or planned developments. This reinforces the importance of social capital as a contributing factor in cluster forming and regional development; the theory has implications for economic development (Putnam, 1993) including forming innovation policies. Knowledge sharing through social networks within the proximity communities may be an essential topic to further understand how the regional innovation processes work (Storper, 1995); and thus stimulate knowledge creation and dissemination beyond the spheres boundaries.

There are three major dimensions in social capital studies (Nahapiet & Ghoshal, 1998). Firstly, the structural dimension is a pattern of connectivity between people such as the density of networks, the uniqueness and bond strength to other actors. Secondly, the relational dimension, which incorporates the relationships of the actors including the personal relationships built with contacts over the years; this is important for trust building between actors. Thirdly, the least measurement of social dimension by Nahapiet and Ghoshal (1998) is the cognitive dimension; referring to the norms, shared language and interpretation. There is another social dimension that is not put forward widely in cluster and regional studies, the social infrastructure (Flora & Flora, 1993). This research will also explore the role of social infrastructure such as how housing and transportation networks influence the social linkages among actors in relation with the proximity and the opportunity for knowledge spill-over to happen. The outcome can provide alternative indicators for policy and economic advisors in strategising effective collaborative relationships between and with universities and industries.

Summing up, therefore, it can be stated that innovation system concept and approaches unmask the crucial benefits of proximity and it may triggers consequences on how the local system (including entrepreneurs) operates from learning (including knowledge spill-over), networking (formal and social), collaboration to innovation process e.g. regional actions and development. However, uncertainty remains on what influences are required for healthy learning and collaborative relationship among system actors in close spatial proximity. Furthermore, there were limited literature that documented the impact of the social dimension as experienced in the early years of Silicon Valley development (Saxenian, 1985). Most studies of collaborative relationship in innovation system (Clark, 1983; Etzkowitz, 2008; Porter, 1998), however, have focused on the relationship in developed nations and in developing countries like Malaysia. This study attempt to address these issue by investigating an MSC as a case to study.

Methodology

Method and Data

The objective of this study is to examine the conditions of Malaysian regional innovation systems focusing on the role of actors and how their collaborative relationships are influenced by the social interactions enabled within a close proximity environment. This is intended to contribute to the understanding of proximity in an innovation system. A case study approach has been used to explore a greater depth explanation of the problem (Tashakkori & Teddie, 2003) and to conduct interview investigations with main actors in a selected innovation system (universities, government agencies, companies (ICT and biotechnology firms), intermediaries and financial institutions) of the new city of Cyberjaya, Malaysia. The case of the MSC region has been chosen for this study due to it being among the first designated regional development initiatives in Malaysia focusing on high technology (including ICT), higher education and biotechnology (Malaysia, 1996). The MSC is among the national initiatives to promote Malaysia to become a developed nation in 2020; further details are explored in the next section. In-depth interviews with system actors have been found to be an appropriate approach when the personal context and experience of system actors are critical (Barratt et al., 2011). This approach is also suitable when studying complex collaborative relationships (Farinha et al., 2016; Lundberg & Andersen, 2012) and has been chosen as the primary data collection method for this study. All 21 interview respondents were carefully selected to represent the main actors in the system, and range from the senior directors of government agencies and officials, local universities professors, CEOs of technology companies (ICT and biotechnology) to senior managers of local banks. The majority of interviewees had experience in collaborative relationship activities and were located within the proximity of Cyberjaya's city and Multimedia Super Corridor (MSC) region. This provides a degree of validation on cross-comparison of the different backgrounds and roles. Interviews were semi-structured and involved a number of open-ended questions intended to elicit views and tease out opinions associated with their experiences of collaborative relationships among their network of system actors in the MSC region. Questions focused on the role of interviewees within their organisation and MSC; condition of the MSC from its role as an innovative cluster enabler, contributions and its uniqueness (or weaknesses) as compare to other successful clusters in developing nations (e.g. Silicon Valley, USA and Cambridge Silicon Fen, United Kingdom); and the synergies of collaborative activities and relationship among key system actors—university, government and industry. The face-to-face interviews were conducted between July and September 2011 and were on average approximately 60 minutes in length. The interviews were digitally recorded with permission and transcribed verbatim.

In terms of data analysis, an abductive approach was utilised to uncover various aspects of reality (Dubois & Gadde, 2002; Jarvensivu & Tornroos, 2010; Lunberg & Andersen, 2012) from innovation literature to collected data and available theory (Dubois & Gadde, 2002). The interviews were summarised using content analysis to help in processing, developing and interpreting the meaning of coded text into themes that were reliable and valid in use for the purpose of this research (Boeije, 2010; Hsieh & Shannon, 2005; Zhang & Wildemuth, 2017). The data analysis begins with understanding the transcribed text using a coding process which looked for commonalities, key patterns and resulted in a range of theoretical concepts (35 concepts) which were later condensed and used as core themes (11 themes e.g. role of government, motives of collaboration, technology cluster status) for this study. Before the coding process began, all transcripts were reviewed and validated by four different qualitative researchers to ensure they were a valid representation of the conversations (O'Connor & Gibson, 2003) for the quality of analytical process. Influence diagrams were used to display, visualise and interpret content analysis of narrative data and provide an opportunity in identifying possible gaps in knowledge associated with this study (Boeije, 2010).

The Malaysian Regional Innovation System: The Case of MSC

The Malaysian government has recognised the cluster-based development approach as one of the strategic development tools for the growth of its economy (Abdullah, 1993; Rahman, 1993). There are selected geographical areas identified as Free Trade Zones (no duty tax on products and services) which aim to boost the growth of local industry clusters, especially the tourism industry in areas such as Labuan Island, Langkawi Island and Tioman Island. Furthermore, there were five new growth corridors identified during the Ninth Malaysia Plan (for the year 2006–2010) which included objectives to balance the regional economic development and focus growth in the selected industry cluster and geographical areas. According to the Tenth Malaysia Plan (for year 2011–2015), the Malaysian government identified the potential economic clusters in selected areas, also known as National Key Economic Areas (NKEAs) of five corridors that have economic and geographic advantages: (1) Iskandar Malaysia is to focus on education, healthcare, finance, creative industry, logistic and tourism industry—launched 2006; (2)

Northern Corridor Economic Region (NCER) to focus on agriculture, manufacturing and services, tourism and logistics industry—launched 2007; (3) East Coast Economic Region (ECER) to focus on tourism, oil, gas and petrochemical manufacturing, agriculture and education industry—launched 2008; (4) Sarawak Corridor Renewable Energy (SCORE) to focus on heavy industry i.e. aluminium, glass, steel and timber industries, agriculture and aquaculture related industry, marine engineering and tourism industry—launched 2008; (5) Sabah Development Corridor (SDC) to focus on tourism, manufacturing (palm oil and related products), oil and gas, agriculture and logistic industry—launched 2008 (Malaysia, 2010).

Other than the five corridors or regions mentioned earlier, focus is also given to the area called Greater Kuala Lumpur (Greater KL) cluster announced in the Economic Transformation Programme in 2010 where this geographic areas contributes eight times the Gross Domestic Product of any other city in Malaysia (EPU, 2010) and cover the areas of Kuala Lumpur (capital city of Malaysia) and its neighbouring cities, previously known as Klang Valley. Parts of Greater KL, an engineered cluster of Multimedia Super Corridor (MSC) was located and created in 1996 to spur the economic growth and introduce information and communication technology (ICT) industry as an industry that can move Malaysia towards high-technology industry with talented skills while attracting foreign investment.

MSC was among the first regional economies projects to concentrate on the ICT industry. Inspired by the success of Silicon Valley in California, coupled with the intention to be a developed nation under its Vision 2020 initiatives (Malaysia, 1992), the policymakers in Malaysia established the Multimedia Super Corridor (MSC) also known as MSC Malaysia in 1996 with a mission to transform Malaysia into a high-technology zone and knowledge-economy. In line with this project, the Malaysian government established the Multimedia Development Corporation (MDeC) now known as Malayisa Digital Economy Corporation (MDEC) to develop, facilitate and oversee the MSC Malaysia project. The MSC covers an area of 50×15 km^2 zone, stretching from the Petronas Twin Towers in Kuala Lumpur which also referred to as the

Kuala Lumpur City Centre (KLCC) to the Kuala Lumpur International Airport (KLIA). This zone includes Putrajaya (the official seat for federal government), Cyberjaya (national hub for information and communication technology (ICT); and research centre), Multimedia University, MSC Central Incubator (focusing on IT and multimedia) and Technology Park Malaysia (focusing on ICT and biotechnology).

The conceptual design of the MSC included a requirement to promote healthy linkages among actors in line with Porter's Cluster concept and the Triple Helix's innovation concept that could drive the innovation contribute to the national competitive advantage of Malaysia and create long term sustainable economic growth. However, there were challenges for Malaysia to pursue this project and it is of interest to this research to explore the motivations and behaviour of the high-technology firms located within the MSC cluster. The Malaysian government has introduced a series of incentives to attract investors including in the 10 Bill of Guarantees (BoG) that gave a privilege status for companies to locate within MSC and city Cyberjaya with tax rebates and less immigration restrictions to employed foreign workers.

Actors and Roles in the MSC Development

The success of high-technology clusters such as Silicon Valley is associated not only with strong linkages among its system actors; active involvement of venture capitalist and advantage of geographical concentration but also through the complex roles played by the system actors within the cluster. Dynamic relationships between the local firms (industry); university and government allow clusters to evolve and develop in a unique way (culture). On the development of the MSC, interviewees indicated that the roles played by government and industry contributed significantly to the MSC development. Overall, nine interviewees were in agreement with the notion that both government and industry are equally important in the development of the cluster. However, the perceived contribution towards the development of the MSC from the university was minimal. Overall, the roles of actors or stakeholders in the MSC were identified in the analyses as emerging issues. Each stakeholder has a particular perspective on the others and it was found that the role of university was perceived as the lesser partner and contributor in the MSC development. The analyses also discovered that the role of government is seen as the dominant contributor in the development of the cluster.

Overall, the role of the university in the MSC is important for social and economic development in the regional or cluster intentionally or unintentionally. However, the role performed is related to the characteristics of the university including its organisational factors such as culture, leadership, structure, management style and motivation. Furthermore, the role of university in the MSC is perceived as generating and supporting the development of the cluster rather than transforming it, leaving it far behind the hybrid type of helix enabling actor. Meanwhile, the role of industry is seen as important in generating the economic growth of the cluster (MSC) including the labour pooling, facilitating agents to university and government, motivator for competition, and to produce competitive indigenous technology for local and global production. The local technology firms are required to upgrade their technological innovation processes, initiate innovative projects and utilise the local resources combined with knowledge-based capacity including experts from other firms, universities and institutions. This leaves an opportunity to investigate for future research the impact of cluster and collaborative relationships in producing indigenous technology.

However, the role of government is in the engineered dimensions of the MSC and is important, not just in providing an economic environment, including local resources and policy initiatives, but also connects to industry and university to foster collaborative relationships. Although, there are changes in the university approach towards the evolution of an Entrepreneurial University and industry involvement with the university in collaborative research activities; the role of government is still maintained as the dominant position in the delivery of the MSC mission. The role of the Malaysian government becomes more challenging when reducing the "red tape" to attract tacit technology knowledge and learning capacities for the local economies as these were found to be barriers to effective collaboration in MSC. This needs innovative policies that fit the requirements of the current economic development as suggest by Porter (1998: 673) that *"government policy must evolve so as to anticipate the needs of an upgrading economy"*. To do so, more investment in the MSC and other similar cluster initiatives are needed for future economic transformation. It seems that the vision of becoming a developed nation by 2020 will be impossible to achieve but perhaps possible in the next 20 years when the region or cluster is at the peak of its life cycle. *The role of intermediaries* in regional and cluster development needs to go beyond knowledge transfer and become adapted to the specific demands of the local priorities in a more mature cluster entity (Smedlund, 2005). Smedlund (2005) also claims that regional level development is the most crucial element for a national system role since it connects the national and local level together with a coherent strategic formation, visioning process and support for the triple helix actors of university, industry and government. Despite the confusion regarding the role of intermediaries in the MSC, interview respondents still indicate that they consider intermediaries as consultants for activities of facilitating, motivating, marketing and commercialising, project management and linkages with university, industry and government. These bridging activities of consultants (Bessant & Rush, 1995) are to primarily support industry and make them aware of current developments.

A summary of roles played by universities, industry (firms), government and intermediaries are presented in Table 3.1. It can be concluded that these are evolving, with the role of universities coming under some pressure from the other actors to improve on their weak collaboration position, while also addressing concerns regarding the quality of the courses offered and the graduates produced. As the main power in the region or cluster, the government, acting through its agencies and intermediaries, has a role to close the communication gap between the universities and industry, However, it has yet to develop the right agency design and policies; Smedlund's (2005) adaptation to local priorities.

Table 3.1 Summary views on role of actors in MSC cluster by interviewes respondents

Role of university	Role of government	Role of intermediaries	Role of industry
• Learning and teaching centre • Source of talent • Research and development centre • Collaborators for research and business • Spin-off and entrepreneur producer • Source of funding • Knowledge sharing provider • Problem solvers • Agent to government	• Source of funding • Policy planner and regulators • Connectors to market • Intermediaries • Provides support to industry and university • Provides economics environment	• Access of funding • Facilitator • Project manager • Agent for government • Problem solver • Marketing and commercialising • Training providers and educators • Business intelligent • Resources agent • Knowledge and technology transfer centre	• Sharing knowledge and resources • Corporate social responsibility • Adviser to government and academic council for university • Seeking and hiring skills and talent • Provides knowledge and technology transfer • Motivator for competition • Provides training for local skills • Engine of growth

(*Source* Authors own)

Social Dimension in MSC

The theories of Porter's Diamond Model and Triple Helix emphasise the influence and importance of strong relationship or linkages between actors for innovation (which were found to be a weakness in the MSC). This weakness is not only because the MSC employs a top-down rather than bottom-up strategic development sequence but due to the lack of provision of social infrastructure as part of social dimension in the cluster space. Interview respondents confirmed that there is nothing interesting to do in Cyberjaya apart from working, this results in a massive swing of population between the day and night. Neither of the foundation concepts (Porter's cluster and triple helix) emphasise the importance of social dimensions of effective social infrastructure for enhancing the linkages among actors in a cluster. This research has found that the weakness in interaction between university and industry not only because of the limited skills, value of research activities, commercialisation difficulties, financial stress, collaboration activities and bureaucracy; but also the limited social infrastructure and services. Thus, the MSC actors have fewer social bonding spaces and opportunities that can enhance the social interaction and knowledge spill-overs among the communities involved in the MSC. The initial planning of the MSC project has neglected the importance of this aspect of social dimension for the MSC communities to interact and socialise. Clearly, the more that is known about the impact of the determinants for cluster development the greater the likelihood that engineered clusters will be successful—not only in the developing countries, but generally. A more comprehensive approach can be devised if cluster engineers and policy designers are aware of the soft determinants that can nurture and produce collaboration as well as the easier to measure and tangible factor conditions such as infrastructure and technology.

The social dimension in cluster building should not be ignored i.e. university, industry and government agency knowledge is in the heads of their employees, and knowledge transfers are matters that contribute significantly to the innovative capability and economic transformation within the cluster. This social dimension not only includes the pattern or structure of the connections, type of relationship between actors and common understanding, but also the provision of social infrastructure that is needed to enable all of these social dimensions to work effectively. Without doubt, the role of government is crucial to utilise the resources available, identify national priorities and set innovative economic programmes that have resilient approaches in order to transform the economic and social condition of the country. This approach implicitly assumes the full engagement of the actors and institutions for cluster development, but generally, the social conditions to enable high trust, social-context, human interactions are lacking in the design of green-field situations. An improved approach for creating a new cluster, i.e. one that has a greater probability of reaching the sustainment phase of the cluster lifecycle model, is to plan the location in a mature social space that offers an attraction to knowledge workers to live and socialise. Attempts to build on low cost, green-field and (usually) remote locations will result in a counterproductive social environment.

The summary of social dimension in the MSC is illustrated in Table 3.2 and this information is useful for the policymaker to understand the social condition of the actors involved in the MSC. This can provide a measure to analyse the appropriate strategy to improve the weakness of linkages among actors in cluster, and in particular, the social interaction between university and industry.

Conclusion

This research has explored, investigated and analysed the relationship dynamics in the localised innovation system represented by the MSC Malaysia regional cluster case. The research has uncovered the possibilities of creating or developing technology clusters for the purpose of economic, social, technology and knowledge transformation for less developed and/or developing countries; and/or any interested regional or sectorial policymakers for strategic local policies framework. The main challenge faced by the MSC are the issues of opportunity for knowledge acquisition and absorptive capacity for the organisations (firms and institutions) to acquire, utilise, transform and exploit the knowledge. In the case of MSC, it was found that the social infrastructure is a matter for the actors including entrepreneurs to interact and connect with their communities. The lack of social infrastructure and low strength of collaboration ties and value result in disappointing impact to the effectiveness of social linkages activities between university and industry in particular. Thus, this has influenced the effectiveness of interaction and linkages among system actors and the dynamics of the cluster in fostering entrepreneurial processes and activities. More comprehensive and robust measures are certainly required for the MSC to further excel and this research can be used as an initial investigation. A mature social space that offers attractions to knowledge workers to live and socialise would probably be an improved approach for developing a new cluster. The outcome from this research and discussion provides new input on both theories

Table 3.2 Social dimensions in the MSC cluster

Social dimension	Feature	MSC's social dimension condition
Structural	Pattern of connectivity, density or size of networks, strength of tie between actors	University and research institution both have low density of connection, government, suppliers, foreign and local firms, financial institutions are all have strong value of connection. Intermediaries have medium value of connection
Relational	Interconnection of relationship build over the years, previous experiences	Trust building start by informal meeting, risk of trust embedded in mutual agreement such as contract or MoU, previous experience counted for smooth business and social networking
Cognitive	Similar norms, shared language and interpretation	Shared similar norms and languages
Social infrastructure	Housing, school, convention centre, sport and recreational centre, health centre, transportation networks	Limited housing and residential area, limited bus services and workers commute with own or share car with colleague. Limited social and recreational centre in Cyberjaya resulting the population at night drop to 10,000 compare during the day which is 50000 people. Access and choices to motorway are easy but charges apply. Commuters facing risk of road traffic during peak office hours linking Kuala Lumpur to main city of Cyberjaya. Transportation networks focus on Kuala Lumpur city centre

(*Source* Authors own)

used i.e. Porter's Diamond model and Triple Helix, thus contributes to the knowledge on the theoretical implications.

References

Abdullah, O. Y. (1993). Human resource development: The key towards a developed and industrialized society. In A. S. A. Hamid (Ed.), *Malaysia's vision 2020: Understanding the concept* (pp. 315–326). Pelanduk Publications.

Barratt, M., Choi, T. Y., & Li, M. (2011). Qualitative case studies in operations management: Trend, research outcomes, and future research implications. *Journal of Operations Management, 29*, 329–342.

Bessant, J., & Rush, H. (1995). Building bridges for innovation: The role of consultants in technology transfer. *Research Policy, 24*(1), 97–114.

Bryant, K., Lombardo, L., Healy, M., Bopage, L., & Hartshom, S. (1996). *Australian business innovation. A strategic analysis.* Measures of Science and Innovation 5, Canberra.

Boeije, H. (2010). *Analysis in qualitative research.* Sage.

Carlsson, B. (1995). *Technological system and economic performance: The case of factory automation.* Kluwer.

Carlsson, B., & Stankiewicz, R. (1995). On the nature, function and composition of technological systems. In B. Carlsson (Eds.), *Technological system and economic performance: The case of factory automation.* Kluwer, Dordrecht.

Carlsson, B., Jacobsson, S., Holmen, M., & Rickne, A. (2002). Innovation systems: Analytical and methodological issues. *Research Policy, 31*, 233–245.

Clark, B. R. (1983). *The higher education system: Academic organization in cross-national perspective.* University of California Press.

Cohen, W. M., & Levinthal, D. A. (1990). Absorptive capacity: A new perspective on learning and innovation. *Administrative Science Quarterly, 35*, 128–152.

Cooke, P. (1996). *Networking for competitive advantage.* National Economic and Social Council, Dublin.

Cooke, P. (2001). Regional innovation systems, clusters and the knowledge economy. *Industrial and Corporate Change, 10*(4), 945–974.

Cooke, P., & Morgan, K. (1994). The regional innovation system in Baden-Wurttemberg. *International Journal of Technology Management, 9*, 394–429.

Cooke, P., Uranga, M. G., & Etxebarria, G. (1997). Regional innovation systems: Institutional and organisational dimensions. *Research Policy, 26*, 475–491.

Department of Trade and Industry. (2004). *Practical guide to cluster development*. DTI Publication.

Dodgson, M. (2000). *The management of technological innovation*. Oxford University Press.

Dubois, A., & Gadde, L. E. (2002). Systematic combining: An abductive approach to case research. *Journal of Business Research, 55*(7), 553–560.

Economic Planning Unit (EPU). (2010). Web access http://www.epu.gov.my/en/undertasking-research-in-malaysia.

Edquist, C. (1997). *System of innovation: Technologies, institutions and organizations*. Pinter.

Etzkowitz, H. (2008). *The triple helix: University-industry-government innovation in action*. Routledge.

Farinha, L., Ferreira, J., & Gouveia, B. (2016). Networks of innovation and competitiveness: A triple helix case study. *Journal of Knowledge Economies, 7*, 259–275.

Flora, C. B., & Flora, J. L. (1993). Entrepreneurial social infrastructure: A necessary ingredient. *Annals of the American Academy of Political and Social Science, 529*, 48–58.

Freeman, C. (1987). *Technology policy and economic performance: Lessons from Japan*. Pinter Publishers.

Hsieh, H. F., & Shannon, S. E. (2005). Three approaches to qualitative content analysis. *Qualitative Health Research, 15*(9), 1277–1288.

Intarakumnerd, P., Chairatana, P., & Tangchitpiboon, T. (2002). National innovation system in less successful developing countries: The case of Thailand. *Research Policy, 31*, 1445–1457.

Jarvensivu, T., & Tornroos, J. A. (2010). Case study research with moderate constructionism: Conceptualization and practical illustration. *Industrial Marketing Management, 39*(1), 100–108.

Lundavall, B. A. (1992). *National innovation systems: Towards a theory of innovation and interactive learning*. Pinter.

Lundberg, H., & Andersen, E. (2012). Cooperation among companies, universities and local government in a Swedish context. *Industrial Marketing Management, 41*, 4429–4437.

Malaysia. (1992). *Vision 2020*. Kuala Lumpur, Percetaken Maziza Sdn. Bhd. For National Print Department.

Malaysia. (1996). *Seventh malaysia plan, 1996–2000*. Kuala Lumpur, National Print. Department.
Malaysia. (2010). *Tenth malaysia plan 2011–2015*. Putrajaya, Economic Planning Unit, Prime Minister's Department.
Malerba, F. (2002). Sectoral system of innovation and production. *Research Policy, 31*, 247–264.
Malerba, F. (2004). Sectoral system of innovation: basic concepts. In F. Malerba (Ed.), *Sectoral system of innovations: Concepts, issues and analyses of six major sectors in Europe*. Cambridge University Press.
Nahapiet, J., & Ghoshal, S. (1998). Social capital, intellectual capital, and the organizational advantage. *Academy of Management Review, 23*(2), 242–266.
Nelson, R. (1993). *National innovation system: A comparative analysis*. Oxford University Press.
Nelson, R. R., & Rosenberg, N. (1993). Technical innovation and national systems. In R. R. Nelson (Ed.), *National innovation systems: A comparative analysis* (pp. 1–18). Oxford University Press.
O'Connor, H., & Gibson, Nancy. (2003). A step-by-step guide to qualitative data analysis. *Pimatisiwin: A Journal of Aboriginal and Indigenous Community Health, 1*, 63–90.
Oprime, P. C., Tristao, H. M., & Pimenta, M. L. (2011). Relationships, cooperation and development in a Brazilian industrial cluster. *International Journal of Productivity and Performance Management, 60*(2), 115–131.
Patel, P., & Pavitt, K. (1994). National innovation system: why they are important and how they might be measured and compared. *Economics of Innovation and New Technology, 3*, 77–95. Porter, M. E. (1990). *The competitive advantage of nations*. Macmillian Inc., Free Press.
Porter, M. E. (1990). *The competitive advantage of nations*. Macmillan Inc., Free Press.
Porter, M. E. (1998, November–December). *Clusters and the new economics of competition*. Harvard Business Review.
Putnam, D. R. (1993). The prosperous community: Social capital and public life. *The American Prospect, 4*(13), 11–18.
Rahman, O. A. (1993). Industrial targets of vision 2020: The science and technology perspective. In A. S. A. Hamid (Ed.), *Malaysia's vision 2020: Understanding the concept* (pp. 271–299). Pelanduk Publications.
Saxenian, A. (1994). *Regional advantage*. Harvard University Press.
Saxenian, A. L. (1985). Silicon valley and route 128: Regional prototypes or historic exceptions. *High Technology, Space and Society, 28*, 81–105.

Smedlund, A. (2005). The role of intermediaries in a regional knowledge system. *Journal of Intellectual Capital, 7*(2), 204–220.

Staber, U., & Sautter, B. (2011). Who we are, and do we need to change? culture identity and life cycle. *Regional Studies, 45*(10), 1349–1362.

Storper, M. (1995). Regional technology coalitions an essential dimension of national technology policy. *Research Policy, 24*(6), 895–911.

Tashakkori, A., & Teddlie, C. (2003). *Handbook of mixed methods in social & behavioral research*. Sage.

Vaz, E., Vaz, T. N., Galindo, P. V., & Nijkamp, P. (2014). Modelling innovation support systems for regional development—Analysis of cluster structures in innovation in Portugal. *Entrepreneurship & Regional Development, 26*(1–2), 23–46.

Zhang, Y., & Wildemuth, B. M. (2017). Qualitative analysis of content. In Wildermuth (Ed.), *Applications of social research methods to questions in information and library science* (2nd Ed.). Libraries Unlimited.

4

Knowledge-Intensive Entrepreneurship

Farahwahida bt Mohd @ Abu Bakar

Introduction to Digital Entrepreneurship

Digital entrepreneurship is a term that describes how entrepreneurship will change, as business and society continue to be transformed by digital technology. Digital entrepreneurship highlights changes in entrepreneurial practice, theory, and education. According to the Malaysia Digital Economy Corp (MDEC) a digital transformation in business executed correctly by corporations could lead to businesses seeing a 10–20 times increase in business volume. In Malaysia, the Jom Transform Programme aims to help at least 100 Malaysian Small Medium Enterprises (SMEs) embrace digitalization to achieve one of the following outcomes: increase in revenue, reduction in business cost, improvement of process time cycle, reduction in man-hours, or creation of new sources of growth.

Farahwahida bt Mohd @ Abu Bakar (✉)
Malaysia Digital Economy Corporation (MDEC), Cyberjaya, Malaysia
e-mail: farahwahidam@unikl.edu.my

© The Author(s), under exclusive license to Springer Nature Switzerland AG 2021
P. Jones et al. (eds.), *Entrepreneurial Activity in Malaysia*,
https://doi.org/10.1007/978-3-030-77753-1_4

The impact of the Covid-19 pandemic gave many organizations, especially SMEs, the imperative to rethink and to reorganize their respective business models. It is now more important than ever for SMEs, who are the backbone of the Malaysian economy, to embrace digital entrepreneurship not only to survive, but to maintain competitiveness. As a digital entrepreneur, they focused exclusively on digital commerce, and digital commerce is "a subset of e-commerce used to delineate companies that create digital products and services that are marketed, delivered, and supported completely online." Such examples of digital commerce products include ebooks, online education, membership sites, downloadable software, web hosting, and software as a service.

Digital entrepreneurs focusing on digital products and services that are marketed, delivered, and supported completely online, therefore the reason to have a good website is a prerequisite for success. There are few elements of the modern marketing website that all digital entrepreneurs need to be thinking about and implementing in a smart way such as email, content and connections. Entrepreneurs and customers need to embrace Internet technologies to enhance productivity, maximize convenience, and improve communications globally.

Digital Darwinism

In today's competitive world, the phenomenon of competition is determined by technological developments. Technology has already made business global. Any new changes or developments with regard to products or processes are inherent with technological components. No doubt even business organizations are shifting from manual record maintenance practice to software or online-based practice, which is facilitating and simplifying various processes carried out on a day-to-day basis. The transition phase from traditional to modern digital methods of carrying out various processes is considered to be difficult due to various shortfalls such as computer skills of system users, quantum of data, cost factors, content, internet connectivity, and many more. These shortfalls might lead to a situation termed Digital Darwinism, a scenario where technology and society are changing faster than organizations can adapt.

This created the need for new business models to ensure economically sustainable businesses.

Internet-enabled industry disruption defined business strategy in the 2010s, but as 2020 begins, that era appears to be winding down. The disruptors have largely become the new establishment, and unlike a decade ago, it doesn't look like the new leaders will be displaced any time soon. Today's internet is a mature and mainstream technology. The music industry has become a streaming industry, with compact discs and digital sales becoming far less important. Today's industry growth is powered by subscriptions. Beginning a few years ago, total revenues have started to grow again after 15 years of decline. The competitive threats to the leader in music streaming, Spotify, come from well-financed competitors with similar offerings, like Apple Music and Amazon Music, rather than a brand-new technology. The music industry may have been the first to be threatened by internet-related disruption in the late 1990s, with the growth of mp3 sharing and Napster, and is now perhaps the first industry to have completed its transformation. The advertising industry has been transformed by Google and social media platforms such as Instagram and Facebook. The literature stresses the importance of facilitators becoming well versed with new technologies and media in order to connect more effectively. First, the entrepreneurs should inhabit the practice of using such innovative tools in their business by which the potential online customer will automatically adapt themselves to the same.

Evolution of the Internet

The Internet began in the late 1960s as an emergency military communications system operated called the ARPANet by the Department of Defense. Gradually, the Internet moved from a military pipeline to a communication tool for scientists to businesses. The Internet is defined as computer networks that pass information from one to another using common computer protocols. Protocol is the standards that specify the format of data as well as the rules to be followed during transmission. There are two events that changed the history of the Internet, first, on August 6, 1991, Tim Berners-Lee built the first Web site using

HTML and HTTP and second, Marc Andreesen built and distributed Mosaic. A World Wide Web (WWW) is a global hypertext system that uses the Internet as its transport mechanism and Hypertext transport protocol (HTTP) is the Internet standard that supports the exchange of information on the WWW.

People often interchange the terms Internet and the WWW, but these terms are not synonymous. The Internet is a global public network of computer networks that pass information from one to another using common computer protocols. However, the WWW is a global hypertext system that uses the Internet as its transport mechanism. By incorporating Internet in your daily lives, it could make your job easy to compile information on products, prices, customers, suppliers, and partners is faster and easier when using the Internet. It has also increased richness of information transferred between customers and business. Businesses and customers can collect and track more detailed information when using the Internet by the increase in reach of the number of people a business can communicate with, on a global basis. Businesses can share information with customers all over the world and make online transaction by improving dynamic relevant content. Those advantages contribute to buyers need to make informed purchases, and sellers use content to properly market and differentiate themselves from the competition.

Knowledge-Intensive Entrepreneurship

Knowledge-Intensive Entrepreneurship (KIE) companies are defined as new learning organizations that use and transform existing knowledge and generate new knowledge in order to innovate within innovation systems (Malerba & McKelvey, 2018). The emerging literature on KIE stresses the relevance of the knowledge-based economy, the central position of innovation in modern industries and services and the essential role of new organizations in the economic growth of countries. Therefore, this chapter argues that KIE provides a modern view of entrepreneurship that links the intense use of knowledge by the new ventures with a high innovative activity related to the economy and markets. KIE are involved in the creation, diffusion, and use of knowledge; introduce new products and technologies; draw resources and ideas from their innovation system; and introduce change and dynamism into the economy.

The field of Entrepreneurship is diverse and expanding, and one where scholars stress the need to continue developing underlying theories to explain the phenomenon (Alvarez et al., 2013; Carlsson et al., 2013). Several studies have attempted to define the wider field of entrepreneurship and characterizing the phenomena for future research. The term entrepreneurship first appeared in 1723 and derives from the French word "Entreprendre" which means "to pursue opportunities" or "to undertake". An entrepreneur is a person devoted to creating something of value for the people, the society, and of course the economy. Apart from the financial reward, an entrepreneur also has a sense of personal pride and satisfaction for his achievements. Taking risks is part of the process but so is the immense reinforcement that furthers entrepreneurial actions. Entrepreneurship in the digital economy entails three components namely business, knowledge and institutional. The knowledge-intensive and disruptive nature of information technology requires entrepreneurs to engage in each form of entrepreneurial practice to create sustainable ventures.

KIE refers to a phenomenon that drives economic competitiveness and innovation capabilities. KIE is irregularly distributed in geographical space, which is largely attributed to heterogeneous endowments in terms of knowledge, institutions, resources, and demand. Different regions are embedded in different contexts and this translates into distinct innovation dynamics. However, the recent rise of digital economy offers extraordinary opportunities for international entrepreneurship by overturning the way start-ups expand into foreign markets.

Innovation ecosystems are characterized by innovative activities that rely on collaborative arrangements between organizations including institutions, universities, research institutes, technology transfer offices, and sources of funding. The justification for the collaborative arrangements is related to the idea of generating innovations, as well as entrepreneurial activity, which are shaped by the internal infrastructure, its externalities, specialized services and levels of trust involved in relationships between agents (Boschma & Frenken, 2011). In this context, voluntary knowledge spillovers take place, favoring open innovation strategies in incumbents. This situation generates fruitful opportunities for entrepreneurs to engage in value co-creation and to participate in established industries in spite of the dominance of large organizations.

The concept of KIE is also relevant for public policy which aims to stimulate knowledge, innovation and entrepreneurship. A community of researchers has been active in defining underlying concepts used by public policy. Initially, the focus was upon research and development (R&D), and its linkages to high-tech, medium-tech, and low-tech industries, including the development of specific indicators and of arguments regarding the relative importance of high-tech industries in the economy. Later work continued the exploration of new indicators and understanding, by focusing upon different types of knowledge prevalent across the economy, such as low-tech industries, services and knowledge-intensive activities (Eurostat, 2014).

The Organization for Economic Cooperation and Development (OECD) has been very active in promoting a view of the importance of knowledge in the economy, using a set of related concepts, for example knowledge economy, knowledge-based economy, learning economy, knowledge-intensive economy. The common denominators of these terms are that they stress that the basis of competitiveness (and jobs) in the wider economy depends upon organizations searching for, developing, and applying different types of knowledge in economic activities; and that organizations act within more holistic context such as innovation systems and entrepreneurial ecosystems. Thus, this volume on KIE is also highly relevant for public policy. As previously mentioned, this volume examines the emerging stream of literature on KIE. The literature reviewed in this chapter frames the broader phenomenon of KIE as a process of learning and problem-solving aiming to benefit from opportunity identification, creation and exploitation and which is conditioned by the linkages and networks related to innovation systems and knowledge-intensive ecosystems.

Role of Entrepreneur as an Innovator

In economic development, the entrepreneur plays a key role. The credit for innovations and the outburst of economic activity goes entirely to the entrepreneur. The word "Innovator" we mean such "Entrepreneur who continuous to make some new changes or creations in his business, like production of new commodity, new technologies of production, new machinery, and equipment, new raw material for searching of new resources of semi-finished commodities, new management system, new organizational setup new markets and many more. The entrepreneur is an agent of economic growth. The role of the entrepreneur as an innovator is highly important in simulating economic stability, industrial awakening and social innovations. The example of the role of the entrepreneur as the innovator is as follows:

1. **To Form Novelty in Society**
   The basic function of the entrepreneur is to create something new. The entrepreneur is the creator and the innovator, so he introduces the new products, new ideas, new markets and new production techniques to the society and living standard is raised, but also execute the research and development activities, for that.
2. **Production of Commodities and Services**
   Since the entrepreneur is also an innovator, they not only carry out innovations in their business activities but also make the production of the products and services according to the requirements of society.
3. **To Use the National Resources for Productive Actions**
   As an innovator, the entrepreneur has an important contribution to the economic progress of the nation by the establishment of new industries and generation of employment and use of national resources for productive activities to satisfy the social and economic needs of the country.
4. **Establishing and Coordinating the Resources of Production**
   As an innovator, the entrepreneur organizes and coordinate the resources of production, to maximize output, at the minimum cost. Entrepreneurs also contribute to increasing National Productivity, by

their managerial capabilities and efficient utilization of unutilized resources.

5. **Base of Industrial Development**
   The innovating entrepreneurs have the readership quality to develop the resources of the enterprise, human capabilities, and generation of new ideas.
6. **Economic Prosperity of the Nation**
   Innovative entrepreneurs start new enterprises to go ahead by removing the hurdles and disturbances arising in their ventures. **Moreover**, they also accept the challenges and improve their own performance by introducing the innovation.

New Knowledge Entrepreneurial Organizations

New entrepreneurial organizations can be found in a variety of sectors from high tech to traditional industries, and new organizations which are also innovative have been a major feature in the economy of most countries. Consequently, these organizations have been the center of attention of many empirical studies both in general and regarding specific typologies, such as new technology-based organizations, academic entrepreneurship and new engineering-based organizations and new organizations active in high technology sectors. The usual conceptual reference for an economic analysis of new innovative organizations is Schumpeter (1934, 1942) Schumpeter's theories and the later Schumpeterian tradition of entrepreneurship have provided vital insights into the entrepreneurial process.

The field of entrepreneurship related to Schumpeter research has evolved quickly, bringing in and analyzing new topics and phenomena (Carlsson et al., 2013; Landström et al., 2012). Some major themes in this tradition are that opportunities are created rather than discovered (Alvarez et al., 2013); entrepreneurs grasp existing opportunities and create new ones (Buenstorf, 2007); and that new organizations challenge incumbents and transform the economic system by creating an entrepreneurial regime (Winter, 1984).

Knowledge entrepreneurship describes the ability to recognize or create an opportunity and take action aimed at realizing an innovative knowledge practice or product. Knowledge entrepreneurship is different from "traditional" economic entrepreneurship in that it does not aim at the realization of monetary profit but focuses on opportunities with the goal to improve the production (research) and throughout of knowledge, rather than to maximize monetary profit. It has been argued that knowledge entrepreneurship is the most suitable form of entrepreneurship for not-for-profit educators, researchers, and educational institutions.

The Three Building Blocks in Knowledge-Intensive Entrepreneurship

KIE rests upon three theoretical building blocks: The Schumpeterian entrepreneur, the evolutionary approach to economic change and innovation systems. Knowledge-intensive entrepreneurial ventures are new learning organizations that use and transform existing knowledge and generate new knowledge in order to innovate within innovation systems.

1. *The Schumpeterian entrepreneur*

The Schumpeterian entrepreneur represents the main first building block for understanding KIE. For the purpose of this chapter, three characteristics of the Schumpeterian entrepreneur are relevant. A first key characteristic is that the entrepreneur is as a visionary and leader, able to implement ideas and inventions into innovations: he/she thereby creates opportunities. A series of debates address whether opportunities are discovered (Kirzner, 1997) or created (Garud & Karnoe, 2001; Lachmann, 1986), or both are active in different contexts. With respect to this topic, studies have been conducted along a variety of perspectives (Short et al., 2010) and have emphasized the differences of the two views in terms of epistemology (Alvarez & Barney, 2007), historical roots, the nature of the entrepreneur and the characteristics of the knowledge involved in the opportunity formation process (Alvarez et al., 2013). In the view of "discovered" opportunities, the opportunities exist, and some individuals and teams can more quickly identify and act upon them. These are often called Kirznerian opportunities. In the view of "created" opportunities, the knowledge and business opportunities do not exist a priori but instead come together through the actions of entrepreneurs. These are often called Schumpeterian opportunities.

A second key characteristic is that the entrepreneur is a risk-taker, who develops new combinations, and often if not always within an organizational context. The Schumpeterian tradition recognizes entrepreneurship as involving an element of risk-taking. In a classic definition, entrepreneurship "pertains to the actions of a risk taker, a creative venturer into a new business or the one who revives an existing business" (Hébert & Link, 1989: 39). In this process of turning ideas and inventions into innovations, Schumpeter was interested in how entrepreneurial individuals act within new companies as well as within large companies—known, respectively, as Mark I and Mark II types. In carrying out their activities, entrepreneurs must act quickly to take advantage of an opportunity before their competitors do.

A third key characteristic is that the entrepreneur challenges incumbents through creative destruction, and thereby transforms the economic system to foster economic growth and development. Here, the role of the entrepreneur is to introduce new technologies, products, production processes, and organizational forms: in this way, they destroy common ways of doing things, established products and existing production processes. Entrepreneurship thus leads to competition between entrants and incumbents as well as changes in market structure, therefore bringing dynamism into the economy. The discussion in Schumpeter (1943) portrays several characteristics and dimensions of this process. More recently, the Schumpeterian tradition has linked entrepreneurship to economic growth, by pointing to its role as a knowledge filter (Acs et al., 2009). According to this view, the knowledge created in the economy is identified and exploited by the entrepreneur, and this process helps create knowledge spillovers and exploits opportunities (Carlsson et al., 2013). In sum, the analysis of the Schumpeterian entrepreneur specifies these key aspects of understanding entrepreneurship:

- Carrying out new combinations.
- Facing uncertainty—and adapting to change.
- Taking risks but also reaping profits.
- Acting as a disruptive, dis-equilibrium force, which arises endogenously in the economy.
- Driving wider processes of innovation and economic growth.

2. *Evolutionary theory of economic change*

The second building block of our conceptualization is the evolutionary theory of economic change. For evolutionary theory, innovation and dynamics are two fundamental aspects necessary to understand the working of the economy. Innovation is the driver of economic change. In addition, three basic processes are at the base of the evolution of an economy: the creation of variety, selection and the retention of some key features. Innovation and entrepreneurship represent fundamental components of the increase in the variety of products, production processes, and organizational settings, and in the selection among companies in industries.

According to evolutionary economic theory, three aspects drive change, namely the creation and use of new knowledge through the exploration and exploitation of scientific and technological opportunities, the learning by individual and organizations, and the search for new ways of doing things.

Within the evolutionary tradition, some contributions have focused on the role of knowledge in entrepreneurship and new firm formation (Loasby, 1999). In particular, entrepreneurs create new knowledge over time and change the opportunity sets available through the interaction with the context (Holmén et al., 2007; Holmén & McKelvey, 2013). One can also consider that the entrepreneurs act as knowledge filters in the economy (Acs et al., 2009). Analyzing the types of knowledge in entrepreneurship has also been linked to the experience and the knowledge accumulated by entrepreneurs in their previous activities. The knowledge referred to is usually education and work experience. Therefore, the knowledge accumulated by the founders and teams within an industry, as well as in scientific organization and in downstream or user activities are vital, because such knowledge diffuse also drives firm entry into industries and spinoff formation (Adams et al., 2016; Klepper, 2016).

Evolutionary theory also claims that different technological regimes—as related to various dimensions of learning and knowledge—characterize the environment in which organizations operate. These regimes in turn affect innovation, entry and the dynamics of industries. The key Schumpeterian distinction between an entrepreneurial setting and a routinized setting is defined in relation to innovation and industrial dynamics. This can be associated with different types of technological regimes in different sectors. The first type is characterized by high technological opportunities, low cumulativeness of technological advance and low appropriability, which generates high rates of new organizations formation and a highly turbulent sectoral environment. The second type is characterized by high technological opportunity but also high cumulativeness and high appropriability, which leads to the much lower entry of new organizations and a more concentrated industrial structure (Winter, 1984).

Finally, the evolutionary theory emphasizes the relevance of co-evolutionary processes in the economy, where co-evolution refers especially to processes that involve knowledge, organizations industrial structure and institutions (Murmann, 2003). As far as entrepreneurship is concerned, the notion of co-evolution involves the knowledge of the entrepreneurs and the knowledge context that surrounds them. For example, McKelvey (1996) analyzes the co-evolution of scientific knowledge and innovation, which involves large organizations and entrepreneurial ventures in order to explain the emergence of a new industry, the biotechnology industry. In sum, evolutionary theory specifies these key aspects of understanding entrepreneurship:

- A process and a dynamic perspective
- Entrepreneurship as a process of searching and generating new knowledge.
- Learning and problem-solving.
- Relevance of previous knowledge and experience in affecting entrepreneurship.

- Importance of the technological and knowledge context (regimes).
- Co-evolution of knowledge, new organizations, industrial structure, and institutions.

3. *The innovation system perspective.*

Finally, the third building block refers to the role that innovation systems have in affecting entrepreneurship. Entrepreneurs do not act in isolation but interact with a variety of other actors within specific institutional settings. In particular, research within the innovation system approach has pointed out that in their innovation process, organizations interact with a wide range of heterogeneous actors ranging from suppliers and users, scientific organizations, government agencies, and financial organizations (Edquist, 1997), each of which has specific knowledge and capabilities, and hence each contributes in a different way to learning and innovation (Lundvall, 2007). These organizations and institutions more broadly shape entrepreneurs' cognition and action and affect their interactions with other agents.

Innovation systems provide the context of learning in terms of sources of knowledge, capabilities that are shared, put together or integrated and channels through which knowledge flows from one actor to another. Therefore, we argue that following this framework, the links and networks of actors are of paramount importance in the innovation process and the formation and development of entrepreneurship. Institutions differ greatly in terms of types of impact upon the behaviour of entrepreneurs. Innovation systems have been studied as primarily consisting of three types, each affecting entrepreneurship in various ways. A first type of innovation system is the national one. National innovation systems have a geographical dimension corresponding to a country including institutions and boundaries, and they were the first ones examined (Lundvall, 1993; Nelson, 1993).

National innovation systems affect the generation and diffusion of knowledge and the formation of entrepreneurship through universities and the educational system, public policy, national regulation and standardization. It has been shown that major differences exist in the national innovation system both among advanced countries and among emerging and developing countries (Lundvall, 2007). The architecture of the national systems may vary in structure and composition: some actors may be missing or do not have the necessary capabilities, some links may not work properly and mismatches among various parts of the systems may block change. All these factors may affect the innovation and entrepreneurship in a country.

Regional innovation systems represent another type of systems. Here the term regional encompasses the regional, local, or cluster level. In regional systems, the focus is on the interaction among local organizations, clusters, and institutions (Boschma & Martin, 2010). In regional systems, knowledge is shared and exchanged in various ways, which in turn affects the creation of entrepreneurship and the formation of industrial clusters. Sectoral systems are a third type of systems. They highlight the major differences across sectors in terms of knowledge, non-firm actors and the institutions that support innovation. These differences among industries generate quite different sectoral systems in terms of knowledge base of innovative activities, role of suppliers, users, universities, financial organizations and government agencies, or institutions in terms of regulation, standards, or labor markets (Malerba, 2002, 2004). Therefore entrepreneurship is affected by the specific sectoral system in terms of availability of knowledge, technological opportunities, supporting actors and institutional setting.

The sectoral dimension of innovation system has been proven to be relevant in both advanced countries and emerging and developing ones (Lee & Malerba, 2016; Malerba & Mani, 2009). Although presented as three types above, national, sectoral, and regional systems interact in their effects on entrepreneurship. Entrepreneurship is affected by national system factors in terms of national policies and regulation, by the sectoral system in terms of the specific sectoral knowledge actors and institutions which shape entrepreneurship, and finally by regional systems in terms of specific clusters in which new organizations operate or regional or local policies and institutions. In summary, the innovation system perspective specifies these key aspects of understanding entrepreneurship:

- The knowledge, supporting and institutional contexts in which entrepreneurs learn and innovate.

- The complementarities in knowledge and capabilities that affect entrepreneurship.
- The networks and channels through which knowledge is communicated, shared or generated.
- The geographical and sectoral dimensions in which entrepreneurs operate and innovate.

The Knowledge-Intensive Sectors

Knowledge-intensive sectors such as biopharmaceuticals, information technology, chemicals, and entertainment increasingly underpin sustainable growth and employment in most OECD countries. It is an association of 35 nations in Europe, the Americas, and the Pacific (see Table 4.1).

Its goal is to promote the economic welfare of its members. It coordinates its efforts to aid developing countries outside of its membership. This is not just a Western phenomenon. Advanced Asian economies such as Japan, the Republic of Korea, Singapore, and Taiwan are having over

Table 4.1 OECD member states

OECD member states	
Australia	Austria
Belgium	Canada
Chile	Czech Republic
Denmark	Estonia
Finland	France
Germany	Greece
Hungary	Iceland
Ireland	Isreal
Italy	Japan
Korea	Luxembourg
Mexico	Netherlands
New Zealand	Norway
Poland	Portugal
Slovakia	Slovenia
Spain	Sweden
Switzerland	Turkey
United Kingdom	United States

(*Source* OECD, 2021)

recent decades moved from agriculture to manufacturing to knowledge-based industries, and China is now charting its own course in this direction. As Malaysia looks to graduate to High Income Country status, it will also need to pay close attention to growing its own knowledge-based industries and participating more meaningfully in global value chains.

Knowledge-Intensive Business Services

Knowledge-Intensive Business Services (commonly known as KIBS) are services and business operations heavily reliant on professional knowledge. They are mainly concerned with providing knowledge-intensive support for the business processes of other organizations. As a result, their employment structures are heavily weighted toward scientists, engineers, and other experts. It is common to distinguish between T-KIBS (those with high use of scientific and technological knowledge—R&D services, engineering services, computer services, etc.), and P-KIBS, who are more traditional professional services—legal, accountancy, and many management consultancy and marketing services.

These services either supply products that are themselves primary sources of information and knowledge or use their specialist knowledge to produce services that facilitate their clients own activities. Consequently, KIBS usually have other businesses as their main clients, though the public sector and sometimes voluntary organisations can be important customers, and to some extent, households will feature as consumers of, for instance, legal and accountancy services. The first discussion of KIBS to use the term seems to have been in a 1995 report to the European Commission "Knowledge-Intensive Business Services: Users, Carriers and Sources of Innovation". In the decade since this appeared these sectors of the economy have continued to outperform most other sectors and have accordingly attracted a good deal of research and policy attention. They are particularly of interest in European countries such as Finland. Care should be taken in reading literature on the topic, since a number of related terms are in wide use. The European Union has recently been referring to a much broader concept of "knowledge-intensive services" recently (extending well beyond the business services) and to "business-related services" (including many services which have large markets among final consumers).

An extract from a description found in Harvard Business Online tells us: "A common characteristic of knowledge-intensive business service (KIBS) organizations is that clients routinely play a critical role in co-producing the service solution along with the service provider. This can have a profound effect on both the quality of the service delivered as well as the client's ultimate satisfaction with the knowledge-based service solution. By strategically managing client co-production, service providers can improve operational efficiency, develop more optimal solutions and generate a sustainable competitive advantage."

Knowledge-Intensive Entrepreneurship in Malaysia

The Government of Malaysia supports the knowledge-intensive entrepreneurship by implementing digital entrepreneurship ecosystem and is committed to transforming Malaysia into a knowledge-based developed economy. Datuk Seri Dr. Wan Azizah Wan Ismail, the ex-Deputy Prime Minister mentioned that the Government aspired for this developed economy to be one which was inclusive and sustainable, as well as one that empowered all levels of the multi-racial society. Dr. Wan Azizah said digital innovation and entrepreneurship have the potential to change how Malaysians interact with the world. Malaysia as a growing nation with great ambitions to join the league of high-income and developed nations. Hence, the digital economy was a new driver for development and was now a major source of growth for the world as it provided an opportunity to boost growth, expand jobs and accelerate innovation. Malaysia has been recognized by many organizations as one of ASEAN's best markets to do business in. The digital population in Malaysia shows high penetration rate of both the internet and smartphones, Malaysia is home to a population that can only be described as "internet savvy." Malaysia estimated about US 1.03 billion for mobile payment transaction value by 2021.

Malaysian Initiatives: Earn Income as a Digital Worker

The Digital Economy is a level playing field offering opportunities to Malaysians from all walks of life. These programs and initiatives are for all Malaysians and designed to open up additional income avenues, provide new skills training and offer opportunities to thrive in the new Digital Economy. The programs are as follows:

1. #eRezeki—Earn extra income from anywhere with an Internet connection.
2. #eUsahawan—Pick up the skills to grow your business in a digital environment.
3. GLOW—Discover your next career move as part of the Global Online Workforce.
4. eCommerce—See how eCommerce is driving the development of Malaysia's Digital Economy.

As advancements in technology continue to disrupt the traditional workspace, it has become increasingly important to futureproof the nation's workforce for the digital era. With Professional Upskilling initiatives, Malaysians can access the necessary tools and knowledge in many of the major sectors of the digital ecosystem—data analytics, artificial intelligence, and cybersecurity. The programs are as follows:

1. Go eCommerce—Discover how we're assisting startups and industry veterans to embrace e-Commerce.
2. Cybersecurity—See how Cybersecurity plays a pivotal role in the country's digital agenda.

The youth of today are the leaders of tomorrow. If Malaysia is to remain a key digital player in the future, the country must begin equipping our youth with the knowledge to do so. Launched in partnership with public and private academic institutions, our Tech Talent Development initiatives aim to empower the nation's youth by providing them access to the digital ecosystem. The goal of this project is to have the youth drive digital innovation in the not-so-distant future.

Knowledge-Based Economy in Malaysia

Knowledge is defined as information combined with experience, context, interpretation, and reflection (Davenport et al., 1998). Knowledge is commonly distinguished from data and information. Knowledge is believed and valued on the basis of the meaningfully organized accumulation of information through experience, communication, or inference. Knowledge can be viewed both as a thing to be stored and manipulated and as a process of simultaneously knowing and acting—that is, applying expertise.

The knowledge-based economy is the basis to sustain a rapid rate of economic growth and enhance international competitiveness so as to achieve Vision 2020. The development thrusts for the knowledge-based economy are based on the following: Building the knowledge manpower base, among others, through a comprehensive review of the education and training system, the implementation/expansion of a system for life-long learning and programs to attract, motivate, and retain the skilled talent needed for a high-income economy; Intensifying efforts in demand-driven Science and Technology and R&D initiatives.

Expanding the development of info structure to facilitate the development of the knowledge-based economy, the financial system which is in line with the development of knowledge-based activities could raise the knowledge content in the agriculture, manufacturing, and services sectors. Getting the small–medium enterprises to prepare themselves with greater urgency for the knowledge-based economy as well as identify and exploit the opportunities in the domain of business. Proficient public sector in acquisition, utilization, dissemination, and management of knowledge goes along with ethical utilization of knowledge by taking affirmative action to bridge the digital divide between income, ethnic and age groups, urban and rural communities, and across regions. In addition, the Knowledge-based Economy Master Plan (KEMP) launched in 2002 contains 136 recommendations encompassing human resource development, information structure, incentives, science and technology development, reorientation of the private and public sectors as well as addressing the digital divide.

The transformation toward a Knowledge-Based Economy has started in Malaysia. Many organizations realize the importance of knowledge and how it will effect their future. Knowledge management will play an increasingly important role in organization production processes rather than labour workforces. Currently, knowledge management is not just restricted to the ICT government sector, it is also widely used in the private hospitality industry. In the service industry, knowledge is very important in order to provide the latest information that customers require immediately. With knowledge, they are able to support customers solve challenging problems in a rapid time period.

Knowledge is not only embodied in goods and services, particularly in high technology industries, but also it is a commodity itself, manifested in forms such as intellectual property rights or in the tacit knowledge of highly mobile key employees. Knowledge includes information regarding how to interact as individuals within a community. In addition, technology breakthrough based on knowledge creates technical platforms that support further innovations and drive economic growth.

Knowledge-Intensive Economy in Malaysia

The currency attacks of mid-1997 and the financial turmoil that followed have seriously undermined Malaysia's economic situation. A few years before the Asian financial crisis hit the Malaysian economy, the Prime Minister of Malaysia announced the establishment of the Multimedia Super Corridor (MSC) to assist in the economic transformation of the country from a production-based economy (P-economy) to a knowledge-based economy (K-economy). Knowledge, in addition to labour, land, and capital, is now accepted as one of the key factors of production that drive the economy. New technologies and innovations are created through the application of knowledge to facilitate economic growth. Acquiring knowledge regarding customer behavior, markets, economics, technology, and other resources not only opens new ways of wealth creation but also ensures the competitiveness of a country's economy. The shift that Malaysia is making toward a knowledge-based economy has a direct implication on the entrepreneurship domain.

Promoting Electronic Commerce and enhancing its use to enable Malaysia to compete more effectively in the global market special focus will be given toward promoting and encouraging wider use of e-commerce as a new way of doing business through the digital network. The Government will also undertake measures to build trust and confidence in e-commerce including security and user privacy. Infrastructure and logistical support, which encompass networks, payment systems and logistics, will also be provided to enhance the development of e-commerce. Business and communities will be encouraged to respond and participate actively in the development and the usage of e-commerce.

In addition, fostering local capabilities in creative content development In developing Malaysia as a competitor in the area of creative multimedia, several initiatives are being undertaken to foster local capabilities in creative content development. To further support and encourage the development of creative content industry locally, the Government will develop clear and precise rules on intellectual property rights protection. This will be complemented by affective enforcement to combat piracy. The implementation of key strategies to propel ICT industry through MSC Malaysia will identify and support the development of niche areas in software and e-solutions, creative multimedia, shared services, and outsourcing as well as e-business. A tiered benefits scheme will be established whereby financial and non-financial benefits will be provided based on the company's needs, size stage of maturity and criteria such as the ability to catalyze the development of SMEs in priority sectors and induce high spill-over effects. The Government will aggressively promote the use of ICT in all industries in parallel with the development of the ICT sector. Cloud computing services will be developed to provide SMEs with critical software applications for customer relations management, enterprise resource planning, supply chain management, human resource management, and financial and accounting management.

Niche areas for applications development include healthcare, education, and financial services especially in Islamic Banking. The National

Transformation Programme or Digital Malaysia is undertaken to stimulate the development of the digital economy by 2020. This programme will create an ecosystem that promotes the pervasive use of ICT in all aspects of the economy to connect communities globally and interact in real-time, resulting in increased Gross National Income (GNI), enhanced productivity and improved standards of living. Overall, the implementation of the Digital Malaysia will benefit the Government and business communities as well as citizens.

Conclusions

One significant part concerning how to generate the knowledge-intensive ventures is to outline and foster innovation ecosystems as to connect technological evolution. The knowledge infrastructure of innovation ecosystems has long been associated with the overall capabilities of organizations. Therefore, an open innovation approaches of incumbents bring opportunities for KIE organizations to emerge and thrive. A main issue regarding the interactions between KIE ventures and the broader innovation ecosystem refers to the dynamics of value co-creation among agents in an environment of open innovation.

As can be gleaned from this chapter, the Malaysian government has been, and continues to be, supportive of entrepreneurship. It has taken various steps to promote the development of entrepreneurs overall (including providing a tax incentives, conducive economic background, various financing and funding schemes, as well as business advisory centers). The government has regarded nurturing entrepreneurs as a way to facilitate and upgrade the industrial structure so as to create industries for the next generation. For this reason, the government has paid special attention to the development of SMIs/SMEs. It is apparent, however, that a paradigm shift and some enhancement in policy-making processes are required for further development to occur. As the Malaysian economy is changed from manufacturing-based to knowledge-based, the kind of businesses and entrepreneurs, as well as their needs and anxieties, are likely to change as well. This gives rise to the need for closer discussion between the private sector, entrepreneurs and the government agencies.

References

Acs, Z., Braunerhjelm, P., Audretsch, D., & Carlsson, B. (2009). The knowledge spillover theory of entrepreneurship. *Small Business Economics, 32*(1), 15–30. https://doi.org/10.1007/s11187-008-9157-3.

Adams, P., Fontana, R., & Malerba, F. (2016). User-industry spinouts: downstream knowledge as a source of entry and survival. *Organization Science, 27*(1), 18–35. https://doi.org/10.1287/orsc.2015.1029.

Alvarez, S., & Barney, J. (2007). The entrepreneurial theory of the firm. *Journal of Management Studies, 44*(7), 1057–1063. https://doi.org/10.1111/j.1467-6486.2007.00721.x.

Alvarez, S., Barney, J., & Anderson, P. (2013). Forming and exploiting opportunities: The implications of discovery and creation processes for entrepreneurial and organizational research. *Organization Science, 24*(1), 301–317. https://doi.org/10.1287/orsc.1110.0727.

Boschma, R., & Frenken, K. (2011). Technological relatedness and regional branching. In H. Bathelt, M. Feldman, & D. Kogler (Eds.), *Beyond territory: Dynamic geographies of knowledge creation, diffusion and innovation* (p. 2011). Routledge.

Boschma, R., & Martin, R. (2010). *The handbook of evolutionary economic geography*. Edward Elgar Publishers.

Breschi, S., Malerba, F., & Orsenigo, L. (2000). Technological regimes and Schumpeterian patterns of innovation. *The Economic Journal, 110*(463), 388–410. https://doi.org/10.1111/1468-0297.00530.

Buenstorf, G. (2007). Creation and pursuit of entrepreneurial opportunities: An evolutionary economics perspective. *Small Business Economics, 28*(4), 323–337. https://doi.org/10.1007/s11187-006-9039-5.

Carlsson, B., Braunerhjelm, P., McKelvey, M., Olofsson, C., Persson, L., & Ylinenpää, H. (2013). The evolving domain of entrepreneurship research. *Small Business Economics, 41*, 913–930. https://doi.org/10.1007/s11187-013-9503-y.

Edquist, C. (1997). *Systems of innovation: Technologies*. Institutions and Organizations, Pinter Publishers/Cassell Academic.

Eurostat. (2014). *Eurostat indicators of high-tech industry and knowledge intensive services*. Eurostat Metadata. http://ec.europa.eu/eurostat/cache/metadata/FR/htec%5C_esms.htm.

Garud, R., & Karnoe, P. (2001). Path creation as a process of mindful deviation. In R. Garud & P. Karnoe (Eds.), *Path Dependence and Path Creation* (pp. 1–38). Mahwah: Lawrence Erlbaum Associates.

Hérbert, R., & Link, A. (1989). Search of the meaning of entrepreneurship. *Small Business Economics, 1*(1), 39–49. https://doi.org/10.1007/BF00389915.

Holmén, M., Magnusson, M., & McKelvey, M. (2007). What are innovative opportunities? *Industry and Innovation, 14*(1), 27–45. https://doi.org/10.1080/13662710601130830.

Holmén, M., & McKelvey, M. (2013). Restless capitalism and the economizing entrepreneur. *Economics of Innovation and New Technology, 22*(7), 684–701. https://doi.org/10.1080/10438599.2013.795780.

Kirzner, I. M. (1997). Entrepreneurial discovery and the competitive market process: an Austrian approach. *Journal of Economic Literature, 35*(1), 60–85.

Klepper, S. (2015). *Experimental capitalism: The nanoeconomics of American high-tech industries*. Princeton University Press.

Lachmann, L. M. (1986). *The market as an economic process*. Oxford, UK: Basil Blackwell.

Landström, H., Harirchi, G., & Åström, F. (2012). Entrepreneurship: Exploring the knowledge base. *Research Policy, 41*(7), 1154–1181. https://doi.org/10.1016/j.respol.2012.03.009.

Lee, K. & Malerba, F. (2016). Catch-up cycles and changes in industrial leadership: Windows of opportunity and responses of firms and countries in the evolution of sectoral systems. Research Policy.

Loasby, B. (1999). *Knowledge, institutions and evolution in economics: The Graz Schumpeter lectures*. Routledge.

Lundvall, B.-Å. (1993). *National systems of innovation: Towards a theory of innovation and interactive learning*. Pinter.

Lundvall, B.-Å. (2007). National innovation systems-analytical concept and development tool. *Industry and Innovation, 14*(1), 95–119. https://doi.org/10.1080/13662710601130863.

Malerba, F. (2002). Sectoral systems of innovation and production. *Research Policy, 31*(2), 247–264. https://doi.org/10.1016/S0048-7333(01)00139-1.

Malerba, F. (2004). *Sectoral systems of innovation*. Cambridge University Press.

Malerba, F., & Mani, S. (2009). *Sectoral systems of innovation and production in developing countries*. Edward Elgar.

Malerba, F., & McKelvey, M. (2018). Knowledge intensive entrepreneurship: Integrating Schumpeter, evolutionary economics and innovation systems. *Small Business Economics, 13*, 1–20. https://doi.org/10.1007/s11187-018-0060-2.

McKelvey, M. (1996). *Evolutionary innovations: The business of biotechnology.* Oxford University Press.

Murmann, P. (2003). *Knowledge and competitive advantage: The co-evolution of firms, technology and national institutions.* Cambridge University Press.

Nelson, R. R. (1993). *National innovation systems: A comparative study.* Oxford University Press.

OECD. (2021). *Where: Global reach.* Available online. https://www.oecd.org/about/members-and-partners/.

Schumpeter, J. A., & Nichol, A. J. (1934). Robinson's economics of imperfect competition. *Journal of Political Economy, 42*(2), 249–259.

Schumpeter, J. (1942). *Capitalism, socialism and democracy.*

Schumpeter, J. A. (1943). Capitalism in the postwar world. In S. E. Harris (Ed.), *Postwar economic problems, in essays* (Schumpeter, 1951).

Winter, S. (1984). Schumpeterian competition in alternative technological regimes. *Journal of Economic Behavior & Organization, 5*(3–4), 287–320.

5

The Role of Government and Higher Education in Developing Social Entrepreneurship in Malaysia

Norasmah Othman
and Radin Siti Aishah Radin A. Rahman

Introduction

Social entrepreneurship in Malaysia has expanded significantly in recent years, adopting a modified approach to traditional entrepreneurship by valuing both social change and the dynamic growth of the national economy (Henley, 2007; Shane & Venkataraman, 2000). This approach has been adopted by entrepreneurs in many developed regions such as the United States and Europe and is increasingly being recognized by those in developing economic regions such as India, Indonesia, Vietnam, the Philippines, and Thailand (Global Entrepreneurship Monitor, 2015). Social entrepreneurship, which focuses on social welfare and developing civic engagement, has become a platform for a variety of educational programs and for people who seek to improve the quality of life in their communities (Light, 2008; Mair & Marti, 2006; Radin A. Rahman,

N. Othman · R. S. A. Radin A. Rahman (✉)
Universiti Kebangsaan Malaysia, Bangi, Malaysia
e-mail: radin@ukm.edu.my

2016). Social entrepreneurs are individuals who have innovative solutions to social problems, and who contribute to economic growth by seeking new and improved ways of implementing solutions with goals that differ from commercial entrepreneurs who associate success with profitability (Johnson, 2002). Social entrepreneurs have the business acumen of traditional entrepreneurs; however, they use this skill to act as an agent of change in their community, often identifying innovative approaches to solving social issues (Ashoka, 2009). The qualities that exist in social entrepreneurship must be developed and nurtured in students to create future leaders with a social outlook.

Social entrepreneurship plays a key role in enhancing a country's socio-economic development by generating diverse innovations and creating new job opportunities (Henley, 2007). Moreover, social entrepreneurship has emerged as a catalyst for the triple bottom line approach—the measurement of success in community development through social, environmental, and economic aspects (Abdul Kadir et al., 2019). The Malaysian government has introduced various support programs for entrepreneurs in the form of business grants, credit financing, and incentives on business tax, particularly during the initial stages of business development (MaGIC, 2015). Recent economic uncertainty has also increased investment in the national development sector (Ministry of Finance, 2020). The implementation of the Malaysian Social Enterprise Blueprint (MSEB), 2015–2018, has succeeded in achieving its objective to promote social entrepreneurship opportunities, demonstrated by an increase in the number of youths interested in becoming social entrepreneurs. In Malaysia context, social enterprise is legally recognized as legitimate business entities seeking to create positive social and environmental impacts and financial sustainability (Social Enterprise Accreditation Guideline, 2019). However, the social entrepreneurial sector is lacking standards and consistent guidelines for compliance and audit purposes.

There are currently approximately 1,000 social enterprises operating in Malaysia that address issues in education, poverty, rural development, environmental sustainability, employment for the marginalized, and at-risk teens (Malaysian Social Enterprise Blueprint 2015–2018). Bacq and

Janssen (2011) focus on the need to drive interest in social entrepreneurship and their research suggests that there are two key factors in attracting potential entrepreneurs: innovation in solving complex social problems (Nicholls, 2010; Weerawardena & Mort, 2006), as demonstrated through the examples of successful local (Amanah Ikhtiar Malaysia) and global (Grameen Bank) social enterprises, and the use of market solutions to address difficult social problems within a community to reduce dependence on the private sector and the government.

Discussion on social entrepreneurship among students requires prioritization to achieve Malaysia's objective of becoming a developed country. Social entrepreneurship in higher education institutions is in its infancy and all related activities are conducted informally (The States of Social Enterprise in Malaysia, 2018). Most institutions offer entrepreneurial business courses that focus on maximizing profit without considering the social impact. Therefore, students seeking involvement in social entrepreneurship activities must join clubs established by non-government organizations (NGOs) such as ENACTUS and Pandemic.

Social entrepreneurship is not an officially recognized field of study in Malaysian vocational training institutions; however, efforts toward developing the field of social entrepreneurship are being pursued by raising awareness of the concept of social entrepreneurship and celebrating students' activities with the community. The effort to nurture students' entrepreneurial skills in Malaysia begins with the involvement of students in club activities such as workshops, competitions, and networking sessions, and some of these clubs have succeeded in establishing social enterprises for at-risk members of the community and providing employment opportunities. The level of interest in social entrepreneurship from young Malaysians is growing, evidenced by the increasing number of social enterprises established each year and youth ownership levels. A report by The States of Social Enterprise in Malaysia, 2019, found that most social enterprises in Malaysia are at least 50% owned by youths under the age of 40. Che Nawi et al. (2018) show that the motivation of young people to become social entrepreneurs is driven by the state of the environment, an interest in business and social activities, and a desire to help and develop the surrounding community.

Defining Social Entrepreneurship

The entrepreneurial process involves the relationship between two phenomena: the existence of profitable opportunities and the presence of enterprising individuals (Shane & Venkataraman, 2000). Profitable opportunities in the context of social entrepreneurship refer to the potential to create social innovations that can transform the lives of marginalized people and sustainably improve the environment while also realizing a profit (Mair & Marti, 2006). While not a new concept, a clear definition of social entrepreneurship is the subject of debate (Okpara & Halkias, 2011). Various definitions exist from previous research depending on the context of the study and demographics. Shaw and Carter (2007) broadly define social entrepreneurship as the communities, volunteers, public organizations, and private companies engaged in social work to achieve social and profitable outcomes. The sustainability of a social enterprise depends on the ability of entrepreneurs to remain profitable while fulfilling their social goals. (Robinson et al., 2009).

Dacin et al. (2010) defined social entrepreneurship as a subfield of entrepreneurship. Moreover, a social entrepreneur identifies a need within a community and develops a social enterprise (Petrella & Riches-Battesti, 2014). Neck et al. (2009) emphasize the issues social entrepreneurs face in trying to simultaneously fulfill social and economic goals. According to Mair and Marti (2006), social entrepreneurs can either be not-for-profit entrepreneurs seeking alternative financing or commercial businesses performing their social responsibility to improve the society in which they operate. There are conceptual differences between the multitude of definitions found within the literature. Table 5.1 provides a comparison of the definitions of social entrepreneurship summarized by characteristics and goals (Radin A. Rahman, 2016). Most researchers define the characteristics of social entrepreneurship as having the business skills to produce social innovations aimed at solving the problems of marginalized groups.

Table 5.1 Definitions of social entrepreneurship

Author	Definition	Characteristics	Objective
Alvord et al. (2004)	Creating innovative solutions to social problems by mobilizing the ideas, capabilities, resources, and social arrangements needed for sustainable social change	Innovative solutions	To solve social problems
Shaw (2004)	Community services, voluntary and public organizations, and private companies working for both social purposes and profit	Community service and volunteerism	To value both social outcomes and profit
Duke University [Fuqua School of Business] (2005)	The art of investment toward both financial and social returns	Investment	To realize social returns
MacMillan (2005)	The process of setting up new business enterprises that lead to an increase in social wealth for the benefit of the community and entrepreneurs	Social wealth	To benefit the community and entrepreneurs
Oxford University Said Business School (2005)	A professional, innovative, and ongoing approach to business that involves systematic changes to solve social market failures and improve opportunities	Innovation	To develop the social market

(continued)

Table 5.1 (continued)

Author	Definition	Characteristics	Objective
Schwab Foundation (2005)	Practical, innovative, and sustainable approaches that benefit the community, especially the marginalized and the poor	Practical and sustainable innovation	To improve the lives of disadvantaged members of the community
New York University [Stern] (2005)	The process of attaining business and entrepreneurial skills to create innovative approaches to tackle social problems	Business and entrepreneurial skills	To solve social problems
Tan et al. (2005)	Involves the benefits of innovation and faces the challenges of communities in which all or some of the benefits are not equally distributed	Innovation and risk	Community benefit
Austin et al. (2006)	Innovative creation of social value activities across the not-for-profit, business, and government sectors	Innovation	To develop the not-for-profit, and government sectors
Mair and Marti (2006)	An innovative model that provides products and services to meet basic needs	Innovation	To meet basic needs

Author	Definition	Characteristics	Objective
Nicholls (2006)	Innovations designed to enhance the well-being of the community, provide a startup position for entrepreneurial organizations, and guide and contribute to positive change in society	Innovation	To improve the well-being of a society
Peredo and McLean (2006)	People or groups that aim to create social value, take the opportunity to innovate, are prepared to take risks in creating and disseminating social values, and are exceptional in utilizing limited resources in pursuit of their social goals	Social values, seeking opportunities, social innovation, taking risks and being exceptional	To achieve social goals
Martin and Osberg (2007)	Identifies the characteristics of instability to improve the lives of those in disadvantaged groups, identifies opportunities and develops new social values to challenge the imbalances in society, and supports a stable ecosystem in the context of reducing injustices to marginalized communities to create a better future	Social value and balance of the community ecosystem	To support disadvantaged groups

(continued)

Table 5.1 (continued)

Author	Definition	Characteristics	Objective
Yusof et al. (2013)	The process of developing social values to meet social needs by seeking and exploiting opportunities in new or existing business innovations	Social value and innovation	To address societal needs
Social Enterprise Accreditation Guideline (2019)	A business entity registered under any written law in the country that proactively creates positive social and environmental impact and is financially sustainable	A business entity registered under any written law	To create social, environmental, and financial impacts

Source Radin A. Rahman (2016)

The Development of Social Entrepreneurship in Malaysia

The development of social entrepreneurship in Malaysia commenced in 1986 in response to the success of Grameen Bank in Bangladesh, which was led by Professor David Gibbons and Professor Sukor Kassim of the University of Science, Malaysia (Amanah Ikhtiar Malaysia, 2011). Grameen Bank was initially established and owned by the borrowers themselves and has been influential in providing microfinance-related services to poor rural areas (Bayulgen, 2008). It has clearly demonstrated that some of the social objectives of a poverty alleviation program can be achieved using a business model. This concept was used to initiate the Ikhtiar Project, now known as Amanah Ikhtiar Malaysia (AIM), which offers micro-credit loans to impoverished people with the objective of reducing rural poverty. Since the establishment of AIM, the concept of social entrepreneurship has gradually been incorporated into the public and private sector agendas as well as not-for-profit organizations nationwide.

Government Support

Global examples have demonstrated the potential of social entrepreneurship to contribute to GDP in the long term. The United Kingdom, for example, has 70,000 social enterprises employing over one million people, contributing over 5% of the nation's GDP (Chong, 2015). The MSEB target of producing 1,000 social enterprises by 2018 was been achieved and the total number is now 2,000 (The State of Social Enterprise in Malaysia, 2018). In addition, Malaysia's New Development Policy (2016–2020) contains a Social Entrepreneurship Action Plan to support the MSEB in achieving a sustainable, fair, and amiable entrepreneurship sector. Moreover, the Malaysian government offers incentives to entities and programs such as the Malaysian Global Innovation and Creativity Center (MaGIC), the 1Malaysia Entrepreneurs (1Met) initiative, and the Graduate Entrepreneur Fund program (Economic Report 2014/2015). The government has also invested USD$5.6 million toward the MaGIC to encourage Malaysian youths to venture into the field of social entrepreneurship and to provide them with a support system.

Social entrepreneurship activities have been incorporated into the programs of many government ministries, as shown in Table 5.1. The Rural Industry Centre was established in 2002 by the Ministry of Information, Communication, and Culture to increase access to information for those in rural communities. The intent of this program was to bridge the digital gap between rural and urban communities through cooperation with the Japan International Cooperation Agency. The program highlighted the local post office as a focal point within the community. As a result, the Ministry, in collaboration with postal service Pos Malaysia Berhad, built 42 additional fully equipped post offices in rural areas. Moreover, the Rural Industry Centre has established social entrepreneur clubs, which include telecentre supervisors, local entrepreneurs, and community members, aimed at carrying out commercial and social activities.

The Ministry of Women, Family, and Community Development, in partnership with the Social Entrepreneurship Foundation, initiated the Economic Generating Family Aspiration program in which women from low-income families can generate income from home through the Small Office, Home Office concept. The Department of Social Welfare allocated USD$2.34 million to launch the Purple DNA Entrepreneurship Programme in May 2012. The program aimed to introduce a business model based on the principles of social entrepreneurship and to empower marginalized groups. The National Entrepreneurial Institute under the Ministry of International Trade and Industry launched the Social Entrepreneurship Project to encourage an entrepreneurial culture among students and established the volunteer program Social Enterprise and Economic Development, aimed at fostering the spirit of volunteerism in tandem with social entrepreneurship in public Higher Education Institutions (HEIs) and universities. The Ministry of Higher Education (MHE) formulated a strategy in 2011 to incorporate the elements of social entrepreneurship as a platform to bridge the economic gap between society and industry. In 2015, the MHE successfully implemented the social entrepreneur program called Women in Social

Enterprise (WISE) to instill entrepreneurial values in students through social entrepreneurship activities, to empower micro-entrepreneurs with business skills that positively impact their socio-economic development, and to enhance strategic partnerships between HEIs and industries in the community development sector. WISE is a national level program and is part of the Ministry's program to enhance the delivery and the contributions of HEIs to society, through the Blue Ocean Strategy in the Government Transformation Programme.

The MHE's 2011 National Higher Education Strategic Plan 2 strengthened the quality and sustainability of community skills through the "My Community Programme" which aimed to produce 1,000 social entrepreneurs in three years. This program has achieved its target. MHE also introduced the "I Am for Youth" program to encourage students to venture into social entrepreneurship. These initiatives highlight the Malaysian government's commitment to promoting the culture of social entrepreneurship, fostering the spirit of volunteerism among young people and providing information to assist youths to understand the goal of producing innovations that benefit society. Most of the social entrepreneurship programs by the government and NGOs in Malaysia involve students, such as the 1Malaysia Young Entrepreneur Challenge Programme, which is a social entrepreneurship concept program in collaboration with the Entrepreneur Development Division, the Ministry of International Trade and Industry and non-profit organization such as ENACTUS Malaysia Foundation. In addition, social entrepreneurship programs are also implemented at the internal level of ministry agencies in Malaysia as shown briefly in (Table 5.2).

The Status of Social Entrepreneurship in Malaysia

The development of a country's social entrepreneurship industry is influenced by current trends and an awareness of the current socio-economic levels of marginalized groups. Social entrepreneurship in European countries developed in Italy in the late 1980s and expanded in the mid-1990s (Defourny & Nyssens, 2008) in response to the success of social

Table 5.2 Emphasis on social entrepreneurship by Malaysian Government Ministries

Agency	Programme	Objective
Ministry of Information, Communication, and Culture	Rural Internet Centre	To establish a telecentre to allow rural communities access to communications information
Ministry of Women, Family, and Community Development	Economics in Generating Family Aspiration	To establish the concept of Small Office, Home Office to enable women entrepreneurs to undertake business from home
	Phase Two Action Plan	To use social entrepreneurship as a platform to bridge the economic gap between society and industry
Ministry of Higher Education Malaysia	National Higher Education Strategic Plan 2 (2011)	To develop social entrepreneurship skills hub through the My Community programme

Agency	Programme	Objective
	Formal Education	To develop knowledge, skills, and competencies in the field of social entrepreneurship. The course also introduces a socially-oriented curriculum including concepts, theories, models, and practices of social entrepreneurship through learning experiences to solve marginalized and environmental issues
	The Bachelor of Social Entrepreneurship programme at Universiti Malaysia Perlis	
	The Social entrepreneurship programmes at Universiti Malaysia Kelantan and Universiti Malaysia Sabah	
	The Centre for Social Entrepreneurship Research at Binary University College and Tun Abdul Razak University (Unirazak)	The specific objectives of these courses are:
• To generate social entrepreneurship ideas and a business plan in the social field
• To actively participate in the local community through both informal and non-formal methods
• To use European best practices;
• To identify and analyze the most realistic and pragmatic strategies for the development of social enterprises

(continued)

Table 5.2 (continued)

Agency	Programme	Objective
	Informal education	
	Entrepreneurial ENACTUS or SIFE in all HEIs The Social Enterprise and Economic Development programme Finishing Schools by the Universiti Teknologi Mara	The specific objectives of these clubs are: • To empower the ideas and aspirations of students and alumni to enable a positive change in society and the environment • To solve issues and explore opportunities in social and environmental sustainability
	Women in Social Enterprise (WISE)	To implement entrepreneurial value in students through social entrepreneurship activities, empowering the micro-entrepreneur community, and enhancing strategic partnerships of HEIs and industry to support community development
Ministry of International Trade and Industry	Social Entrepreneurship Project (2012)	To encourage the culture of entrepreneurship among students in HEIs through National Entrepreneurship Institute
Department of Prime Minister	I Am For Youth programme	To encourage volunteerism among the youth through social entrepreneurship activities
Department of Social Welfare	Purple DNA Entrepreneurship Programme	To assist those in need through community-based rehabilitation programmes

Source Radin A. Rahman (2016)

enterprises in Bangladesh. It subsequently expanded to Latin America, Japan, and South Korea. According to a report by the 2015 Global Entrepreneurship Monitor, the growth of social entrepreneurship activities in Malaysia is low, at only 0.3%. Social entrepreneurship in Malaysia is in its infancy (MSEB, 2015–2018) with courses offered only at certain HEIs through clubs and associations. The development of these social entrepreneurship activities is measured by an increase in any type of activity, organization, or initiative which has social, environmental, or community goals. The 2013 reports by Mhd Sarif, Ismail, and Sarwar and the 2018 reports by The State of Social Enterprise in Malaysia found that most Malaysians are still unaware of the emergence of social entrepreneurship and how to benefit from such activities.

Psychological research has shown that social entrepreneurship is capable of transforming entrepreneurs with the sole motivation of generating profit, into volunteering-oriented entrepreneurs (Ernst, 2011) with a willingness to provide human resources, financing, and premises to meet needs that cannot be addressed by the national welfare system (Thompson et al., 2000). While the role of the Ministry of Youth and Sports Malaysia is to plan volunteer programs to improve the lives of marginalized people, the 2016 Malaysian Youth Index survey shows that Malaysian youths' interest in entrepreneurship is at a moderate level, with a score of 62.95 in 2015 and 64.36 in 2016. An increase of 1.41 demonstrates that the government and NGOs are committed to implementing entrepreneurship programs and introducing platforms and places for the youth to enter the entrepreneurship field.

The results of the 2011 MHE Graduate Detection Survey for the Research and Planning Division show that interest in starting a business has significantly increased among public university graduates from 3.8% in 2009 to 45.9% in 2011 and private university graduates from 5.1% in 2011 to 28.7% in 2013. Meanwhile, the 2013–2014 Global University Entrepreneurial Spirit Students' Survey International Report shows that the value of students' interest in entrepreneurship in Malaysia is 5.0, which is above the global average value of 3.7 and higher than Singapore (3.9) and many other developed countries. These findings show that there is an increase in interest in entrepreneurial businesses among Malaysian youths and that a focus on social entrepreneurship is appropriate.

Social Entrepreneurship Activities in Malaysia

The government's encouragement to expand the social entrepreneurship sector has been welcomed by Malaysian people. This is evident in the establishment of social enterprises such as the AIM, Mangkuk Tingkat.Com, Scholarlist, TechnoCount, and Tandemic. The establishment of social enterprises is driven by the motivation of business owners to offer products or services to disadvantaged members of the community and to provide new job opportunities for those most in need.

Aim

AIM plays a role in addressing farmers' poverty issues through micro-credit offerings in rural areas. Professor Eunuch and Professor David Gibbon started the AIM Project using the same approach as Grameen Bank in Bangladesh. This financing enables agricultural activities to be undertaken to increase the income of the marginalized. The role of AIM is not only to help the poor but also to indirectly contribute to the country's economic development. AIM sets out three main objectives: to reduce poverty among poor households in Malaysia through micro-credit financing and by financing activities that increase and raise income; to provide continuous financial aid to social entrepreneurs; and to provide ongoing guidance and training to the poor and extremely poor and also to entrepreneurs (Amanah Ikhtiar Malaysia, 2011).

Mangkuk Tingkat.Com

Mangkuk Tingkat.Com was founded by Ameer Soekre Ishak in 2006 with the aim to start a profit-oriented business. The founders adhere to the principle of teaching people to be self-sufficient rather than relying on others. The project has grown by offering free training and skills courses to orphans, unemployed graduates, secondary school graduates, and low-income groups in collaboration with the State Islamic Religious Council. Business is conducted online by supplying and delivering lunch and dinner to customers who book the service. The company has been effective in alleviating the financial burden of the less fortunate (Sharuddin, 2008) and its success has gained attention in print and electronic media.

Scholarlist

Social enterprises were also developed in 2012 through the success of the 'Scholar-list' established by Brian Law, an ENACTUS Alumni and a graduate of the Universiti Utara Malaysia. 'Scholar-list' is a consulting firm that conducts educational programs for Malaysian secondary school students, such as the Scholarlist Education Carnival, the Tour De Future, and the Edutainment Tour. These programs assist students to make informed decisions regarding their career pathways and employment based on their talents and interests. The business also offers career advisory services from industry professionals and has received a positive response with 15,000 participants from 60 schools.

Technocount

The Technocount project, founded in 2013 by Engku Zaida Engku Abdul Rahman from Universiti Kebangsaan Malaysia, specializes in computerized accounting systems and accounting development and is managed by Technocount Consulting Services. The project offers simplified and systematic QNE Accounting System services without the need for business owners to own the entire system, alleviating the problems faced by small and medium-sized enterprises that often have trouble maintaining accounting records. The service costs as little as USD$11.7 per month for six months. In addition, the firm manages 11 business consultants with a target of 200 consultants.

Tandemic

There are other examples of programs that mirror social entrepreneurship under the management of Tandemic, an NGO founded in 2015 by Kal Joffres and Gwen Yi. This organization has been successful in many social enterprise programs among the youth including EPICHomes and Do Something Good. Tandemic has helped in developing the community through social and volunteer innovation. The project uses a technology platform to enable the creation of products, processes, and systems that support marginalized groups.

The EPIC Homes program has the ultimate goal of bridging the inequity between urban and rural areas through the simple home building. The company trains and empowers people with no previous experience in construction or engineering to build homes for indigenous families living in rural areas, with an aim to provide 12,000 homes for indigenous families. Do Something Good is a one-stop hub program designed to transform volunteering in Malaysia, stating that volunteering activities should facilitate the society, be enjoyable, and provide meaningful experiences for each volunteer. Volunteers are responsible for finding and choosing NGOs based on their interests and location. The program includes 30,000 registered individual users and 300 organizations and generates revenue through licensing volunteers' technology and helping firms manage volunteering work opportunities across a variety of target groups including education, homelessness, and welfare.

ENACTUS

ENACTUS is one of the key social entrepreneurship-based education programs in Malaysia and is designed to shape the personal characteristics of social entrepreneurs with a learning approach that empowers students to be resilient and competitive. The ENACTUS program has a high participation rate within HEIs and serves as a benchmark in developing quality, resilience, competitiveness, and competence through a social entrepreneurship approach.

ENACTUS is responsible for organizing and implementing programs that encourage students to participate in economic and social activities within the local community. This organization, formerly known as Students in Free Enterprise (SIFE), was founded in Texas, USA, by Robert T. Davis on behalf of the National Leadership Institute, and was introduced in Malaysia in 2000 under the management of Universiti Teknologi Mara through the Malaysian Entrepreneur Development Centre. ENACTUS is a not-for-profit organization that works closely with business leaders and HEIs to mobilize university students to make changes in the community. Students of ENACTUS programs can develop the skills to become business leaders with an understanding of social responsibility and with the ability to affect change in society. Universities are encouraged to implement their own ENACTUS programs and apply the business concepts to develop projects that will enhance the quality and standard of living of people who are in need.

ENACTUS trains students to plan and manage their programs from start to finish within a specific timeframe. Through this platform, students can engage with, and network within, the corporate sector while delivering programs or projects. ENACTUS students are encouraged to leverage classroom experiences, faculty and business advisors' expertise, and university-based resources to build projects that empower people to improve their situation. Their projects cover a wide range of topics such as economic markets, entrepreneurship, financial literacy, personal success skills, environmental sustainability, and business ethics.

In addition to managing a project, participants are encouraged to work within a specified framework of these topics and adapt their approach to meet the requirements of diverse communities. ENACTUS students have undertaken projects that provide the unemployed with the necessary skills to obtain productive jobs, teach families how to obtain financial security, and bring economic development to marginalized communities. Although the projects pioneered by ENACTUS are on a small scale and only beneficial toward a limited number of communities, it is an example of the impact of economic and social change that can be enjoyed by the regional community if these efforts are continuously implemented at various levels.

The programs organized by ENACTUS produce community-based organizations with a global outlook, flexibility of purpose, and accountability. The highlight of the ENACTUS program is a series of annual competitions that provide forums for participating groups to present their projects, where they are evaluated by business leaders. Groups compete at a national level, with the winner competing at an international level in the ENACTUS World Cup. The ENACTUS program benefits the community and instills a healthy competitive spirit in students that will help build their talents and motivation to pursue excellence while strengthening their resilience and competitiveness.

The growth of social enterprises since the inception of social entrepreneurship in 1986 illustrates that the field of social entrepreneurship is relevant to the current needs of the people of Malaysia. Many of these firms have been established by HEI graduates and offer consulting services, credit financing, and food products. As the field of social entrepreneurship contributes to the growth of GDP in Malaysia, educators must leverage students' talent as early as possible during their education so that their social entrepreneurship desire does not diminish after graduation.

The Application of Social Entrepreneurship in Technical and Vocational Education and Training (TVET)

There has been a global emphasis on developing entrepreneurial education ever since entrepreneurship was recognized as a source of economic prosperity and competitiveness (Martinez et al., 2010). Entrepreneurship is one of the key elements emphasized in the TVET process. The implementation of TVET aims to produce quality students who meet the needs of the industry, creating a highly skilled labor force. The development of a holistic exemplary model requires the integration of knowledge and entrepreneurial skills through lifelong education, training, and learning processes. Social entrepreneurship forms an integral part of TVET and is recognized by the United Nations Educational,

Scientific, and Cultural Organization—International Centre for TVET. The TVET system identifies skills required for learning, provides social entrepreneurship support, and offers a broad range of teaching tools in a variety of environments. It supports aspects of the educational process involving, in addition to general education, the study of technologies and related sciences, the acquisition of practical skills and attitudes, and knowledge related to occupations in various sectors of economic and social life (UNESCO, 2002). TVET in Malaysia is implemented in school-based centers, non-school-based centers, and within enterprises (Ab Rahim, 2011).

According to Ernst (2011), the challenge of producing quality social entrepreneurs depends on an individual's interests and motivations, which is driven by a commitment and willingness to improve the welfare of marginalized people in the community. TVET activities in Malaysia must, therefore, align with the goals of the National Philosophy of Education, including the application of values in the curriculum, strengthening soft skills in financial management (Nicholls, 2010), developing leadership attitudes in addressing community issues (Bornstein, 2007), and displaying an openness to innovation (Scholtz, 2011). The need to increase societal-based innovation has led to the targeted development of students' competence in social entrepreneurship skills.

Scholtz (2011) argues that social entrepreneurship in TVET reinforces the element of sustainability in existing entrepreneurial education. Social entrepreneurship education can provide students with different career paths and provide entrepreneurial skills to students who aspire to start a social-oriented business. Social entrepreneurship skills need to be identified and applied to students so that they can explore new social innovations before entering the workforce. The field of social entrepreneurship has grown exponentially with the availability of relevant courses in top universities globally (Bornstein, 2007; Global Entrepreneurship Monitor, 2013) and is increasingly relevant in Malaysia's TVET process. The adoption of social entrepreneurship activities in teaching and research is now an expectation, to enhance students' entrepreneurial motivation and desire to generate socio-economic change. As such, the role of education is related to the status of ENACTUS members including HEIs and Alumni who act as moderators of entrepreneurial personalities and exemplars of social entrepreneurial aspirations. Therefore, social entrepreneurship is a critical inclusion in TVET in Malaysia.

Social Entrepreneurship Issues

Research has demonstrated that social entrepreneurship activities have contributed to a reduction in poverty rates and the improvement of large-scale economic development (Alvord et al., 2004; Anderson & Dees, 2006; Borzaga & Defourny, 2001; Dean & McMullen, 2007; Dees, 2008; Mair & Seelos, 2006; Zahra et al., 2009). However, the individual desire to become a socially oriented entrepreneur requires further investigation. The topic of desire and its association with entrepreneurial interest has been discussed by many researchers in recent years (e.g., Ernst, 2011; Noorseha et al., 2013). In addition, considering Fowler's (2000) view of social entrepreneurship as an activity that combines social goals and profits by diversifying the role of not-for-profit organizations, significant differences in various forms of social entrepreneurship activities exist (Johannisson & Olaison, 2007).

Students' potential in the field of social entrepreneurship should be consistently encouraged to ensure they are constantly motivated and trained to create new social innovations after graduating. Encouraging students to venture into this field of study is important for the potential social entrepreneurs, not only to understand and be aware of the problems faced by the community but also to produce social innovations and improve the living standard of the community including the economic, welfare, education and health sectors (New Year's Mandate, 2012). Although social entrepreneurship research is increasing, there is minimal research being undertaken on factors underlying the motivation of social entrepreneurship (Short et al., 2009; Ab. Wahid, 2014).

The Malaysian Social Enterprise Blueprint (2015–2018) encourages citizens, especially the youth, to venture into the social entrepreneurship field to drive the economy and enrich the peoples' lives. Social business grants are offered by MaGIC to young entrepreneurs in the early stages of social innovation, and education has been formally and informally offered with the aim of exposing students to a broader field of social entrepreneurship across multiple disciplines. The level of social entrepreneurship and volunteer participation in Malaysia is still low (Malaysian Youth Index, 2016). In a study of German students, Ernst (2011) found that the success of social entrepreneurship activities is related to enthusiasm toward volunteerism. Malaysia's entrepreneurial career offerings need to be expanded, to meet not only the needs of the community but also the needs of the marginalized.

The challenges identified in expanding the social entrepreneurship industry in Malaysia are a lack of institutional awareness of social entrepreneurship, a deficiency in recognition of existing laws and policy structures, negative public perception toward social entrepreneurship, an absence of quality exemplary models, limited access to large financial capital, and minimal support to expand. To improve economic development and increase employment opportunities, a mechanism must be established to increase the number of social enterprises (Bacq et al., 2011).

Social Entrepreneurship Interest Level Among Malaysian Students

There is currently a gap in understanding how to encourage students to change their goals from solely maximizing profitability to social orientation when they start a business (Ab. Wahid, 2014). However, as the desire to contribute to society grows stronger, individuals are more likely to engage and act. This desire is described by the theory of organizational behavior (Ajzen, 1991); an interest in social activities can be determined by investigating desire as a predictor of behavior. Most previous studies have found that Malaysian students' desire to engage in social entrepreneurship is at a moderate level (Ab. Wahid et al., 2013; Baierl et al., 2012; Ernst, 2011; Mair & Noboa, 2003, 2006; Moorthy & Annamalah, 2014; Nga & Shamuganathan, 2010; Noorseha et al., 2013; Prieto, 2011; Tan & Yoo, 2011; Youssry, 2007). This finding was driven by the lack of a supportive environment (Ab. Wahid et al., 2013; Mhd Sarif et al., 2013) and limited education (Scholtz, 2010), which hinders efforts to increase the number of social entrepreneurs in Malaysia.

The level of entrepreneurship aspiration is based on the interpretation of the mean score values by Nunnally (1978). According to this interpretation, a low level is defined by a mean value of 1 to 2, a moderate-low level is defined by a mean of 2 to 3, a moderate-high level is defined by a mean of 3 to 4, and a high level is indicated by a mean value of 4 to 5. Noorseha et al. (2013) found that Malaysian undergraduate students majoring in economics and business have moderate-high levels of interest in social entrepreneurship, with a mean value of 3.32. Moreover, a study by Prieto (2010) found that the interest in social entrepreneurship in undergraduate students in Africa, North America, and Latin America was moderate-high (mean value 3.11). Similarly, Radin A. Rahman (2016) found that ENACTUS students' social entrepreneurial interest was moderate-high (mean value 3.5).

This finding is in contrast with Ernst (2011) who discovered moderate-low interest levels (mean value 2.12) among German undergraduate students. However, Ab. Wahid (2014) found that the combination of social entrepreneurship characteristics of SIFE students in Malaysia, including characteristics that identify opportunities, collaborative leaders, teamwork, and community orientation, were at a high level (mean value 4). Therefore, all findings indicate that the students' social entrepreneurial interest is between moderate-low and high with results showing low levels of social entrepreneurship interest.

Moorthy and Annamalah (2014) state that a high degree of enthusiasm and determination is required to enable the success of social enterprises. Their results show a strong relationship between the element of determination and the desire to be a social entrepreneur ($r = 0.951$) in Malaysia. Furthermore, students with a strong interest in social entrepreneurship can be ideal candidates to work within the field of corporate social responsibility in Malaysia. Corporate social responsibility projects have a significant impact on the quality of life in communities (Prieto, 2010). Mair and Noboa (2006) and Robinson (2006) emphasize that personal characteristics can shape interest in social entrepreneurship opportunities. Specifically, demographic aspects of business students can influence their potential to become entrepreneurs (Krueger et al., 2000). Radin A. Rahman (2016) found that 49.7% of respondents between the ages of 22 and 25 engaged in entrepreneurial activities, showing that young people are more inclined to engage in social entrepreneurial activities. In addition, research conducted by MaGIC toward owners of social enterprises found that 55% of respondents were between the ages of 18–40 (The State of Social Enterprise in Malaysia, 2018). University administrators need to incorporate compulsory elements of social entrepreneurship in undergraduate and postgraduate courses. Moreover, cooperation in research and development expertise with private universities should be intensified and the social entrepreneurship module should be used to evaluate its effectiveness toward students.

Conclusions

Social entrepreneurship education for students should continue regardless of some studies showing that the desire among students is at a moderate-low level (Radin A. Rahman, 2016; Ab. Wahid, 2014). The potential of students who are likely to be interested in social entrepreneurship activities should be encouraged through education (Radin A. Rahman et al., 2019; Rahman et al., 2019). The young generation is becoming more aware of their responsibility in developing the community around them through job creation and social innovation. The aspirations of social entrepreneurs are expected to increase with the presence of existing social entrepreneurs acting as mentors among graduates, which will raise the level of social entrepreneurship activity in Malaysia and lead to a higher standard of living for marginalized people.

The level of social entrepreneurship activity in Malaysia, based on the growth of new social enterprises, is still low (0.3%), indicating that Malaysians' awareness of social entrepreneurship is also low. The Malaysian government seeks to encourage young people to venture into the social entrepreneurship sector by providing social entrepreneurship grants, developing socially oriented programs within ministry agencies, and offering formal and informal undergraduate programs. In addition, the launch of the MSEB 2015–2018 has successfully created the SEA Guideline which contains definitions, procedures, and criteria for the accreditation process and matters related to social entrepreneurship.

Industry leaders such as ENACTUS and Pandemic have been able to attract young people by promoting social-oriented activities and projects at an international level and have attracted investors to fund social projects. Education is one of the most important mediums for young people to ensure that a planned project reaches its target. Most youths who are involved in social entrepreneurship projects have gained knowledge about social entrepreneurship through formal education or informally by being active in clubs and NGOs. In addition to government and NGO efforts to encourage social entrepreneurship activities through mass media platforms, funding should be allocated to support viable social entrepreneurship projects. Funding is critical for new social entrepreneurs and students committed to implementing social entrepreneurship projects. Furthermore, Legal provisions to recognize the social enterprise sector must be established to ensure that social enterprises are viable in the market and accepted by commercial financial institutions. Finally, social entrepreneurship programs must be expanded into formal courses and integrated into existing HEIs to foster student awareness. In the early stages of education, schools should be encouraged to conduct strategic cooperation programs with successful social entrepreneurs to educate students on the existence and role of social entrepreneurs in society, the economy, and the environment.

References

Ab Wahid, H., Othman, N., & Mohd Salleh, S. (2013). *Social entrepreneurship contributions on the competitiveness of active students in the Students in Free Enterprise Program (SIFE) Malaysia*. Proceedings of 6th International Seminar on Regional Education UKM-UNRI2013, 19191-1929.

Ab Wahid, H. (2014). *Keusahawanan social, daya tahan dan daya saing pelajar Institusi Pengajian Tinggi di Malaysia* (Doctoral thesis). Universiti Kebangsaan Malaysia: Bangi.

Abdul Kadir, M. A. B., Zainudin, A. H., Harun, U. S., & Muhammad, N. A. (2019). Malaysian Social Enterprise Blueprint 2015–2018: What's Next? *ASEAN Entrepreneurship Journal*, 5(2), 1–7. https://www.researchg

ate.net/publication/336990745_Malaysian_Social_Enterprise_Blueprint_2015-2018_What%27s_next

Ab Rahim, B. (2011). *Preparing Malaysian youth for the world of work: Role of TVET*. Universiti Putra Malaysia Press.

Ajzen, I. (1991). The theory of planned behavior. *Organizational Behavior and Human Decision Processes, 50*, 179–211.

Alvord, S. H., Brown, L. D., & Letts, C. W. (2004). Social entrepreneurship and societal transformation. *Journal of Applied Behavioral Science, 40*(3), 260–282.

Amanah Ikhtiar Malaysia. (2011). *Corporate information*. http://www.aim.gov.my/index.php/kenali-kami/2013-03-14-14-2042/maklumatkorporat.html

Anderson, B. B., & Dees, J. G. (2006). Rhetoric, reality, and research: Building a solid foundation for the practice of social entrepreneurship. In A. Nicholls (Ed.), *Social entrepreneurship—New models of sustainable social change*. Oxford University Press.

Ashoka. (2009). *What is a social entrepreneur?* http://www.ashoka.org/social_entrepreneur

Austin, J., Stevenson, H., & Wei-Skillern, J. (2006). Social and commercial entrepreneurship: Same, different, or both? *Entrepreneurship: Theory & Practice, 30*(1), 1–22.

Bacq, S., Hartog, C., Hoogendoorn, B., & Lepoutre, J. (2011). *Social entrepreneurship: Exploring individual and organizational characteristics*. EIM Research Reports. www.entrepreneurship-sme.eu/index.cfm/12,html?nxt=ctm_publikatie&bestelnummer=H20110.

Bacq, S., & Janssen, F. (2011). The multiple faces of social entrepreneurship: A review of definitional issues based on geographical and thematic criteria. *Entrepreneurship & Regional Development, 23*(5/6), 373–403.

Baierl, R., Grichnik, D., Sporrle, M., & Welpe, I. (2012). *Formation of social entrepreneurial intentions: The role of an individual's general social appraisal*. Research project: Experimental Entrepreneurship in Entrepreneurial Decision-Making. TIE 2012—14th Annual Conference of the Scientific Committee of Technology, Innovation, and Entrepreneurship, Hamburg-Harburg, Germany.

Bayulgen, O. (2008). Muhammad Yunus, Grameen Bank and the nobel peace price: What political science can contribute to and learn from the study of microcredit. *International Studies Review, 10*(3) (September, 2008), 525–547

Bornstein, D. (2007). *How to change the world: Social entrepreneurs and the power of new ideas*. Oxford University Press.

Borzaga, C., & Defourny, J. (2001). *The emergence of social enterprise*. Routledge.
Che Nawi, N. R., Arsyad, M. M., Krauss, S. E., & Ahmad Ismail, I. (2018). Social entrepreneur as career: Why it attracts youth in Malaysia? *International Journal of Academic Research in Business and Social Sciences, 8*(6), 24–36.
Chong, T. (2015). *Pelan Pembangunan Keusahawanan Sosial bertujuan melonjak jumlah perusahaan sosial Berjaya*. http://www.utusan.com.my/berita/nasional/pelan-pembangunan-keusahawanan-sosial-1.91618.
Dacin, P. A., Dacin, M. T., & Matear, M. (2010). Social entrepreneurship: Why we don't need a new theory and how we move forward from here. *Academy of Management Perspectives, 24*(3), 37–57.
Dean, T. J., & McMullen, J. S. (2007). Toward a theory of sustainable entrepreneurship: Reducing environmental degradation through entrepreneurial action. *Journal of Business Venturing, 22*(1), 50–76.
Dees, J. G. (2008). Philanthropy and enterprise: Harnessing the power of business and social entrepreneurship for development. *Innovations: Technology, Governance, Globalization, 3*(3), 119–132. https://doi.org/10.1162/itgg.2008.3.3.11
Defourney, J., & Nyssens, M. (2008). *Social enterprise in Europe: Recent trend and developments* (Working Paper—08/01). Liège: EMES.
Duke University [Fuqua School of Business]. (2005). *Social entrepreneur and education*. http://www.fuqua.duke.edu/centers/case/knowledgeitems/social-entrepreneurs-and-education/
Ernst, K. (2011). *Heart over mind-an empirical analysis of social entrepreneurial intention formation on the basis of the theory of planned behaviour* (Doctoral thesis). University of Wuppertal, Berlin.
Fowler, A. (2000). NGDOs as a moment in history: Beyond aid to social entrepreneurship or civic innovation? *Third World Quarterly, 21*(4): 637–654.
Global Entrepreneurship Monitor. (2013). *Global report on social entrepreneurship: executive summary*. http://www.babson.edu/Academics/centers/blank-center/global-research/gem/documents/GEM%202013%20Global%20Report.pdf
Global Entrepreneurship Monitor. (2015). *Special topic report: Social entrepreneurship*. https://www.gemconsortium.org/file/open?fileId=49542
Henley, A. (2007). Entrepreneurial aspiration and transition into self-employment: Evidence from British longitudinal data. *Entrepreneurship and Regional Development, 19*(3), 253–280.

Johannisson, B., & Olaison, L. (2007). The moment of truth- reconstructing entrepreneurship and social capital in the eye of the storm. *Review of Social Economy, 65*(1), 55–78.

Johnson, S. (2002). Social entrepreneurship literature review. *Canadian Centre for Social Entrepreneurship.*

Krueger, N. F., Reilly, M. D., & Carsrud, A. L. (2000). Competing models of entrepreneurial intentions. *Journal of Business Venturing, 15*(5/6), 411–432.

Light, P. C. (2008). *The search for social entrepreneurship.* The Brookings Institution.

MacMillan, I. A. (2005). *Social entrepreneurs: Playing the role of agents in society.* http://knowledge.wharton.upenn.edu/index.cfm?fa=viewfeature&id=766

MaGIC. (2015). *Malaysian social entrepreneurship blueprint 2015–2018.* Cyberjaya, Malaysia. http://se.mymagic.my/en/publications

Mair, J., & Marti, I. (2006). Social entrepreneurship research: A source of explanation, prediction and delight. *Journal of World Business, 41,* 32–44.

Mair, J., & Noboa, E. (2003*).* Social entrepreneurship: How intentions to create a social enterprise get formed (Paper work). IESE Business School.

Mair, J., & Noboa, E. (2006). Social entrepreneurship: How intentions to create a social enterprise get formed. In J. Mair, J. A. Robinson, & K. Hockerts (Eds.), *Social entrepreneurship* (pp 121–135). Palgrave Macmillan.

Mair, J., & Seelos, C. (2006). Social entrepreneurship: The contribution of individual entrepreneurs to sustainable development the ICFAI. *Journal of Entrepreneurship Development, 3,* 30–46.

Malaysian Social Enterprise Blueprint 2015–2018. (2015). *Unleashing the power of social entrepreneurship.* Malaysian Global Innovation and Creativity Centre (MaGIC). Social Entrepreneurship Unit.

Malaysian Youth Index. (2016). *Institut Penyelidikan Pembangunan Belia Malaysia.* Kementerian Belia dan Sukan Malaysia.

Martin, R. L., & Osberg, S. (2007). Social entrepreneurship: The case for definition. *Stanford Social Innovation Review* (Spring), 28–39.

Martinez, A.C., Levie, J., Kelley, D.J., Saemundsson, R.J., & Schott, T. (2010). Global entrepreneurship monitor special report: A global perspective on entrepreneurship education and training. Global Entrepreneurship Monitor, United States.

Mhd Sarif, S., Ismail, Y., & Sarwar, A. (2013). Creating wealth through social entrepreneurship: A case study from Malaysia. *Journal of Basic and Applied Scientific Research, 3*(3), 345–353.

Ministry of Finance. 2020. *Economy stimulus package 2020.* Putrajaya, Malaysia.

Moorthy, R., & Annamalah, S. (2014). Consumers' perceptions towards motivational intentions of social entrepreneurs in Malaysia. *Review of Integrative Business and Economics Research, 3*(1), 257–287.

Neck, H., Brush, C., & Allen, E. (2009). The landscape of social entrepreneurship. *Business Horizons, 52*(1), 13–19.

New Year Mandate. (2012). 'Berfikiran global bertindak glokal'. From Y. B. Dato' Seri Mohamed Khaled Nordin, Menteri Pengajian Tinggi Malaysia. Dewan A, Pusat Konvensyen Antarabangsa Putrajaya.

New York University [Stern]. (2005). *Berkley Center for social entrepreneurship & innovation.* http://w4.stern.nyu.edu/berkley/social.cfm

Nga, J. K. H., & Shamuganathan, G. (2010). The influence of personality traits and demographic factors on social entrepreneurship start up intentions. *Journal of Business Ethics, 95*(2), 259–282.

Nicholls, A. (2006). *Social entrepreneurship: New models of sustainable social change.* Oxford University Press.

Nichols, A. (2010). The legitimacy of social entrepreneurship: Reflexive isomorphism in preparadigmatic field. *Entrepreneurship Theory and Practice, 34*(4), 611–633.

Noorseha, A., Yap, C. S., Dewi, A. S., & Md Zabid, A. R. (2013). Social entrepreneurial intention among business undergraduates: An emerging economy perspective. *Gadjah Mada International Journal of Business, 15*(3), 249–267.

Nunnally, J. C. (1978). *Psychometric theory* (2nd ed.). McGraw-Hill.

Okpara, J. O., & Halkias, D. (2011). Social entrepreneurship: An overview of its theoretical evolution and proposed research model. *International Journal of Social Entrepreneurship and Innovation, 1*(1), 4–20.

Oxford University Said Business School. (2005). *Who are social entrepreneurs?* https://www.sbs.ox.ac.uk/research/skoll-centre-social-entrepreneurship/who-are-social-entrepreneurs

Peredo, A. M., & McLean, M. (2006). Social entrepreneurship: A critical review of the concept. *Journal of World Business, 41*(1), 56–65.

Petrella, F., & Riches-Battesti, N. (2014). Social entrepreneur, social entrepreneurship and social enterprise: Semantic and controversies. *Journal of Innovation Economics & Management, 2*(14), 143–156. https://www.cairn.info/revue-journal-of-innovation-economics-2014-2-page-143.htm

Prieto, L. C. (2010). *The influence of proactive personality on social entrepreneurial intentions among African American and Hispanic undergraduate students: The moderating role of hope* (Doctoral thesis). Graduate Faculty of the Louisiana State University and Agricultural and Mechanical College.

Prieto, L. C. (2011). The influence of proactive personality on social entrepreneurial intentions among African-American and Hispanic undergraduate students: The moderating role of hope. *Academy of Entrepreneurship Journal, 17*(2), 77–96.

Radin A. Rahman, R. S. A. (2016). *The moderating effects of ENACTUS members' status between entrepreneurial personality, human capital and social capital, and social entrepreneurial intention in Higher Education Institutions* (Doctoral thesis). Universiti Putra Malaysia, Serdang, Malaysia.

Radin A Rahman, R. S. A, Kutty, F. M., & Othman, N. (2019). Gender and family background as antecedents on the social entrepreneurial strategic domain of university students. *International Journal of Innovation, Creativity and Change, 7*(6), 336–346.

Rahman, R. S. A. R. A., Ismail, M. F., & Sahid, S. (2019). Strategic domains of social entrepreneurship among students in Malaysian higher education institutions. *Academy of Strategic Management Journal, 18*(1), 1–7.

Robinson, J. A., Mair, J., & Hockerts, K. (2009). *International perspectives of social entrepreneurship*. Palgrave Macmillan.

Robinson, J. A. (2006). Navigating social and institutional barriers to markets: How social entrepreneurs identify and evaluate opportunities. In J. Mair, J. A. Robinson, & K. Hockerts (Eds.), *Social entrepreneurship* (pp. 95–120). Palgrave Macmillan.

Scholtz, L. M. (2010). Factors that impact on the successful functioning of social entrepreneurs in the informal sector of the Nelson Mandela Metropole. *Nelson Mandela Metropolitan University*, South Africa.

Scholtz, L. M. (2011). Impact of social entrepreneurs' education and business skills training on the success of non-profit organisations (Magister Commercial Dissertation). Nelson Mandela Metropolitan University, South Africa.

Schwab Foundation. (2005). *Skoll Centre for social entrepreneurship*. http://www.schwabfound.org

Shane, S., & Venkatraman, S. (2000). The promise of entrepreneurship as a field of research. *Academy of Management Journal, 25*, 217–226.

Sharuddin, Z. (2008). *Mangkuktingkat.com*. Berita Harian- 7 Ogos. Diambil daripada. https://hamydy.wordpress.com/tag/mangkuktingkat.com/

Shaw, E. (2004). Marketing in the social enterprise context: Is it entrepreneurial? *Qualitative Marketing Research: An International Journal, 7*(3), 194–205.

Shaw, E., & Carter, S. (2007). Social entrepreneurship: Theoretical antecedents and empirical analysis of entrepreneurial processes and outcomes. *Journal of Small Business and Enterprise Development, 14*(3), 418–434.

Social Enterprise Accreditation Guidelines. (2019). Ministry of Entrepreneur Development, Malaysia, Retrieved June 14, 2019, https://s3-ap-southeast1.amazonaws.com/mymagic-misc/SEA_Guidelineen.pdf

Short, J. C., Moss, T. W., & Lumpkin, G. T. (2009). Research in social entrepreneurship: Past contributions and future opportunities. *Strategic Entrepreneurship Journal, 3*(2), 161–194.

Tan, W. L., & Yoo, S. J. (2011). *Non-profits and social entrepreneurship intentions: Examining the role of organizational attributes*. Paper presented at the ICSB.

Tan, W. L., Williams, J., & Tan, T.-M. (2005). Defining the 'social' in 'social entrepreneurship': Altruism and entrepreneurship. *International Entrepreneurship and Management Journal, 1*, 353–365.

The State of Social Enterprise in Malaysia. (2018). https://www.britishcouncil.org/sites/default/files/the_state_of_social_enterprise_in_malaysia_british_council_low_res.pdf

Thompson, J., Alvy, G., & Lees, A. (2000). Social entrepreneurship: A new look at the people and the potential. *Management Decision, 38*(5), 328–338.

United Nations Educational, Scientific and Cultural Organization. (2002). *Records of the thirty-first session of the General Conference: Resolutions*, 28. Paris: UNESCO. https://unesdoc.unesco.org/images/0012/001246/124687e.pdf

Weerawardena, J., & Mort, G. S. (2006). Investigating social entrepreneurship: A multidimensional model. *Journal of World Business, 41*(1), 21–35.

Youssry, A. (2007). *Social entrepreneur and enterprise development*. Research on YES, Egypt: Alexandria.

Yusof, M. Z., Ibrahim, I. A., & Abdul Hamid, M. (2013). *Who is the social entrepreneur? Easy question, difficult answer*. 4th International Conference on Business and Economic Research (4th ICBER 2013) Proceeding, Golden Flower Hotel, Bandung, Indonesia. ISBN: 978-967-5705-10-6.

Zahra, S. A., Gedajlovic, E., Neubaum, D. O., & Shulman, J. M. (2009). A typology of social entrepreneurs: Motives, search processes and ethical challenges. *Journal of Business Venturing, 24*(5), 519–532.

6

Social Entrepreneurship: Policies and Practice in Malaysia

Yasmin Rasyid and Robert Bowen

Introduction

The aim of this chapter is to evaluate social entrepreneurship in Malaysia. Although not a new phenomenon, Social Entrepreneurship (SE) is a complex issue that is hard to define (Banks, 2016). Indeed, entrepreneurship is difficult to define (Chell et al., 2016). Phillips et al. (2015: 430) point to social entrepreneurship as the drive for the creation of social value, with social entrepreneurs focussed on "bringing about improved social outcomes for a particular community or group of stakeholders". According to Thompson (2002), social entrepreneurs do not merely aim to make a profit, but also seek to resolve society failures by generating income-making opportunities for the benefit of everyone in their locality.

Y. Rasyid
EcoKnights, Kuala Lumpur, Malaysia

R. Bowen (✉)
School of Management, Swansea University, Swansea, Wales, UK
e-mail: robert.bowen@swansea.ac.uk

Globally, interest in the SE sector has grown exponentially in the last decade, especially among policy makers, funders, investors, academics and civil society organizations (CSOs). A Social Enterprise UK (2015) report argues that social enterprises have an important role to play in the achievement of the United Nations Sustainable Development Goals (SDGs). However, with 17 SDGs and no less than 169 associated targets, understanding how social enterprises can contribute to the achievement of these goals remains challenging, particularly given the diversity of social enterprise models that exist globally.

The focus of this chapter on Malaysia is significant in understanding the role of social entrepreneurship in an emerging economy. Social entrepreneurship remains a new concept in Malaysia; however, it is emerging through cooperation, non-profit organisations, and government (Adnan et al., 2018). Abdul Kadir and Sarif (2016) point to the 2015 Malaysian Social Enterprise Blueprint as an approach to accelerate the social enterprise sector, outlining social enterprises across the country working on issues relating to education, poverty, and rural development. This chapter seeks to evaluate the most prominent issues of social entrepreneurship in Malaysia, focussing on the actions of policymakers in furthering the reach of SE, as well as analysing working examples of SE across Malaysia. Given the geography of the country, divided between Peninsular Malaysia and Borneo, this study investigates different case studies of social entrepreneurship across the Peninsular, Sarawak and Sabah areas. This allows place-specific issues to be evaluated, in understanding social entrepreneurship across Malaysia, and how these can inform knowledge in this field. Hereafter, the chapter discusses social entrepreneurship in a Malaysian context, outlines the case studies, and develops a critical evaluation of social entrepreneurship in Malaysia.

The Rise of Social Entrepreneurship in Malaysia

In Malaysia, there is a recognition among key stakeholders that social entrepreneurship, as a concept and activity, has the potential to solve many social challenges by utilising the best of for-profit and non-profit sectors, and as such has been growing in importance (MaGIC, 2015). Social enterprises are expected to contribute to a range of areas, including uplifting minority communities, employment creation, and contributing to achieving the sustainable goals set by the United Nations (EPU, 2017). Apart from these social benefits, social entrepreneurship is also expected to build the country's economy.

The perceived importance of social entrepreneurship is evidenced by the growing diverse policies and programmes that are initiated by government, such as funding (e.g. the PUSH (Pemangkin Usahawan Social Hebat) scale-up and funding programmes for social enterprises to benefit B40 communities), physical infrastructure (B477 coworking space in Kuching, Sarawak managed by MaGIC), and business advisory services (MaGIC's online mentorship platform). The potential of social entrepreneurship was on the radar of the government and saw the first initiative in 2013 when Malaysia hosted the Global Social Business Summit. Launched by the then Malaysian Prime Minister, YAB Dato' Sri Najib Razak, RM20 million was announced to be allocated for the establishment of a Social Entrepreneurship Unit under the Malaysian Global Innovation and Creativity Centre (MaGIC).

With the launch of MaGIC in 2015, social entrepreneurship development became one of the key agendas the government-linked agency drove in terms of policy-making, advocacy, training and skills development. The vision of the MaGIC social entrepreneurship unit is to make Malaysia the regional leader for a people economy. However, there was a lack of a legal definition and recognition of social enterprise as a business entity during this time. In addition, the initiatives alone were inadequate to fully realise the potential of this sector. When the political governance of Malaysia changed in 2018, the Ministry of Entrepreneur Development (MED) was re-established in July 2018, and the Ministry was tasked to lead the Government's efforts in developing Malaysian social enterprises through its agency, MaGIC. Through the National Entrepreneurship Framework, MED and MaGIC are to spearhead the effort to address the challenges that exist within the social entrepreneurship sector. In addition, the MED is also tasked to formulate and execute the required strategies to empower social enterprises to drive and deliver long-term benefits for society and environment.

The Malaysian Social Enterprise Blueprint

The Malaysian Social Enterprise Blueprint, published by MaGIC in 2015, is a three-year roadmap that describes strategic thrusts required to accelerate the development of the sector. The blueprint's aim is for the Malaysian social enterprise sector to be self-sustaining, equitable, and people-centric in order to empower impact-driven entrepreneurs. The Blueprint reported that there are over 100 social enterprises operating mostly in the areas of education, poverty, rural development, environmental sustainability, employment for the marginalised and at-risk youth. The document also noted that several challenges and missed opportunities need to be unlocked to unleash the full potential of social entrepreneurship in Malaysia. These include rigidity and lack of institutional awareness, limited legal recognition and policy structure, negative public perception and recognition, a limited access to quality human capital, insufficient financial capital and inadequate support to grow and upscale.

Following the recent change in government, this blueprint has been replaced with more recent innovative policies to enhance the SE ecosystem in the country. Similarly, another international organization at the forefront of advocacy and promotion of social entrepreneurship in Malaysia is the British Council Malaysia. In 2018, the State of Social Enterprise in Malaysia report was published by British Council Malaysia (2018), in partnership with United Nations Economic and Social Commission for Asia and the Pacific (UN ESCAP), Ministry of Entrepreneur Development Malaysia and Yayasan Hasanah. Based on 132 survey responses, the report estimates that there are more than 20,000 social enterprises in Malaysia that exist formally as either medium SMEs, Non-Government Organisations (NGOs) or cooperatives. Most social enterprises (66%) were noted to be operating from major city centres such as Kuala Lumpur and Petaling Jaya. Approximately 54% of SE leadership are led by females and 46% by males. Within these social enterprises, leadership was noted to be young with 36% of the SE leaders aged between 31–40 years old, 30% between 41–50, while 7% of them are between 18–25 years old.

The British Council (2018) report noted that some of the social enterprises surveyed were in existence since 1998, however it was reported that 36% were established between 2015 and 2016. The growth in SE existence seen in 2016 could be attributed to the establishment of MaGIC the previous year, thus, there could have been greater awareness and education programmes delivered on the SE ecosystem by then. As such, more entities could have been aware of the SE definition, and thus acknowledging their SE status. The British Council also reported that 22% of respondents were focussed on education; 16% on sustainability; 13% on food and beverage, and 11% on art, culture and heritage. In terms of the missions and goals, 34% were focussed on creating employment opportunities; 31% on supporting vulnerable and marginalized communities; 27% on improving a particular community; and 24% on environmental protection.

Policy Development on Social Entrepreneurship in Malaysia

The MED continues to support SE through MaGIC, the implementation agency for all matters pertaining to social entrepreneurship. MED has taken various steps to promote the development of SE, such as the provision of a national guideline and definition of social entrepreneurship, an accreditation and tax-exemption programme, and grants for scale-up activities. The operationalization of the SE agenda for the country is part of the Ministry's effort to operationalize one of the key strategic thrusts of the National Entrepreneurship Policy 2030 (Kementerian Pembangunan Usahawan, 2019). Additionally, the Ministry provides accredited social enterprises with training and access to the government procurement platform, a one-stop entrepreneurship digital information centre, and industry exposure of social enterprises to other Ministries and corporates.

The British Council (2018) report highlights the lack of knowledge among these enterprises about an existing and workable social business model. This could be a barrier for them to grow as they seek a sustainable model that balances making a profit with making an impact. The report points to low access to investors due to limited capital supply (46%) as a significant financial challenge for social enterprises. It notes that investors remain cautious to investing in social enterprises due to a lack of reliable information and data on the sector. Additionally, the Malaysian market is smaller than other ASEAN countries such as Indonesia or the Philippines, therefore, investors are also moving their funding and investments to these countries. Hence, growing a robust SE ecosystem in Malaysia requires inclusive and comprehensive policy development efforts to solve the problem of scale. Appropriate policies need to be implemented to grow the social enterprises into companies that are sustainable financially and scalable, with measurable social and/or environmental impact on society.

A recent MED policy initiative was the launch of the National Social Entrepreneurship Guidelines and Accreditation programme in April 2019, aimed to provide the public and private sectors with the national definition of a social enterprise. Under the Guidelines, a "social enterprise" is defined as *"a business entity registered under any written law in Malaysia that creates social impact or positive environmental impact in a proactive manner and financially sustainable"* (Zakaria, 2019). Organisations fulfilling this criteria are encouraged to apply for the recognition of their organisation as social enterprise on MaGIC's SE microsite. For the accreditation programme, social enterprises needs to be in existence for two years, and be willing to declare and submit their financial audited reports to MaGIC for an audit and assessment on their organization. Additionally, each social enterprise is required to provide quantitative and qualitative evidence of their SE impact. Following a positive evaluation, social enterprises is acknowledged with a certificate of recognition valid for three years.

Overall, MaGIC is tasked with growing a vibrant SE ecosystem, including ensuring an increase in public awareness and knowledge on SE. One of its flagship programmes is the SE Knowledge Day, where academics, students, entrepreneurs and the general public are able to register for a one-day knowledge session on SE, in which they can learn the definition of social enterprise, understand various business models the sector utilizes, discuss with local social entrepreneurs, and gain a strong understanding of the importance of impact-driven businesses. MaGIC delivers annual boot camps and accelerator programmes for nascent social entrepreneurs in which the objective is to accelerate the ideation process and support the growth of new social enterprises. MaGIC is also currently implementing a SE scale-up programme called PUSH (Pemangkin Usahawan Social Hebat), in which 35 social enterprises undergo training and capacity building modules to scale their social enterprises, with the support of a RM100,000 grant by government.

Cases of Social Entrepreneurship Efforts in Malaysia

Given the objectives of understanding and evaluating social entrepreneurship, the study adopts a case study approach, as a way of examining different cases of social entrepreneurship across various parts of Malaysia. Case studies are a method of advancing understanding of a particular phenomenon, through the collection of data from multiple sources, whether quantitative or qualitative (Ghauri, 2004). This allows for a depth of focus on the specific situation, with sufficient information. Yin (2009) supports a multiple case design over single cases, as this provides a stronger basis for theoretical generalisation. Thus, five case studies are presented and discussed from the Klang Valley, Sarawak and Sabah, selected with a view to accounting for the different place-specific issues, as well as reflecting the different types of social entrepreneurship evident in Malaysia. This includes NGOs, social enterprises and SMEs focussed on social entrepreneurship:

- Community Service Centre for the Deaf (Klang Valley)
- Biji-Biji (Klang Valley)
- EcoKnights (Klang Valley)
- Tanoti Crafts (Sarawak)
- Eco Yap (Sabah)

The vast majority of social enterprises are located in the Klang Valley area, encompassing Kuala Lumpur (39% of Malaysian social enterprises) and Selangor (27%), with Sarawak and Sabah accounting for 7% each.

Case Study 1: Community Service Centre of the Deaf (CSCD)

CSCD is a non-profit NGO with a mission to ensure that children (aged 5–18) with hearing disabilities acquire necessary skills to succeed in a life full of challenges, by providing them with life skills training based on the philosophy of helping them support themselves. CSCD realized that to improve and enhance the accomplishment of their mission, they could not depend solely on funding help from the public so they decided to start working on self-help projects. The main idea of these self-help projects is to operate sustainable long-term programmes that can generate income, in tandem with providing employment opportunities to the Deaf. One of the self-help projects is known as the Silent Teddies Bakery, which today is a full-fledged Halal-certified bakery that not only bakes for corporate clients in the city, but also employs trained beneficiaries from CSCD. Today, after five years of operations, the Silent Teddies Bakery is a social enterprise specializing in a variety of bread, cookies, muffins and tarts, which are supplied to local and international brands such as Starbucks Malaysia and AirAsia. All proceeds from sales go directly into enhancing CSCD beneficiaries in their vocational and entrepreneurial skills.

Case Study 2: Biji-Biji

Biji-Biji was formed as a NGO in December 2012, beginning by tackling environmental issues through up-cycling and repurposing waste into gifts and products, mainly through woodworking and metalworking activities. Over the years, the NGO has spun off several social enterprises; among them are Biji-Biji Ethical Fashion, and Me.re.ka. Later in 2015, a second Open Workshop was opened, centred on electronics, stitching and tailoring. Besides that, Biji-Biji also practices open source ideas, which is an idea and information sharing.

According to Co-Founder, Rashvin Pal Singh: "One of biggest challenges has been managing our cash-flow with significant corporate orders and managing the scale of our growth. We have grown from a team of 4 people to 40 in 5 years. The very real business challenges of having to start work first to secure the sale, delayed payment terms with big corporates, and a team that is growing with higher salary expenses. This multi-faceted challenge has been at the crux of our biggest stress and struggles. In dealing with this, we had to get the entire teams buy-in and shared with them transparently all our challenges. We practice a strong code of open-book finance with the entire team. By sharing honestly with the entire team our situation and the options presented to us, we would explore the possible solutions together: (1) Delaying our salaries and taking temporary pay-cuts, (2) Borrowing money from close relatives/friends, and (3) Chasing previous clients that owed us money. In return, we adopted a profit-sharing mechanism with the entire team, that a fixed percentage of profits will be channelled back with everyone. This ultimately created a set-up of 'we-are-all-in-this-together' mentality, and we were able to ride the difficult waves on entrepreneurship and come out stronger".

Case Study 3: EcoKnights

One of the locally well-known social enterprises in Malaysia, Pertubuhan Alam Sekitar EcoKnights Kuala Lumpur dan Selangor, or EcoKnights for short, aims to mainstream sustainable living in Malaysia through education and awareness programmes, volunteerism and youth development activities, and community development interventions. Based in the Klang Valley, EcoKnights serves the requirements of communities, governments and educational institutes all over the country. Over the years, the organization has been featured and mentioned in many social entrepreneurship efforts, especially in the media, and apart from demonstrating that an NGO can be viable and financially sustainable using the SE business model, EcoKnights, is also perceived as a mentor, influencer and advocate within the social entrepreneurship ecosystem. EcoKnights was awarded the Impact-Driven Enterprise Accreditation (IDEA) by MaGIC in 2017, and now maintains its SE Basic recognition under the MED's National Social Entrepreneurship Guidelines and Accreditation programme.

Case Study 4: Tanoti Crafts

Tanoti Crafts is a social enterprise reaching out to women in rural communities in Sarawak to help them "weave" an enhanced future. What began as a simple workshop to preserve the traditional art of songket weaving in 2008 has grown to become a notable social enterprise based in Kuching, Sarawak. Today, Tanoti is a congregation of Sarawakian women weavers and artisans dedicated towards the production, promotion and proliferation of handcrafted fabrics. Tanoti aims to make good the vision of the foundation; that is to improve the lives and livelihoods of womenfolk and rural communities through the ancient art of songket weaving. According to Co-founder, Jacqueline Fong: "To do work in social impact, one really must be driven by passion otherwise there will be no long term commitment for the cause. It is not an easy journey and financial returns are low. Only grit will ensure you carry on. SEs exist to solve social issues. Government policies should be in place to support SEs' work".

Case Study 5: Eco Yap

Eco Yap is a recognised brand of fresh milk from Sabah, produced on an eco-friendly farm near Keningau, a rural community approximately 100 km south of Kota Kinabalu. Founded in 1982 by Datuk Yap Yun Fook, the dairy farm has grown from two cows, to over 5,000, producing in excess of four million litres of milk a year, now the largest supplier of fresh milk in Malaysia. The operations of the farm are based on a zero-waste policy, in which the various activities of the farm co-exist to develop sustainable practices. This is reflected in the business' mission statement: "Demonstrating and adopting zero waste management practices, recycling, composting, reusing products wherever possible and educating society as to the importance of green living".

This philosophy means that grass is grown specifically for animal feed, and animal waste is used to fertilise the land. Additional activities of the farm include growing pineapples and durian, rice fields, and a fish farm. The operations of the farm have increased as the farm has grown, bringing employment to the local population. Following this success, Datuk Yap Yun Fook has been appointed as a mentor for agri-entrepreneurs by the Ministry of Agriculture, and as a lecturer at Universiti Malaysia Sabah. This integrated approach to sustainable farming has brought interest to the farm from everywhere, with visitors coming to discover the farms best practice. The success of the business has led to the opening of restaurants in local communities and plans to build a hotel.

Case Studies Evaluation

Many NGOs in Malaysia have embraced the social entrepreneurship business model, and have been gradually known as social enterprises (Abdul Kadir & Sarif, 2016). Some of these NGOs, like CSCD, even have a profit-making business entity formed separately to the parent NGO, while others like Biji-Biji have spin-off enterprises established. The reality is that NGOs are challenged in acquiring donations and funds especially when the donor sector fluctuates in its generosity, and there are more NGOs in existence today, each competing to access the same funds. Over the last decade, there has been a realization that the traditional non-profit NGO model is not a viable model to sustain the efforts of an organization. In order to continue delivering impact to communities and the environment, NGOs are required to adopt innovative approaches to sustain its efforts. One of the key social innovations observed is the transition of a donor-dependent business model to one that relies on the NGO's professional capacity to generate income to fund its impact areas and programmes.

While the SE ecosystem is growing nationally, as evidenced in the British Council (2018) report, much of this growth is documented and recorded in Peninsular Malaysia, with 66% of social enterprises located in the Klang Valley. This heavy concentration could be because Kuala Lumpur offers more access to customers, clients, and the market for business opportunities. Alternatively, it could be due to the multidimensional social and environmental challenges and issues that need to be addressed in an urban setting. Generally, SE-related activities such as events, networking sessions and training programmes are heavily concentrated in the Klang Valley. Yet in recent years, social entrepreneurship interest has attracted greater attention from the states of Sarawak and Sabah. Even MaGIC has programmes that primarily focus on growing, building and supporting the SE ecosystem in Sarawak since 2015, starting with its nationwide programme, SEHATI 2015, centred on knowledge-sharing and capacity building, exposing the target audience to the potential of social entrepreneurship in driving long-term benefits for the society and environment.

What can be observed from SE in Sabah and Sarawak is that the social enterprises are localized in their reach and participation. Most SE prominent in Sabah and Sarawak focus on using local culture, arts and heritage to create employment, and enhance skills and capacities of the community. This is evident by the artisans and weavers of the Tanoti Crafts case study, as well as the local heritage and emphasis on sustainable agriculture in the Eco Yap case. Despite their isolated location, and distance from the main activities in the Klang Valley, social entrepreneurship has developed significantly in Borneo, both with the support of policy initiatives, such as in the Tanoti Crafts case, and through organic means in the Eco Yap case.

Challenges Ahead

Social entrepreneurship embraces a multidimensional model (Weerawardena & Mort, 2006) and while it has emerged as an area of academic interest and investigation, the sector is fragmented and there is no coherent theoretical framework. This is evident across Asia, as countries like Thailand, Malaysia, Singapore and Indonesia have various legal and unofficial definitions for social entrepreneurship, and are at different stages of growth and evolution. While these gaps and challenges exist, there are also growing opportunities for stakeholders to participate in growing this sector. The common challenges of social enterprises in Malaysia were noted by the British Council (2018) report, in which 36% mentioned a serious lack of awareness on social entrepreneurship and social enterprises in the country; 33% pointed to the challenge of acquiring and retaining talent in their organization, and 31% indicated a lack financial support. Some of these challenges are being addressed by the Malaysian government, while many challenges require the concerted effort of all stakeholders in the ecosystem. The following section outlines and discusses the main challenges in the Malaysian SE ecosystem.

Social Entrepreneurship Awareness

Although SE is growing rapidly, people are still not aware of these enterprises. This lack of knowledge could hamper entrepreneurs who want to make a social impact while being sustainable. It also lowers their chances of gaining support from investors to scale their enterprise. Additionally, low public awareness on the sector makes it difficult for these companies to gather support from consumers and investors, which also makes it difficult for them to scale up. The local Malaysian media has recorded a surge of stories on social entrepreneurship since 2010, while MaGIC is also working with the media, educational institutes and with corporate partners in crafting and delivering crafting programmes to further enhance the public's awareness on social entrepreneurship.

Legal Definition

One of the significant hurdles social enterprises encountered is the lack of a legal definition and recognition of social enterprise as a business entity in Malaysia. This issue has led to many social entrepreneurs operating under a variety of legal forms, which are governed by different acts and regulations. Be it NGOs or foundations, SMEs or cooperatives, SE in Malaysia lacks an official recognition in its form and functions. Realizing this, the MED launched the National Social Entrepreneurship Guidelines and Accreditation programme in April 2019; however, there is still a need to ensure that social enterprises are given the option to be registered as a legal social enterprise with the Registrar of Companies.

Access to Capital, Funding and Investments

Malaysia has a variety of financial institutions and sources of capital that are open to social entrepreneurs, including the banking system, development finance institutes, venture capital funds and other special funds, such as impact investment funds (Adnan et al., 2018). However, access to such sources of capital or funding for social entrepreneurs is noted to be difficult. According to the British Council (2018) report, 21% of respondents indicated a lack financial support, 27% pointed to insufficient grants offered to assist them in scaling up, while 55% said they still face challenges in managing cash flow. These findings suggest that social entrepreneurs are uncertain about their business models and sustainability of their firms (Ladin et al., 2017). Moreover, the report found that social enterprises in Malaysia are largely viable and successful businesses, with 37% of respondents making profits, and 32% breaking even. The case studies also point to successful examples of social enterprises, such as Biji-Biji, EcoKnights and Eco Yap, who are experiencing growth in developing new products and services, acquiring customers and expanding geographically.

While growth is beneficial, the industry and government are more focussed on the scale of the SE. PUSH is one government initiative aimed at scaling social enterprises that are currently benefiting the B40 communities either through employment or as beneficiaries. The assumption is that if social enterprises are already delivering good impact on the ground in a specific community, with more training and funding, these enterprises are able to scale or replicate their efforts in other geographical boundaries. There is also the need to be cautious of the fact that not all social enterprises require funding or access to capital to scale in order to deliver impact. Some enterprises may be addressing a very specific community-centric or geographical-based challenge in which scaling may not necessarily be the best option to enhance organization impact. Therefore, a conducive financing ecosystem is required for social enterprises to accelerate growth. While many social enterprises serve a very localized need, there are aspirations for them to scale or replicate their business model and impact across the country. Growth is pertinent to social enterprises not just in terms of profitability but also in increasing their impacts on the environment and/or society. In the British Council study (2018), 68% of respondents noted that they require access to funding and capital to develop and launch new products and services; 66% of them want to attract new customers and clients; 38% want to expand into new geographic areas, and 38% want to attract investment to expand their business.

Building Enablers Across All Stakeholders

It is recognized that to build an inclusive and vibrant SE sector requires developing ecosystem enablers across all stakeholders (Roundy, 2017). The Malaysian government has been very encouraging thus far with the current policies in place and with initiatives such as tax breaks for donors of SEs. There is still room to improve and enhance greater alignment between various policy measures. For instance, the government needs to initiate discussions and initiatives with financial institutions to cater some of their financing options and opportunities to social enterprises. Currently, most of the financial institutions have products and services only cater to SMEs or larger corporations. Regulators would need to be engaged by the government to design financial services that meet the requirements of social enterprises.

Another tool that will assist the ecosystem is to develop impact assessment practices and tools. Impact investors currently note an acute lack of information for assessing social impact, and policymakers are increasingly interested to see improved data to monitor the impact of the

SE sector. Now, investors develop their own metrics, some of which may be confusing and complicated for social enterprises to implement. Several government agencies such as MaGIC, and IMPACT Malaysia are currently working with social enterprises and other stakeholders to develop impact measurement tools to facilitate the monitoring and assessment of the work the social enterprises embark on.

Talent Acquisition and Retention

With the lack of institutional and community support available, this sector faces difficulty in attracting and retaining quality talents. Significant support and resources must be given to train and develop knowledge, capability, and skills of quality talent in social enterprises. This will help social enterprises to grow their businesses and increase their impact. In order to acquire the relevant talents and skills, education needs to be positioned at various levels to ensure that entrepreneurial education is accessible to all.

Conclusions

While still in its infancy, Malaysia has the potential to build a vibrant SE ecosystem, which can address numerous social issues. Existing policies have generated higher public interest in social entrepreneurship and created more opportunities for social entrepreneurs to grow, expand and scale their business and impact. Indeed, many local SE champions, such as Eco Yap, have also made global footprints and are paving their way in the global arena through speaking engagements, workshops and participation in global entrepreneurship programmes. Nevertheless, the quality and impact of SE can be further escalated so that social enterprises can build resiliency in areas related to positive cash flow and financial gains, and measurable and quantifiable impacts on communities or the environment. There is a need to ensure the social enterprises are resilient so that they are not reliant on government grants, funding or support. Recognising the importance of growing resilient enterprises,

SE ecosystem players focus on SE leadership empowerment and early entrepreneurship education. However, there is evidence of a paradigm shift in Malaysia and there have been many advancements in the policy-making processes in promoting and growing the local SE ecosystem. As the Malaysian economy begins to evolve towards a future where businesses are required to be impact-driven and more responsible to people and the planet, this gives rise to the need for closer engagement and consultation between the private sector, social entrepreneurs and the government and its agencies. This is a lesson for other emerging economies, especially ASEAN nations, such as Indonesia or Thailand, as a manner in promoting the development of social entrepreneurship and addressing various social issues. Further research may focus on the challenges facing social enterprises in emerging economies, notably questions over awareness of social enterprises, their legal registration, access to resources and talent, and engagement with stakeholders. In the Malaysian context, future research may also investigate factors that influence the high concentration of social enterprises around Kuala Lumpur.

References

Abdul Kadir, M. A. B., & Sarif, S. M. (2016). Social entrepreneurship, social entrepreneur and social enterprise: A review of concepts, definitions and development in Malaysia. *Journal of Emerging Economies & Islamic Research, 4*(2), 1–16.

Adnan, R. M., Yusoff, W. F. W., & Ghazali, N. (2018). The role of social entrepreneurship in Malaysia: A preliminary analysis. *Advanced Science Letters, 24*(5), 3264–3269.

Banks, K. (2016). *Social entrepreneurship and innovation: International case studies and practice.* Kogan Page Publishers.

British Council. (2018). *The state of social enterprises in Malaysia.* https://www.britishcouncil.org/sites/default/files/the_state_of_social_enterprise_in_malaysia_british_council_low_res.pdf. Accessed 5 December 2019.

Chell, E., Spence, L. J., Perrini, F., & Harris, J. D. (2016). Social entrepreneurship and business ethics: Does social equal ethical? *Journal of Business Ethics, 133*(4), 619–625.

Economic Planning Unit. (2017). *Malaysia: Sustainable development goals. Voluntary national review 2017. High-level political forum*. Economic Planning Unit, Putrajaya, Malaysia. https://sustainabledevelopment.un.org/content/documents/15881Malaysia.pdf. Accessed 1 February 2020.

Ghauri, P. (2004). Designing and conducting case studies in international business research. *Handbook of qualitative research methods for international business, 1*(1), 109–124.

Kementerian Pembangunan Usahawan. (2019). *Dasar Keusahawanan Nasional 2030*. http://www.med.gov.my/admin/files/med/image/portal/Dasar%20Keusahawanan%20Nasional%20(DKN)%202030.pdf. Accessed 6 December 2019.

Ladin, M. R. M., Abdullah, S., & Abdulsomad, K. (2017). A concept in promoting social entrepreneurship through Malaysian innovation and creativity centre for sustainability economic development Malaysia. *Journal of Education and Social Sciences, 8*(1), 105–109.

MaGIC (Malaysian Global Innovation and Creativity Center). (2015). *Unleashing the power of social entrepreneurship. The Malaysian social enterprise blueprint. 2015–2018*. https://mymagic-misc.s3.amazonaws.com/SE%20BLUEPRINT.pdf. Accessed 6 December 2019.

Phillips, W., Lee, H., Ghobadian, A., O'Regan, N., & James, P. (2015). Social innovation and social entrepreneurship: A systematic review. *Group & Organization Management, 40*(3), 428–461.

Roundy, P. T. (2017). Social entrepreneurship and entrepreneurial ecosystems: Complementary or disjointed phenomena? *International Journal of Social Economics, 44*(9), 1–18.

Social Enterprise UK. (2015). *Think global, trade social: How business with a social purpose can deliver more equitable and sustainable development for the 21st century*. https://www.britishcouncil.org/research-policy-insight/research-reports/think-global-trade-social. Accessed 6 December 2019.

Thompson, J. (2002). The world of the social entrepreneur. *International Journal of Public Sector Management, 15*(5), 412–431.

Weerawardena, J., & Mort, G. S. (2006). Investigating social entrepreneurship: A multidimensional model. *Journal of World Business, 41*(1), 21–35.

Yin, R. K. (2009). *Case study research: Design and methods* (4th ed.). Sage.

Zakaria, I. (2019). *Overview of social enterprise accreditation guidelines: Definitions and criteria (Part 1)*. https://www.izwanpartners.com/articles/overview-of-social-enterprise-accreditation-guidelines-defining-social-enterprise-part-1/. Accessed 10 December 2019.

7

From Producer to Entrepreneur: Entrepreneurial Learning Process of Smallholders in Sabah

Jane Chang, Ainurul Rosli, and Steward Giman Stephen

Introduction

This chapter investigates the rural smallholders' entrepreneurial learning process leading to the development of entrepreneurial skills, by developing their entrepreneurial capacity, while at the same time creating value at their own community level. This research is particularly important as much work in this area, focuses on entrepreneurial skills (Chang & Rieple, 2013), assuming the entrepreneurial learning process are the same for those in urban and rural areas. Some early studies that examine the context of the entrepreneurial journey (Chang et al., 2014)

J. Chang
Gritse CIC, London, UK

A. Rosli (✉)
Brunel University London, Uxbridge, UK
e-mail: ainurul.rosli@brunel.ac.uk

S. G. Stephen
AMC College, Kota Kinabalu, Malaysia

© The Author(s), under exclusive license to Springer Nature Switzerland AG 2021
P. Jones et al. (eds.), *Entrepreneurial Activity in Malaysia*,
https://doi.org/10.1007/978-3-030-77753-1_7

place minimal emphasis on the role of community in enabling the entrepreneurial journey. Moreover, there is limited understanding of the development of alternative entrepreneurial ventures of small farmers in developing countries, particularly concerning poor and less educated farmers, who rely on their community to survive.

Since social construction plays a significant role to influence rural entrepreneurship (Aldrich & Martinez, 2003), research in the field has turned explicitly to the process on how to and apply the concept as a process, or as a practice (Jack et al., 2004). It has been argued that the localness of rural community can help with the community-led local development, particularly across Europe (Bosworth et al., 2016), as they recirculate resources locally and multiplies benefits for the local community through entrepreneurship (Korsching & Allen, 2004). This is part of iconic symbol of embedded relationships (de Bruin et al., 2017; Muhammad et al., 2017), often associated with the smallness of rural settlements (Kalantaridis & Bika, 2006), which can also be found in many areas outside Europe, particularly in rural Asia and Africa (Muhammad et al., 2017).

McElwee and Annibal (2010) suggests that they have difficulty in accessing appropriately skilled labour and also are weak in skills such as business and management. What they are good at are skills related to social resources, social ties or networks which can be taken as to improving their social embeddedness (Pyysiäinen et al., 2006). This socially constructed way of working carries several influences on their rural engagement, including behaviour, of roles and practices (Bock, 2004, 2015). The entrepreneurial learning process has been identified as an essential element (Oreszczyn et al., 2010; Pyysiäinen et al., 2006), and understanding its factors within the study context can help with the change processes required to progress into an alternative enterprise (Seuneke et al., 2013).

This chapter contributes to the call for more research in the context of everyday entrepreneurs (Welter et al., 2017), in order to understand the combination of entrepreneurial learning and the circumstances in which it arises. It contributes to the rural entrepreneurship literature by providing unique empirical evidence of factors underlying the entrepreneurial learning process of 14 independent palm oil smallholders of Sapi Nangoh in the rural part of Borneo. The remainder of this chapter is structured as follows. We first present our literature review by elaborating on the context of our study and discussing the concept of entrepreneurial learning. The following section describes the empirical basis of this study. A considerable part of the paper is devoted to the presentation of our main findings. The chapter closes by drawing out and discussing the main conclusions and by proposing some possible avenues for further research.

Independent Smallholders as Entrepreneurs

In this study, we consider the development of new and non-farming business activities by smallholders as a form of entrepreneurship (Martin et al., 2015). Blank et al. (2002) were one of the first scholars to use the concept of entrepreneurship in the context of agriculture. Stathopoulou and colleagues (2004) offers a good example, explaining the rural context with three components: geographic, social and economical, which interact with different stages of the entrepreneurial process. For example, the geography of being rural, distances from markets and small customer base have profound effects in entrepreneurial practice (Anderson & Obeng, 2017).

Researching on farmers behaviour, McElwee (2008) identifies two pertinent types of smallholders. First, the "farmer as a farmer", who tends to engage in limited diversification and depends on push factors. Their strategic orientation is based on cost-price reduction with little awareness of market opportunities and individualistic orientation. Second, the "farmer as an entrepreneur", who identifies and exploits non-agricultural or high-value opportunities based on the farm's resources in flexible and innovative ways. Developing entrepreneurial competency in the agricultural sector means bringing the smallholders from the "farmer as farmer" position to the "farmer as entrepreneur" level through an educational process based upon entrepreneurial learning concept. This process of "engine of change" in the rural area (Dodd et al., 2016) requires an understanding of how to change-making via entrepreneurial practice in a rural context works. Oreszczyn et al. (2010) highlights that rural smallholders have a particular type of network of practice, particularly communities of practice in which entrepreneurial learning may occur. In researching farmer-to-farmer learning videos, Zossou et al. (2009) found that the learning process can trigger creativity and help rural people to innovate. It also shows that apart of learning via the community of practice, their access to many useful physicals, human and social resources which are often required to start new businesses.

Contextualising the Development of Alternative Businesses for Smallholders

The smallholders studied in this study are creating businesses in the specific context of the transition from production-oriented to entrepreneurship (McElwee, 2006, 2008; Mustaffa & Singaravelloo, 2019). In the context of agriculture, smallholders are like farmers, McElwee (2006) discovered limited literature in farm diversification and farmers' enterprise skills. Farming is not a homogeneous sector; smallholders too operate in a tightly constrained and regulated, complex and multi-faceted environment, which acts as a significant barrier to entrepreneurial activity (Martin et al., 2015).

Entrepreneurial skill incorporates behaviour which may be tactical at the individual level (Chell, 2013). Within the agricultural sector, important entrepreneurial attitudes and skills also include aspects that can be found in general entrepreneurship literature, which are entrepreneurial orientation and market orientation (Baker & Sinkula, 2009; Slater & Narver, 1995). Entrepreneurial orientation is the "*processes, practices, and decision-making activities that lead to new entry*" (Lumpkin & Dess, 1996: 136). By contrast, market orientation looks into an individual willingness to continuously deliver higher value to its customers (McElwee, 2006). Both entrepreneurial and market orientation assist the entrepreneur identify new business opportunities, which, according to McElwee, 2008 (b) are major requirements for smallholders to compete successfully. Individuals and community with high entrepreneurial orientation constantly innovate their products and markets, involves in proactive decision making, and take a risk in business (Basso et al., 2009). The entrepreneurial skill in the rural area incorporates activities that can be changed through communication or experience (Pyysiäinen et al., 2006). This includes skills related to social resources, social ties/networks which are crucial for improving social embeddedness (Pyysiäinen et al., 2006). More importantly, smallholders' entrepreneurial actions can be related to situational and personal factors (Pyysiäinen et al., 2006).

Organisational competency is also essential in the Sabah palm oil sector. In our case, the majority of smallholders owning between one and 20 hectares of land, they are bound to work together in order to present a united front to protect their interests, especially when dealing with buyers, intermediaries, and in achieving more efficient production models, such as those achieving economies of scale (Martin et al., 2015). Hence, community plays a significant role that influences how entrepreneurship is being practised in a rural area, which may be itself an important social resource that can help to create value. (Gaddefors & Anderson, 2019). This is also known as a social network, focuses on the interpersonal relationship, based in the local community (Pato & Teixeira, 2016). This can act as a vehicle for smallholders to help the weaker smallholders to attain collective efficiency in order to overcome infrastructure constraints for market entries (Mesquita & Lazzarini, 2008). Previous literature has shown that community of smallholders embrace inter-organisational networks in order to remain competitive in today's markets (Johnston & Huggins, 2016).

Smallholders must develop the capacity for entrepreneurial and market orientation including organisational competency as well as the ability to use the social network to compete in the free market for sustainable development to alleviate poverty (Martin et al., 2015; McKague & Oliver, 2012). It is hoped that the process of developing these competencies, the smallholders will become less dependent on government subsidies, respond to the growing demand for quality and conform to the social and environmental policies (Martin et al., 2015). Developing entrepreneurial and business competency of smallholders is challenging and stressful. Martin et al. (2015) discovered the lack of entrepreneurial and business skills is one of the obstacles to innovaion which hinders potential investment. In order to develop these critical entrepreneurial and business cognitive skills, learning by doing method has been shown can be more effective through entrepreneurial learning approach (Chang & Rieple, 2013; Chang et al., 2014).

The Role of Entrepreneurial Learning

Entrepreneurial learning is described as an experiential approach where an entrepreneur's individual experience is transformed into knowledge, which can then be utilised to select new experiences (Politis, 2005). It could also be learning that informs the search for new opportunities by an entrepreneur (Clinton & Gamble, 2019). In order to drive business success and growth among these palm oil smallholders, there is a need for entrepreneurial learning to develop entrepreneurial skills. There has been a lot of focus on entrepreneurial learning within entrepreneurship research (Krakowiak-Bal et al., 2017). This growing interest is due to the notion that experience, entrepreneurship education and training programmes can enhance the learning and development of entrepreneurial competencies (McElwee, 2006; Krakowiak-Bal et al., 2017).

Entrepreneurial learning is a situated phenomenon, embedded and influenced by social dynamics of the entrepreneur's work environment (Cope, 2003; Rae, 2006). These studies stem from the notion of situated learning (Lave & Wenger, 1991) which claims that learning is a social process beyond the thinking process of the learner. In this chapter, we adopt the situated standpoint on entrepreneurial learning using Rae's (2006) framework, which captures the complexity of the process by connecting the cognitive and social dimensions. Rae's framework, based upon technological-based entrepreneurship, can be used to focus on transforming entrepreneurship in the agriculture sector. Five elements of entrepreneurial learning underpin Rae's works are:

1. Is dynamic process of awareness, reflection, association and application that involves transforming experience and knowledge into functional learning outcomes (Cope & Watts, 2000).
2. Comprises knowledge, behaviour and affective or emotional learning.

3. Is affected by the context in which learning occurs, and it includes the content of what is learned as well as the processes through which learning takes place (Politis, 2005).
4. Both individual, with personal differences in ability producing different learning outcomes, as well as social and organisational (Corbett, 2005).
5. Close relationship between the processes of entrepreneurial learning and of opportunity recognition, exploitation, creativity and innovation (Lumpkin & Lichtenstein, 2005).

Rae's framework has three themes of learning processes (1) personal and social emergence of entrepreneurial identity, (2) contextual learning and (3) the negotiated enterprise. The personal and social emergence of entrepreneurial identity is the enactment of being and assuming the role of an entrepreneur (Rae, 2006). The act of doing what entrepreneurs do assume the identity of being an entrepreneur (Chang et al., 2019). Contextual learning involves the participation of the community, industry and other relevant stakeholders which the learner experiences are related and compared to and shared meaning is constructed (Chang & Rieple, 2018). This situated experience provides the social network for learning and developing new opportunities (Chang et al., 2019) The final theme, negotiated enterprise refers to the construction of new ventures that occurs through the participation of negotiated relationships (Rae, 2006). The ideas and aspirations of individuals are realised through interactive processes of exchange with others within and around the enterprise (Chang & Rieple, 2018).

This chapter considers the smallholders can be transformed into entrepreneurs, by developing new businesses on their existing land, they do not only become more entrepreneurial but also develop different ways of developing their acreage. The transition from producer to different business revenue models of agriculture is furthermore considered as an important background to this study. Finally, the development of the entrepreneurial competencies and business skills required for the smallholder's new role in agriculture is explored using the concept of entrepreneurial learning, this being the core of our theoretical framework.

Research Method

We intended to understand the factors of the entrepreneurial learning process of smallholders who participated in the Effective Entrepreneurship Training programme using mobile technology (supported by the Newton Mobility Fund). Understanding the entrepreneurial learning cognitive and social influences on these processes, and how they change over time, requires longitudinal qualitative data and an interpretive epistemology (Cope, 2011). The smallholders were tasked to set up a new business without any prior budget. This took place in a rural village, Sapi Nangoh, Beluran nestled among large corporation palm oil estates of Borneo Island. The village is six-hour drive from the local investigators over treacherous Mount Kinabalu and hills the local investigators. The training lasted for 12 months (March 2017–March 2018) instead of four months contributed by the slow adoption of smartphone for learning, poor road infrastructure and poor weather conditions. The training programme consists of five site visits for face to face team coaching sessions. The smallholders were not required to have any prior knowledge of entrepreneurship concepts or theory in order or business experience. Our objectives were to enable smallholders to be immersed in developing their businesses, a form of "learning by doing" (Pittaway & Cope, 2007). Adopting from Chang and Rieple (2018), microcosm, would allow smallholders to learn the skills that entrepreneurs do.

Coaching was provided by trained academic staff in coaching, who met weekly via the smartphone using facebook and whatsapp with the smallholders in order to provide feedback and discuss options. A total of 14 smallholders participated in the training programme, and each team coach is allocated three smallholders for weekly coaching. The business activities included raising swiftlet for their bird-nest, goat rearing, fishpond rearing, street food kiosk, café, as seen in Table 7.1. Each smallholder was required to report on their progress weekly on facebook, reflecting on what they had done, and why, and what had worked and what had not (Lindh & Thorgren, 2016). These social media comprise our primary data, onto which we subsequently were used to mapping Rae's entrepreneurial learning framework and the contextual influences

Table 7.1 Participants background information

Participants	Orientation	Age	Education level	Ethnic	New business
AA	Male	61	Low level Education	Jawa	Bird-nest production
BB	Male	70	Completed Junior School	Sungai	Meat production
CC	Male	62	Low level Education	Sungai	Banana products
RR	Male	46	Completed High School	Sungai	Meat and bird-nest production
DD	Male	60	Low level Education	Sungai	Duck farming
EE	Male	48	Completed High School	Dusun	Fishpond farming
FF	Male	56	Completed High School	Sungai	Ferm farming
GG	Male	44	Low level Education	Sukang	Transport business
HH	Male	52	Completed High School	Sungai	Homestay business
II	Male	57	No formal education	Sungai	Homestay business
JJ	Male	50	No formal education	Sungai	Auto service business
KK	Male	51	Completed High School	Jawa	Street food kiosk
LL	Male	44	Low level Education	Sungai	Poultry
MM	Female	61	No formal education	Brunei	Grocery store

All participants' names are anonymised
Source Authors own

on them (Pittaway & Cope, 2007). All the participants gave permission for their data to be used for research purposes. The data from the facebook and whatsapp account were supplemented by information from site visits, observation of smallholder's interactions, discussions with smallholders, all of which were recorded and discussed between the teaching and research team. These helped to inform the analysis and judgement of why and how smallholders behaved as they did. We used Rae's entrepreneurial learning framework to identify the use of the different behaviours within the facebooks and documents from observations inductively.

Smallholders were not asked to categorise their entrepreneurial learning process; instead, the authors went through the transcripts and categorised any behaviours that could be identified. They agreed on the themes and the entrepreneurial learning process identified. Where there were differences of interpretation, these were discussed and a common conclusion reached. There was no attempt to measure the degree of disagreement or inter-coder reliability ratings; all classifications were discussed, and an agreed decision reached. Each learning process was allocated exclusively to one of Rae's EL themes: (1) personal and social emergence of entrepreneurial identity, (2) contextual learning and (3) the negotiated enterprise, described in the "Findings" section. Almost all of our data could be fitted into one of the categories. Factors which appeared to fit into two or more categories were also noted and allocated to what appeared to be the most appropriate. Of the most frequently recurring and notable sub-themes, at the point of writing this chapter, we contextualise three themes.

Findings

This section narrates the three main factors driving entrepreneurial learning among the participating smallholders which correspond to the three entrepreneurial learning frameworks of (1) personal and social emergence of entrepreneurial identity, (2) contextual learning and (3) the negotiated enterprise.

Embodying the Entrepreneurial Identity

Rae (2006) argues that simply acquiring entrepreneurial skills and knowledge is not sufficient (p. 45) but requires the individual to act and assume the identity of an entrepreneur. In our context, identity plays an essential role in transforming smallholders into entrepreneurs. The majority of the smallholders saw themselves as producers at the start of the programme and let fate decides their livelihood and relied on government subsidies for help. Their learning experiences with the development of their new businesses has compelled the smallholders to think practices they have developed and to define entrepreneurship. All the smallholders expressed that the development of the new businesses had made them aware, reflect, associate and apply the knowledge to transform their ideas into a venture.

Some of them still think as palm oil producer complaining about low yield due to the rainy season. They look forward to the govern extension officer to help them to maximise the yield.

Not all smallholders assume the identity as an entrepreneur at the same rate. In particular, we notice that smallholders who adopt the use of smartphone are much faster in developing the identity of entrepreneurs. They feel in touch with the real market and use social media network to reach out to potential customers as they are so out of the mainstream. The smallholders generally find difficulty to develop entrepreneurial identity as they perceived that the word entrepreneur (or Usahawan in the Malay language) is associated with people who are more educated, and of those who know to develop new business. They also assumed that these very much require a certain level of education, by attending an entrepreneurship course offered in the local university. Therefore, it is difficult for the smallholders to break free from the norm, regarding themselves only as a palm oil producer. These smallholders tend to have less self-confidence and are not void of family's disapproval for business.

The smallholder that exhibits strong leadership in persuading others to participate in this action research showed a high level of entrepreneurial activities. The entrepreneur displayed entrepreneurial identity as they overcome doubt and uncertainty. They had a vision for their children to set up a business. They were the first person in the village to start a canteen business in front of the palm oil mill recognising the opportunity to serve lorry drivers and passers-by with food. In addition, the entrepreneur persuaded his fellow smallholders to join this project to become entrepreneurs. They understand the benefit of the project and rallied other smallholders to take on this opportunity to learn by doing.

Crossing the Boundary of Palm Oil Dependency

Entrepreneurial learning is the outcome of the process of contextual learning as pointed out by Rae (2006) and Cope (2003). The contextual learning includes social participation in the community, industry and other networks through which individual experiences are related and compared, and shared meaning is constructed (p. 47). In the context of our educational programme, the focus was on the social participation and interaction of the participants. The social interaction in the work environment develops the smallholders' entrepreneurial propensity, knowledge and skills in shaping new business activities. During the second block of the educational programme, the smallholders have to interact with relevant stakeholders such as customers to identify their needs and create demand, the suppliers to calculate the cost, government officials to find out the compliance and so on. Smallholders are moving into non-palm oil activities such as food production (bird-nest, meat and poultry), grocery store and hospitality service provider, depending on the availability of the individual resources of the smallholders. For example, Mr AA started the canteen business, which then influences Mr KK to operate the grilled chicken business as his supplier. Mr AA passed on the canteen business to other friends so that he can focus on the swiftlet farming to produce bird-nest. The training session allows actors in the work environment that influence each to take action upon their business ideas.

Learning a New Trade: Entrepreneurship with Smartphone

During the second block of site training, smallholders were required to do individual SWOT analysis based on the resources they possess. Identifying their own resources (such as physical, network, social resources, etc.). Indeed all 14 participants have learnt a new trade, as shown in Table 7.1 as they venture into different activities within their palm oil land. The common expression was learning a new trade focusing on entrepreneurship using a smartphone with social media, e.g. Facebook and WhatsApp, to do business. They were excited and stressed the development of their new activities increasingly requires them to leave their palm oil activities for more social participation for their new business venture. This includes, for example, finding the requirements of customers and meeting with potential suppliers. The smallholders contend with themselves that crossing the physical boundaries of the normal activities have broadened their horizons and connections and operate beyond the palm oil domain. Eventually establishing new trade has given them extra income to help support the family. Learning new trade has also given them family members to acquire the experience as they require to assist with the business activities to ensure sustainability.

Space for Learning

For all smallholders, existing palm oil production forms the basis for new activities as the training programme enabled them to evaluate their existing resources to develop new business ideas closely associated with their interests. This is to minimise reliance on external resources. Dealing with a limit in the availability of labour, the smallholder families have to find a way to integrate current palm oil production with the development of new business activities. For example, during the second site training, participant EE's identified his fish-rearing hobby could be turned into a business. They then created a pond and the push to have the confidence to turn it into a business. By the third visit, they were overjoyed that their product was already booked six months ahead by clients (restaurants) outside the village using Whatsapp. Similar observations were noted for participant JJ who enjoyed repairing his pickup to transport the palm oil harvest to the milling factory. Their reputation allowed them to start-up a auto-repair garage.

Using the team coaching learning approach in the programme undoubtedly created a space for contextual learning. During the third block of teaching, smallholders, were asked to identify issues and challenges they faced in setting up and running new business activities.

Creating the space for learning during team coaching sessions were received well by all the participants as they were all very open to sharing the challenges and issues faced. The coaches facilitated them to come out with their own solutions. For example, they identified several challenges that impeded their business activities such as finance as there were no banks within the village, the nearest being about three hours drive. To illustrate this, participant EE's fish-rearing business is gaining demand, however, they find it difficult to obtain funds to scale up as the nearest bank is three hours drive from the village and most of them do not have a commercial bank account and the likelihood of obtaining finance is almost negligible. As the village business activities are becoming rigorous, the values of their goods increase and the reports of theft become prevalent.

Collaboration Behaviour to Increase Community Capacity

Engagement with others is a crucial aspect of developing new business as it is the culmination of the outcome through a negotiated relationship with others (Rae, 2006: 49). We find this is evident in the collaborative behaviour for developing community capacity. The collaborative behaviour to increase the community capacity was particularly prevalent with participants with a stronger vision for growth and scaling up their businesses. The stronger entrepreneurial participants exhibited their influence in creating more room for manoeuvring their limited resources to increase the community capacity. The new dynamics created through the collaborative behaviour in solving the challenges raised in the previous section shows the significant importance of the notion of negotiated enterprise in this context. We will focus on the relationship between the smallholders' learning and the community dynamics in the introduction of "Dana" in Malays language that means the collective investment fund, and developing a market place, where local businesses can combine and trade openly and encourage other smallholders to be like them.

Devise Funding System Called Dana

By the third site visit training, all smallholders were aware that in order to realise their ambitions to scale up their business activities, they needed to work together collectively. For smallholder EE, who wanted to scale up his fish business and smallholder JJ who desired to franchise his BBQ chicken wing recipe for street food. Having mentioned the availability of financial assistance, collectively, they devised a financial process known as "Dana" to help the participating smallholders who urgently required the money to run their business activities. Thus, whoever is having a financial problem, they can sell palm oil harvest to the Dana to obtain the necessary finance. Then, Dana sells it to the harvest accordingly. All transactions were recorded and reported to all members of the community through their smartphone. This demonstrates the high level of trust that has developed through this negotiated relationship which enables them to use the fund to repair roads which are damaged by frequent flooding.

Wearing Hats with Different Colours

The introduction of the funding system, the organisation of the palm oil smallholders community, extends to the whole village. This changing context forces the participating smallholders to assume different roles and positions with the village. As the village faces security and access to police authority may be limited due to the remoteness of this village. They have decided to set up the village watch voluntarily. Rota was set up and distributed via WhatsApp to all individuals who participated in the neighbourhood watch. They will use smartphones to contact the network if there is crime on the site. They also take a step back when they notice that not all participants were motivated to run their business activities. Participants like AA, who was highly motivated and experienced mentored participant RR, who was less experienced. When they run out of ideas for mentoring, they watched motivational video using the smartphone to become the subject of the mentoring relationship. Similarly, we also observe that not all participants are agile with the smartphone and the younger participants like GG and LL mentored the smartphone illiterate participants. This took quite a while to learn. Once all the participants become savvy smartphone users, they supported each other to gather information on the weather so that they managed the business operation as the roads in the village were not sealed with recurring floods.

Developing a Market to Help Others to Be in Business

One of the unexpected outcomes of the negotiated relationship is the recognition of the collective action in setting up a market place to encourage other smallholders to sell their produce. The smallholders realise that the market place will create the pull factor for potential customers to visit the village, and they seem to want to create a brand for their village. The head of the village donated part of his land to the business venture.

Conclusions

The smallholders' flexible behaviour to the environmental, social and economic crisis has resulted in an increase in research for entrepreneurship in the agriculture sector in Malaysia. Although extensive research has been carried out on smallholders' entrepreneurial skills, the existing body of literature has not provided adequate information on the learning process underlying the development of these skills. This chapter has contributed to this gap by exploring the learning process that enables the development of entrepreneurial and business skills. By looking at smallholders who started businesses on their existing palm oil land, we focused on the learning processes of producers to entrepreneurs. We applied the concept of entrepreneurial learning (Cope, 2003; Politis, 2005; Rae, 2006), with the objective to identify the factors that drive this process in the rural agriculture setting of entrepreneurship. Using Rae (2006) entrepreneurial learning framework, we unfold three major themes that become the driving force of the change of the behaviours of the smallholders from individual to collective behaviours: (1) the embodiment of entrepreneurial identity, (2) crossing the boundary of palm oil dependency and (3) community collaboration. The case highlights the importance of active community engagement and leadership in persuading others in the community to take up a new business, as they recirculate resources locally (e.g. Dana) and multiplies benefits for the local community through entrepreneurship (Korsching & Allen, 2004).

This research provides excellent insights for policymakers that deals with rural development. Our work illustrates a different way of capacity building of rural community via entrepreneurial learning, that is not focusing on the reliance of government aids, but instead allowing the individuals in the rural community to realise their local strengths, and becoming the owner of their own transformation (i.e. ownership of change). By taking into consideration the interests of individual participants (needs, desires and aspirations), and the social-economic context (conflicts, crises, opportunities and challenges), the individual initiatives take hold, and there will be a local community governance arrangement emerged. This transformation will lead to a high level, overarching outcomes, such as sustainability, resilience and societal well-being. Nevertheless, not all entrepreneurship initiatives are transformative. Our research showed that the transformation of the community, involved the creation of their community support governance, triggered by embodying individual entrepreneurial identity, crossing the boundary of palm oil dependency. Hence, any government aids made into the community can be used as a catalyst to facilitate ongoing entrepreneurial activities for rural development.

This research has limitations to consider. First, the evidence was collected in a single community—a rural village in Borneo Island, Malaysia. This helped with the control of the national context, and also with the type of engagement on which we focused. Future research from other countries, within a different context (non-palm-related villagers), would be able to provide more insights on the topic. Secondly, this research is highly contextual, that requires a high level of local knowledge. Hence, the involvement of local researchers is vital to the success of the study. There is potential for future research to investigate the value derived by the collaborators of the investigation.

References

Aldrich, H. E., & Martinez, M. (2003). Entrepreneurship as social construction: A multi-level evolutionary approach. In *Handbook of entrepreneurship research* (pp. 359–399). Springer.

Anderson, A. R., & Obeng, B. A. (2017). Enterprise as socially situated in a rural poor fishing community. *Journal of Rural Studies, 49*, 23–31.

Baker, W. E., & Sinkula, J. M. (2009). The complementary effects of market orientation and entrepreneurial orientation on profitability in small businesses. *Journal of Small Business Management, 47*(4), 443–464.

Basso, O., Fayolle, A., & Bouchard, V. (2009). Entrepreneurial orientation: The making of a concept. *The International Journal of Entrepreneurship and Innovation, 10*(4), 313–321.

Blank, H. G., Mutero, C. M., & Murray-Rust, H. (2002). *The changing face of irrigation in Kenya: Opportunities for anticipating changes in Eastern and Southern Africa* (No. H030816). International Water Management Institute.

Bock, B. B. (2004). Fitting in and multi-tasking: Dutch farm women's strategies in rural entrepreneurship. *Sociologia Ruralis, 44*(3), 245–260.

Bock, B. B. (2015). Gender mainstreaming and rural development policy: The trivialisation of rural gender issues. *Gender, Place & Culture, 22*(5), 731–745.

Bosworth, G., Rizzo, F., Marquardt, D., Strijker, D., Haartsen, T., & Aagaard Thuesen, A. (2016). Identifying social innovations in European local rural development initiatives. *Innovation: The European Journal of Social Science Research, 29*(4), 442–461.

Chang, J., & Rieple, A. (2013). Assessing students' entrepreneurial skills development in live projects. *Journal of Small Business and Enterprise Development, 20*(1), 225–241.

Chang, J., & Rieple, A. (2018). Entrepreneurial decision-making in a microcosm. *Management Learning, 49*(4), 471–497.

Chang, J., Benamraoui, A., & Rieple, A. (2014). Stimulating learning about social entrepreneurship through income generation projects. *International Journal of Entrepreneurial Behavior & Research, 20*(5), 417–437.

Chang, J., Rosli, A., & Jackson, A. (2019). Entrepreneurship education in developing student entrepreneurs: A practice theory perspective. In *Academy of management proceedings* (Vol. 2019, No. 1, p. 15510). Academy of Management.

Chell, E. (2013). Review of skill and the entrepreneurial process. *International Journal of Entrepreneurial Behavior & Research, 19*(1), 6–31.

Clinton, E., & Gamble, J. R. (2019). Entrepreneurial behaviour as learning processes in a transgenerational entrepreneurial family. In *Entrepreneurial behaviour* (pp. 237–260). Palgrave Macmillan.

Cope, J. (2003). Entrepreneurial learning and critical reflection: Discontinuous events as triggers for 'higher-level' learning. *Management Learning, 34*(4), 429–450.

Cope, J. (2011). Entrepreneurial learning from failure: An interpretative phenomenological analysis. *Journal of Business Venturing, 26*(6), 604–623.

Cope, J., & Watts, G. (2000). Learning by doing–an exploration of experience, critical incidents and reflection in entrepreneurial learning. *International Journal of Entrepreneurial Behavior & Research, 6*(3), 104–124.

Corbett, A. C. (2005). Experiential learning within the process of opportunity identification and exploitation. *Entrepreneurship Theory and Practice, 29*(4), 473–491.

de Bruin, A., Shaw, E., & Lewis, K. V. (2017). The collaborative dynamic in social entrepreneurship. *Entrepreneurship & Regional Development, 29*(7–8), 575–585.

Dodd, S. D., Pret, T., & Shaw, E. (2016). Advancing understanding of entrepreneurial embeddedness: Forms of capital, social contexts and time. In *A research agenda for entrepreneurship and context* (pp. 120–133). Edward Elgar.

Gaddefors, J., & Anderson, A. R. (2019). Romancing the rural: Reconceptualizing rural entrepreneurship as engagement with context (s). *The International Journal of Entrepreneurship and Innovation, 20*(3), 159–169.

Jack, S. L., Dodd, S. D., & Anderson, A. R. (2004). Social structures and entrepreneurial networks: The strength of strong ties. *The International Journal of Entrepreneurship and Innovation, 5*(2), 107–120.

Johnston, A., & Huggins, R. (2016). Drivers of university–industry links: The case of knowledge-intensive business service firms in rural locations. *Regional Studies, 50*(8), 1330–1345.

Kalantaridis, C., & Bika, Z. (2006). In-migrant entrepreneurship in rural England: Beyond local embeddedness. *Entrepreneurship and Regional Development, 18*(2), 109–131.

Korsching, P. F., & Allen, J. C. (2004). Locality based entrepreneurship: A strategy for community economic vitality. *Community Development Journal, 39*(4), 385–400.

Krakowiak-Bal, A., Ziemianczyk, U., & Wozniak, A. (2017). Building entrepreneurial capacity in rural areas: The use of AHP analysis for infrastructure evaluation. *International Journal of Entrepreneurial Behavior & Research, 23*(6), 903–918.

Lave, J., & Wenger, E. (1991). *Situated learning: Legitimate peripheral participation.* Cambridge, UK: Cambridge university press.

Lindh, I., & Thorgren, S. (2016). Critical event recognition: An extended view of reflective learning. *Management Learning, 47*(5), 525–542.

Lumpkin, G. T., & Dess, G. G. (1996). Clarifying the entrepreneurial orientation construct and linking it to performance. *Academy of Management Review, 21*(1), 135–172.

Lumpkin, G. T., & Lichtenstein, B. B. (2005). The role of organizational learning in the opportunity–recognition process. *Entrepreneurship Theory and Practice, 29*(4), 451–472.

Martin, S., Rieple, A., Chang, J., Boniface, B., & Ahmed, A. (2015). Small farmers and sustainability: Institutional barriers to investment and innovation in the Malaysian palm oil industry in Sabah. *Journal of Rural Studies, 40,* 46–58.

McElwee, G. (2006). Farmers as entrepreneurs: Developing competitive skills. *Journal of Developmental Entrepreneurship, 11*(3), 187–206.

McElwee, G. (2008). A taxonomy of entrepreneurial farmers. *International Journal of Entrepreneurship and Small Business, 6*(3), 465–478.

McElwee, G., & Annibal, I. (2010). Business support for farmers: An evaluation of the Farm Cornwall project. *Journal of Small Business and Enterprise Development, 17*(3), 475–491.

McKague, K., & Oliver, C. (2012). Enhanced market practices: Poverty alleviation for poor producers in developing countries. *California Management Review, 55*(1), 98–129.

Mesquita, L. F., & Lazzarini, S. G. (2008). Horizontal and vertical relationships in developing economies: Implications for SMEs' access to global markets. *Academy of Management Journal, 51*(2), 359–380.

Muhammad, N., McElwee, G., & Dana, L. P. (2017). Barriers to the development and progress of entrepreneurship in rural Pakistan. *International Journal of Entrepreneurial Behavior & Research, 23*(2), 279–295.

Mustaffa, F., & Singaravelloo, K. (2019). Multiplicity in entrepreneurship economic development of Malaysian smallholder farmers. *Academy of Entrepreneurship Journal, 25*(1), online.

Oreszczyn, S., Lane, A., & Carr, S. (2010). The role of networks of practice and webs of influencers on farmers' engagement with and learning about agricultural innovations. *Journal of Rural Studies, 26*(4), 404–417.

Pato, M. L., & Teixeira, A. A. (2016). Twenty years of rural entrepreneurship: A bibliometric survey. *Sociologia Ruralis, 56*(1), 3–28.

Pittaway, L., & Cope, J. (2007). Simulating entrepreneurial learning: Integrating experiential and collaborative approaches to learning. *Management Learning, 38*(2), 211–233.

Politis, D. (2005). The process of entrepreneurial learning: A conceptual framework. *Entrepreneurship Theory and Practice, 29*(4), 399–424.

Pyysiäinen, J., Anderson, A., McElwee, G., & Vesala, K. (2006). Developing the entrepreneurial skills of farmers: Some myths explored. *International Journal of Entrepreneurial Behavior & Research, 12*(1), 21–39.

Rae, D. (2006). Entrepreneurial learning: A conceptual framework for technology-based enterprise. *Technology Analysis & Strategic Management, 18*(1), 39–56.

Seuneke, P., Lans, T., & Wiskerke, J. S. (2013). Moving beyond entrepreneurial skills: Key factors driving entrepreneurial learning in multifunctional agriculture. *Journal of Rural Studies, 32*, 208–219.

Slater, S. F., & Narver, J. C. (1995). Market orientation and the learning organization. *Journal of Marketing, 59*(3), 63–74.

Stathopoulou, S., Psaltopoulos, D., & Skuras, D. (2004). Rural entrepreneurship in Europe: A research framework and agenda. *International Journal of Entrepreneurial Behavior & Research, 10*(6), 404–425.

Welter, F., Baker, T., Audretsch, D. B., & Gartner, W. B. (2017). Everyday entrepreneurship—A call for entrepreneurship research to embrace entrepreneurial diversity. *Entrepreneurship Theory and Practice, 41*(3), 311–321.

Zossou, E., Van Mele, P., Vodouhe, S. D., & Wanvoeke, J. (2009). Comparing farmer-to-farmer video with workshops to train rural women in improved rice parboiling in central Benin. *Journal of Agricultural Education and Extension, 15*(4), 329–339.

8

Exploring SME Women Entrepreneurs' Work–Family Conflict in Malaysia

Wendy Ming-Yen Teoh, Chin Wei Chong, Yee Yen Yuen, and Siong Choy Chong

Introduction

Women typically undertake multiple roles as a spouse, parent and employer, often carrying out their work and family responsibilities simultaneously. Hence, they are amongst the groups that tend to experience higher work–family conflict compared to those employed (König & Cesinger, 2015). According to Simmons (2013), women entrepreneurs, on their own accord, should work between 70 and 100 hours per week to ensure a successful business. However, according to the Malaysian Labour Force Survey Report (2011), women entrepreneurs spent an

---

W. M.-Y. Teoh (✉) · Y. Y. Yuen
Multimedia University, Malacca, Malaysia
e-mail: myteoh@mmu.edu.my

C. W. Chong
Multimedia University, Cyberjaya, Malaysia

S. C. Chong
Finance Accreditation Agency, Kuala Lumpur, Malaysia

© The Author(s), under exclusive license to Springer Nature Switzerland AG 2021
P. Jones et al. (eds.), *Entrepreneurial Activity in Malaysia*,
https://doi.org/10.1007/978-3-030-77753-1_8

average of 50.2 hours per week at work only, implying the challenges they experienced when attempting to balance both home and business demands (Agarwal & Lenka, 2014). Minimal research attention has been paid to the life stage changes of married women with children and their entrepreneurial careers. Further, how work–life balance impacts on individual career paths and outcomes has rarely been considered in the Malaysian context (Ahmad, 2005; Nasurdin et al., 2013; Teoh et al., 2016). These serve as the motivation for this research to be carried out.

Literature Review

Work–Family Conflict

Due to the changing work and demographic trends of families in Malaysia and across the world, many women reported that their work interferes with their family responsibilities (Aazami et al., 2016). Prior research has demonstrated that work-to-family conflict has a greater effect on job satisfaction than family-to-work conflict (Kossek & Ozeki, 1998). Since most of the women entrepreneurs were not able to balance their work life and family life, when they feel dissatisfied with their work life, they are more likely not to succeed in their businesses (Mohamad & Bakar, 2017).

Work Schedule Flexibility

Work schedule flexibility has been investigated as a motivator for entrepreneurs (Kirkwood & Tootell, 2008). Based on the work–family conflict model by Lee and Choo (2001), amongst the job characteristics (e.g. work schedule flexibility, number of hours worked and work stressors), it has been found that work schedule inflexibility and work stressors were the most significant factors contributing to work–family conflict. According to the conservation of resources (COR) theory (Hobfoll, 2001), individuals place the highest value on reducing work–family conflict by acquiring work schedule flexibility that moves them toward higher job satisfaction. However, work schedule flexibility is vague according to various researchers, with some postulating that schedule flexibility reduces work–family conflict when individuals frequently encountered conflicts with family obligations (Kossek & Michel, 2011). There is yet other research which found work–family conflict to be independent of schedule flexibility (Kossek et al., 2006), showing that the evidence available is mixed.

Role Ambiguity

Role ambiguity represents the uncertainties arising when individuals have no clear direction about what is expected of them and how to perform (Palomino & Frezatti, 2016; Rizzo et al., 1970). Insufficient resources and poor communication could be potential stressors for entrepreneurs (Buttner, 1992; Khairuddin, 2015) in fulfilling their obligations, leading to role ambiguity. Entrepreneurs should respond proactively by avoiding ambiguities in potential role conflicts and addressing role overload when factors from either side of the divide threaten to disrupt operations on the other (Teoh et al., 2016). It has been found that role ambiguity has direct and indirect effects on work–family conflict (Boles et al., 2003). Role ambiguity is seen not only as the precursor of work–family conflict, but it is also associated with higher levels of role conflicts (Aryee, 1992; Chin et al., 2012; Grandey & Cropanzano, 1999). These studies imply that when people experience ambiguity in their jobs and lack precise knowledge of the goals they must accomplish, they tend to feel the pressure and fatigue and hence hesitate to make decisions. Hence, individuals perceived to experience ambiguity in their roles were less satisfied in their work (Tremblay & Roger, 2004). According to Kahn et al. (1964), the vague expectations may cause ambiguity, particularly for women entrepreneurs mainly due to the societal expectation that the role of a woman is to attend to family matters instead of being the "breadwinner". These dual roles that women entrepreneurs take on cause role ambiguity and consequently dissatisfaction at work.

Spousal Support

Having a spouse is a major asset for women entrepreneurs since spouses form an integral part of the support network (Lee & Choo, 2001; Rehman & Roomi, 2012). Support extended to entrepreneurs can be emotional or instrumental (Bodenmann et al., 2006; Lapierre & Allen, 2006; Semerci, 2016). Emotional support (e.g. love, empathy and respect) seems to be even more crucial than the relief from household responsibilities (Vadnjal & Vadnjal, 2013) since it helps to reduce the occurrence of conflicts. Instrumental support (e.g. tools, money or care services) is the provision of actual assistance to complete or at least help in task accomplishment and can at least reduce the pressures pertaining to time and also parental demands (Lee & Choo, 2001).

Despite the existence of many studies reiterating the relevance of spousal support, there are some which demonstrated inconsistent results between spousal support and work–family conflict (Gudmunson et al., 2009). Parasuraman et al. (1996) for one, discovered the effects of spousal support on work–family conflict and found no buffering effect between the two. Their work found support from another study by Gudmunson et al. (2009) on family business owners which examined the emotional effects of spousal support on work–family conflict using the COR theory (Hobfoll, 1989, 2001). The findings suggest that no direct effect is found between spousal support and work–family balance, implying a mixed conclusion. Khan (2016) suggests that a male spouse who is much more willing to provide support to his wife, will possibly pave the way for a positive impact towards the career of his wife, lead his wife to work satisfactorily and become committed to her goals for her enterprise.

Core Self-Evaluations

Core Self-Evaluations is personified by four traits: "*self-esteem*, the overall value that one places on oneself as a person (Harter, 1990); *generalised self-efficacy*, an evaluation of how well one can perform across a variety of situations (Locke et al., 1996); *neuroticism*, the tendency to have a negativistic cognitive/explanatory style and to focus on the negative aspects of one's self (Watson, 2000); and *locus of control*, beliefs about the causes of events in one's life—locus is internal when individuals see events as being contingent in their own behavior" (Judge et al., 2003: 303–304). In general, core self-evaluation traits refer to the basic beliefs that people hold about themselves, their ability to succeed and their sense of control over their lives (Judge et al., 1997, 2003).

Amongst the four individual core traits, Wan Rashid et al. (2012) found that the higher the self-esteem of an individual, the greater is his or her capability to cope with the conflicting demands of work and family. However, Richter et al. (2014) found that individuals demonstrating a strong performance-based self-esteem (Hallsten, 2005; Hallsten et al., 2005) are at an increased risk of suffering from stress due to the imbalance between work and family demands. Self-efficacy has also been found to be negatively related to work–family conflict (Hennessy & Lent, 2008), whereas neuroticism was consistently related to both directions of work–family conflict (Michel & Clark, 2012; Wayne et al., 2004). In addition, Judge (2009) observes that those with high core self-evaluations were more productive at work and more successful in their careers, experienced greater job and life satisfaction. Srivastava et al. (2010) reported that those with lesser stress and conflict are able to cope effectively with obstacles and can capitalise on advantages and opportunities. This situation is best suited and applied on the women entrepreneurs. From the entrepreneurial perspective, those having positive core self-evaluations may minimise negative situations and are more able to seize opportunities for themselves, innovate and create change (Judge et al., 2010). Subsequently, this would impact significantly on job satisfaction of the women entrepreneurs.

Research Methodology

Research Model and Hypotheses Development

The proposed research model measures the causal relationships between work–family conflict and job satisfaction amongst women entrepreneurs.

Generally, the predictors in the model can be classified as job characteristics (e.g. work schedule flexibility and role ambiguity), family characteristics (e.g. spousal support) and individual characteristics (e.g. CSEs). The mediating variables for the study is work–family conflict, whilst the dependent variable is job satisfaction of women entrepreneurs. These variables and their interrelationships were identified based on the extant literature.

Generally, the model developed was based on two theories, i.e. role theory (Kahn et al., 1964), and the COR theory (Hobfoll, 1989). The distinct feature of this research model is that the studies by Lee and Choo (2001) and Aminah (2008), which were adapted in this study, was broadened to make specific references to the perspective of women entrepreneurship. The former study examines work–family conflict of married women entrepreneurs in Singapore, whilst the latter study proposes a new model of work–family conflict which incorporated variables like emotional exhaustion, job satisfaction and job performance for future development in management studies. The latter model has yet to be tested; hence, an objective of this study was to enhance knowledge on the validity of that model as well as the current model. A key issue to be examined in this research is how the proposed predictors affect job satisfaction of women entrepreneurs in Malaysia, and whether there are variables that significantly mediate the relationship between work–family conflict and job satisfaction. The proposed model depicted in Fig. 8.1 reflects the relationship amongst the variables.

Aligned with the research model, the following hypotheses are proposed to be tested:

H1: Work schedule flexibility is negatively related to work–family conflict.
H2: Role ambiguity is positively related to work–family conflict.
H3: Spousal support is negatively related to work–family conflict.
H4: Core self-evaluations is negatively related to work–family conflict.
H5: Work schedule flexibility is positively related to job satisfaction.
H6: Role ambiguity is negatively related to job satisfaction.
H7: Spousal support is positively related to job satisfaction.

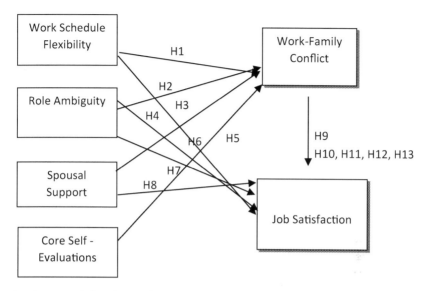

Fig. 8.1 Work-family conflict and job satisfaction of women entrepreneurs (*Source* Authors own)

H8: Core self-evaluations are positively related to job satisfaction.
H9: Work–family conflict is negatively related to job satisfaction.
H10: The effect of work schedule flexibility on job satisfaction is mediated by work–family conflict.
H11: The effect of role ambiguity on job satisfaction is mediated by work–family conflict.
H12: The effect of spousal support on job satisfaction is mediated by work–family conflict.
H13: The effect of core self-evaluations on job satisfaction is mediated by work–family conflict.

Sampling Method

Using a purposive sampling method, the sample of this study consisted women entrepreneurs who are married with at least one child. These criteria were established to ensure that the women in the sample had similar responsibilities in terms of family and work roles. Moreover, women entrepreneurs are significantly more likely than employed women to be married (Budig, 2006; Lombard, 2001). The respondents were asked to return the survey form through the envelope addressed to the researcher provided to increase participation in the study. From the questionnaires returned, 332 questionnaires (66.4% response rate) were usable. This exceeded the acceptable level of response rate of 30% (Sekaran, 2000). After data cleaning, the data from 304 women entrepreneurs were used for further analysis using Partial Least Square (PLS) analysis using the SmartPLS version 2.0 software. Goodness-of-Fit (GoF) indices for PLS path modelling were obtained to assess model fit. Importance-performance map analysis was also used to extend the findings of the basic PLS-SEM outcomes using the latent variables scores for managerial implications (Hair et al., 2017). Table 8.1 shows the descriptive statistics of this research.

Measurement Model Assessment

The measurement model was verified in terms of its convergent and discriminant validity. The convergent validity of the measurement model can be established by examining the factor loadings, average variance extracted (AVE) and composite reliability (CR) (Gholami et al., 2013; Hair et al., 2014, 2017). In Table 8.2, the results show that all of the items were above the cut-off values where loadings of all the constructs exceeded 0.70 (Hair et al., 2014), the AVE was superior to the acceptable limit of 0.50 (Bagozzi & Yi, 1988; Fornell & Larcker, 1981) and that the CR was also higher than the recommended value of between 0.70 and 0.90 (Hair et al., 2014), suggesting that the parameter estimates are sound (Garrity et al., 2009). This indicates that the measures have sufficient convergent validity (Gefen et al., 2000). Most of the factor loadings were greater than the minimum acceptable level of 0.40, which demonstrates the reliability of the measurement scale.

Table 8.1 Descriptive statistics

Variables		Frequency	
		N	%
Age	Less than 20	2	0.7
	20–29	61	20.1
	30–39	117	38.5
	40–49	98	32.2
	50–59	24	7.9
	60 or more	2	0.7
	Total	**304**	**100.0**
Ethnicity	Malay	54	17.8
	Chinese	217	71.4
	Indian	33	10.9
	Others	0	0.0
	Total	**304**	**100.0**
Education level	Less than primary education	15	4.9
	Primary education	21	6.9
	Secondary education	41	13.5
	GCE/STPM/Pre-university	13	4.3
	Diploma	61	20.1
	Advance diploma	6	2.0
	University	120	39.5
	Postgraduate education	13	4.3
	Others	14	4.6
	Total	**304**	**100.0**
Number of Children	1	102	33.6
	2	94	30.9
	3	89	29.3
	4	19	6.3
	5 and above	0	0.0
	Total	**304**	**100.0**
Business ownership	Founder	126	41.4
	Purchased	11	3.6
	Join/Inherited family business	162	53.3
	Others	5	1.6
	Total	**304**	**100.0**
Business sector	Trading	81	26.6
	Services	182	59.9
	Construction/mining	3	1.0

(continued)

Table 8.1 (continued)

Variables		Frequency	
		N	%
	Manufacturing	3	1.0
	Others	35	11.5
	Total	304	100.0
Years in business	5 or less	88	28.9
	6–10	155	51.0
	11–15	52	17.1
	16–20	9	3.0
	21–25	0	0.0
	25 or more	0	0.0
	Total	304	100.0
Work hours per week	20 hours or less	4	1.3
	21–35 hours	122	40.1
	36–45 hours	140	46.1
	46–55 hours	35	11.5
	56 hours or more	3	1.0
	Total	304	100.0
Family hours per week	20 hours or less	58	19.1
	21–35 hours	175	57.6
	36–45 hours	44	14.5
	46–55 hours	17	5.6
	56 hours or more	10	3.3
	Total	304	100.0

Source Authors own

Discriminant Validity

The discriminant validity of the measures was examined using the criteria established by Fornell and Larcker (1981) by comparing the correlations between the constructs and the squared root of the AVE (as shown on the diagonal, in bold) for that construct in Table 8.3. Since all the values on the diagonals exceeded the values of the corresponding row and columns, i.e. greater than the recommended 0.50 level, this indicated that the discriminant validity of the measures exists (Hair et al., 2014).

Table 8.2 Measurement Model

Construct	Item	Loadings	AVE	CR
CSE	CSE1	0.839	0.688	0.964
	CSE2	0.843		
	CSE3	0.824		
	CSE4	0.888		
	CSE5	0.867		
	CSE6	0.842		
	CSE7	0.802		
	CSE8	0.767		
	CSE9	0.801		
	CSE10	0.778		
	CSE11	0.886		
	CSE12	0.810		
JS	JS1	0.784	0.647	0.969
	JS2	0.780		
	JS3	0.697		
	JS4	0.759		
	JS5	0.727		
	JS6	0.702		
	JS7	0.728		
	JS8	0.736		
	JS9	0.734		
SS	SS1	0.950	0.887	0.984
	SS2	0.959		
	SS3	0.926		
	SS4	0.933		
	SS5	0.934		
	SS6	0.949		
	SS7	0.952		
	SS8	0.932		
WFC	WFC1	0.969	0.823	0.958
	WFC2	0.971		
	WFC3	0.949		
	WFC4	0.838		
	WFC5	0.794		
RA	RA1	0.936	0.897	0.981
	RA2	0.942		
	RA3	0.962		
	RA4	0.941		

(continued)

Table 8.2 (continued)

Construct	Item	Loadings	AVE	CR
	RA5	0.959		
	RA6	0.943		
WSF	WSF1	0.940	0.824	0.966
	WSF2	0.942		
	WSF3	0.923		
	WSF4	0.884		
	WSS5	0.890		
	WSF6	0.866		

Source Authors own

Table 8.3 Fornell-Larcker Criterion analysis for checking discriminant validity

	CSE	JS	SS	WFC	RA	WSF	Discriminant validity met? (Squared root of AVE > LVC?)
CSE	**0.830**						Yes
JS	0.258	**0.805**					Yes
SS	0.292	0.464	**0.942**				Yes
WFC	0.194	0.304	0.287	**0.907**			Yes
RA	0.262	0.299	0.222	0.017	**0.947**		Yes
WSF	0.146	0.193	0.229	0.103	0.303	**0.908**	Yes

Note Values in the diagonal (bolded) represent the square root of the AVE while the off-diagonals represent the latent variable correlations (LVC)
Source Developed by the author using data from SmartPLS v.2.0

Structural Model Assessment

Figure 8.2 shows the use of standardised path coefficients (β), significance level (t-statistics), and R^2 estimates to create a structural model, by analysing the inner model as proposed by Henseler and Sardtedt (2013). T-statistics is used to identify significance between constructs (Wong, 2013) and a 5000 bootstrapping procedure was used to test for significance as used by Hair et al. (2011). It shows that not all the constructs tested were significant.

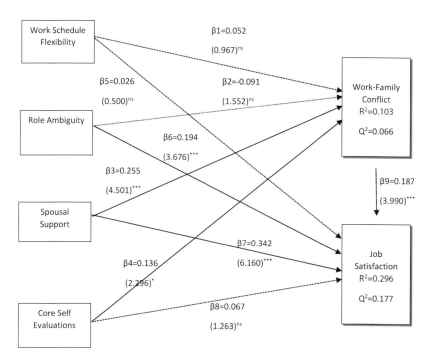

Fig. 8.2 Structural model (*Note* ***p < 0.001, **p < 0.01, *p < 0.05, ns &: not significant. *Source* Developed by the author using data from SmartPLS v.2.0)

Hypotheses Testing

Bootstrapping method (5000 re-samples) was performed using SmartPLS 2.0 to determine the significance of the path co-efficient, standard beta, standard error and t-values to test the hypothesised relationships between the constructs. Using a two-tailed t-test with a significance level of 5%, the path coefficient will be significant if the T-statistics is larger than 1.96. It was found that role ambiguity, spousal support and work–family conflict were significantly and positively related to job satisfaction. Moreover, spousal support and CSEs were found to be positively significant with work–family conflict. The findings also revealed that work schedule flexibility and CSEs were not significantly related to job satisfaction. Work schedule flexibility and role ambiguity also showed no significant relationships with work–family conflict. Therefore, all the hypotheses are supported, except for H1, H2, H5 and H8 (see Table 8.3).

The Mediating Effect

Table 8.4 shows the results of mediation effect, with work–family conflict as the mediator. The bootstrapping analysis showed that only two out of four were indirect effects, with $\beta = 0.069$ and $\beta = 0.039$ significant with t-values of 3.045 and 2.316, respectively. The indirect effects of 95% Boot CI Bias Corrected: [LL = 0.03, UL = 0.117], and [LL = 0.006, UL = 0.07] did not straddle at 0 in between, indicating there is a mediation effect (Preacher & Hayes, 2004, 2008). Hence, H12 and H13 are supported, confirming the mediation effects of work–family conflict between spousal support, CSEs and job satisfaction.

Table 8.4 Significance testing results of the structural model path coefficients

Hypothesis	Relationship	Standard beta	Standard error	t-value	p-value	Decision
H1	WSF -> WFC	0.052	0.054	0.967 ns	0.334	Not Supported
H2	RA -> WFC	−0.091	0.059	1.552 ns	0.122	Not Supported
H3	SS -> WFC	0.255	0.057	4.501***	0.000	Supported
H4	CSE -> WFC	0.136	0.059	2.296*	0.022	Supported
H5	WSF -> JS	0.026	0.052	0.500 ns	0.617	Not Supported
H6	RA -> JS	0.194	0.053	3.676***	0.000	Supported
H7	SS -> JS	0.342	0.055	6.160***	0.000	Supported
H8	CSE -> JS	0.067	0.053	1.263 ns	0.208	Not Supported
H9	WFC -> JS	0.187	0.047	3.990***	0.000	Supported

Note ***$p<0.001$, **$p<0.01$, *$p<0.05$
Source Developed by the author using data from SmartPLS v.2.0

Table 8.5 Mediation analysis results with work-family conflict as the Mediator

No	Relationship	Std. beta	Std. error	t-value	Confidence interval (BC) LL	Confidence interval (BC) UL	Decision
H10	Work Schedule Flexibility -> Work Family Conflict -> Job Satisfaction	0.019	0.022	0.872	−0.087	0.038	Not supported
H11	Role Ambiguity -> Work Family Conflict -> Job Satisfaction	−0.023	0.021	1.067	−0.059	0.022	Not supported
H12	Spousal Support -> Work Family Conflict -> Job Satisfaction	0.069	0.023	3.045***	0.03	0.117	Supported
H13	Core Self-evaluations -> Work Family Conflict -> Job Satisfaction	0.039	0.017	2.316*	0.006	0.07	Supported

Note ***$p < 0.001$, **$p < 0.01$, *$p < 0.05$, BC = Bias Corrected, UL = Upper Level, LL = Lower Level
Source Developed by the author using data from SmartPLS v.2.0

Brief Summary of Hypothesis Results from the Study

Table 8.5 portrays the overall summary of the hypotheses tested in the study. From the results, only seven hypotheses were supported, whilst the rest were rejected.

Importance-performance matrix analysis (IPMA) introduced by Martilla and James (1977) is a robust methodology that is useful in extending the findings of basic PLS-SEM outcomes using the latent variable scores (Hair et al., 2014; Hock et al., 2010; Ringle & Sarstedt, 2016; Völckner et al., 2010). IPMA is used to identify relevant and even the most specific areas of improvement (Hair, Hult et al., 2017), in which the implications are beneficial for the practitioners. Specifically, it can provide guidance in improving the performance of women entrepreneurs in their business ventures as this analysis is a simple tool for formulating strategic development solutions (Slack, 1994) and allows for constructs to be prioritised to improve on a certain target construct (Ringle & Sarstedt, 2016) for managerial actions.

In Table 8.6, the IPMA of job satisfaction revealed that spousal support was of primary importance for establishing job satisfaction. Spousal support showed the highest performance (index value = 81.889) when compared with the other constructs. This is followed by work schedule flexibility which scored the second-highest performance (index value = 57.490) and importance (total effect = 0.036). However, work–family conflict (index value = 49.896) showed a relatively low performance, amongst others. Work schedule flexibility itself showed the lowest importance (total effect = 0.036) and core self-evaluations showed little relevance with job satisfaction.

Discussion

This study has examined the postulated connection between work–family conflict and job satisfaction amongst women entrepreneurs in the Malaysian context. It has also provided a more precise description of work–family conflict amongst women entrepreneurs with children, who strive to balance their work and personal lives. It is vital for the

Table 8.6 Summary of results of hypotheses

Hypotheses		Supported (Yes/No)
H1	Work schedule flexibility is negatively related to work-family conflict	No
H2	Role ambiguity is positively related to work-family conflict	No
H3	Spousal support is negatively related to work-family conflict	Yes
H4	Core self-evaluations is negatively related to work-family conflict	Yes
H5	Work schedule flexibility is positively related to job satisfaction	No
H6	Role ambiguity is negatively related to job satisfaction	Yes
H7	Spousal support is positively related to job satisfaction	Yes
H8	Core self-evaluations is positively related to job satisfaction	No
H9	Work-family conflict is negatively related to job satisfaction	Yes
H10	The effect of work schedule flexibility on job satisfaction is mediated by work-family conflict	No
H11	The effect of role ambiguity on job satisfaction is mediated by work-family conflict	No
H12	The effect of spousal support on job satisfaction is mediated by work-family conflict	Yes
H13	The effect of core self-evaluations on job satisfaction is mediated by work-family conflict	Yes

Importance-Performance Matrix Analysis
Source Authors own

women entrepreneurs themselves to have an improved understanding of the relationship between work and family to ensure they can achieve better satisfaction in operating their businesses.

The results demonstrated that work schedule flexibility did not significantly reduce work–family conflict or make the women entrepreneurs studied more satisfied with their careers although it ranked second in terms of performance as indicated in the IPMA. Congruent with Kossek et al. (2006), as most entrepreneurs work independently and do not take orders, the women entrepreneurs are expected to be able to organise their work and home schedules and establish boundaries between the two as seen from the time they spent on family and work in Table 8.7.

However, contrary to the literature, the study found that role ambiguity showed a positive influence on job satisfaction although it was not significantly related to work–family conflict. It seems to suggest that the women entrepreneurs view their roles as a new normal, having prior expectations and are prepared for the changes and challenges in their roles as they commence and settle down in their businesses. In addition, their experiences in running businesses would have allowed them to get used to their roles as well. Their ability to balance both work interests and family demands would have brought greater satisfaction to them. As Ionescu (2004) indicates, women entrepreneurs tend to devote more time and effort to doing what is of benefit for their businesses due to their interest regardless of the level of ambiguity they face, more so when many of them founded or inherited the business.

What appears to be important in this study is spousal support, which was significantly linked to both work–family conflict and job satisfaction. Spouses serve as an important source of support for women entrepreneurs where such support enables them to achieve satisfaction in their careers. However, the findings also indicate that the more spousal support given to women entrepreneurs, the more likely it is that they will feel strained (work–family conflict) and therefore unable to manage their work–life balance well. This will have important implications on managing their relationships with their spouses.

Table 8.7 Index value and total effects for the IPMA of JS

	Importance (total effects)	Performance (index values)
WSF	0.036	57.490
RA	0.177	54.879
SS	0.389	81.889
CSE	0.092	54.409
WFC	0.187	49.896

Note WSF = Work Schedule Flexibility; RA = Role Ambiguity; SS = Spousal Support; CSE = Core Self-Evaluations; WFC = Work-Family Conflict; JS = Job Satisfaction
Source Developed by the author using data from SmartPLS v.2.0

In contrast to role ambiguity, core self-evaluations were found to be significantly and positively related to work–family conflict but not significant on job satisfaction. Those women entrepreneurs with higher levels of performance-based self-esteem will typically experience high levels of work–family conflict as they strive to achieve more on their businesses (Richter et al., 2014). An implication of this study is that high core self-evaluations do not necessarily lead to greater job satisfaction. This suggests that an adjustment to the personality traits of the women entrepreneurs might help in addressing work–family conflict.

The results indicated that work–family conflict was positively correlated with job satisfaction, the logic of which can be observed in the interplay between spousal support, role ambiguity and core self-evaluations. The ability to manage work–family conflict is an important driver of satisfaction of the women entrepreneurs toward their careers. The findings point to the need to address what matter most to reduce work–family conflict and to enhance the job satisfaction of the women entrepreneurs. In the context of the current study, this means a deeper understanding of the roles played by spousal support, role ambiguity and core self-evaluations is required. On the other hand, work schedule flexibility does not appear to be a priority for attention to be paid on, either to enhance job satisfaction or to address work–family conflict.

Conclusions

This study has achieved its objectives of identifying the factors that influence work–family conflict and job satisfaction amongst women entrepreneurs and determining the extent to which work–family conflict mediates the relationship between the predictors and job satisfaction of such women entrepreneurs in Malaysia. It also contributes to the literature on women entrepreneurship, particularly in Malaysia. The success of women entrepreneurial ventures would, of course, be of great value to an SME-dominated economy such as that of Malaysia. It is hoped that the findings provide insights to the women entrepreneurs and various stakeholders, as well as encouraging further in this area.

The theoretical implications are manifold. There has been little theoretical research on work–family conflict and job satisfaction amongst women entrepreneurs in Malaysia. This study has extended previous research since it considered four exogenous factors in a single setting. In addition, this study has also broadened understanding of the relationships amongst spousal support, core self-evaluations, job satisfaction and work–family conflict from the perspective of women entrepreneurs, particularly in the context of a country with a promising growth in women entrepreneurship. The validated instrument makes it possible to conduct similar research in different types of economies to determine whether the findings will vary according to economic context.

From the practical perspective, the findings confirmed the importance of variables, particularly spousal support, role ambiguity and core self-evaluations investigated to identify ways of addressing work–family conflict, as well as in ensuring greater job satisfaction amongst the women entrepreneurs. Since spousal support appeared to be a significant factor, it should warrant extra attention. It implies open communication on the expectations and responsibilities of both parties so that appropriate boundaries can be set. This is because too little or too much support may actually do more harm, especially to the women entrepreneurs with high core self-evaluations. What is considered enough will depend on the individuals concerned. Perhaps the women entrepreneur associations could play a role to provide advice to the women entrepreneurs on how to balance work–family conflict and seek appropriate spousal support.

In terms of role ambiguity, the women entrepreneurs should be motivated to treat role ambiguity as a positive stress (eustress) which can help them to achieve better satisfaction with their careers, the source of motivation which can come from their spouse, women entrepreneur networks or associations. Since core self-evaluations are significantly related to work–family conflict but not job satisfaction, an examination of the personality traits of the women entrepreneurs might be necessary so that adjustments to expectations can be made. This gives rise to the possible role played by role models or mentors influencing the women entrepreneurs who might possess certain traits that could be emulated.

Having said so, work–family conflict is not a bad thing after all, since it has been found to influence job satisfaction in a positive direction. With the role of women entrepreneurs increasingly becoming a new normal, the crux lies in the ability of the women entrepreneurs to manage it well with appropriate support and expectations based on their personality traits. There are no formulae cast in stone. One possible area that future research could examine is the moderating and mediating effects of core self-evaluations in the study of work–family conflict and job satisfaction amongst the women entrepreneurs, particularly those who exhibit high core self-evaluations to gain a better understanding on the relationships between them. This model could also be tested to address the heterogeneity of male and female entrepreneurs who are single parents and/or co-entrepreneurial couples by using a range of methods and data sources to capture accurately the reality of experiences of these entrepreneurs.

Acknowledgements This research was funded by the Fundamental Research Grant Scheme (FRGS), Ministry of Higher Education Malaysia with project code: FRGS/2/2014/SS05/MMU/03/2.

References

Aazami, S., Mozafari, M., Shamsuddin, K., & Akmal, S. (2016). Work-family conflict and sleep disturbance: The Malaysian working women study. *Industrial Health, 54,* 50–57.

Ahmad, F. (2005). *Sources of work-family conflict: A study of Malay women entrepreneurs in Kedah, Malaysia* (Doctoral thesis). University of South Australia [online]. Available at: http://melayu.library.uitm.edu.my/id/eprint/1928. Accessed 2 February 2017.

Aminah, A. (2008). Job, family and individual factors as predictors of work-family. *The Journal of Human Resource and Adult Learning, 4*(1), 57–65.

Agarwal, S., & Lenka, U. (2014). Study on work-life balance of women entrepreneurs—Review and research agenda. *Industrial and Commercial Training, 47*(7), 356–362.

Aryee, S. (1992). Antecedents and outcomes of work-family conflict among married professional women: Evidence from Singapore. *Human Relations, 45*(8), 813–837.

Bagozzi, R. P., & Yi, Y. (1988). On the evaluation of structural equation models. *Journal of the Academy of Marketing Science, 16*(1), 74–94.

Bodenmann, G., Pihet, S., & Kayser, K. (2006). The relationship between dyadic coping and marital quality: A 2-year longitudinal study. *Journal of Family Psychology, 20*, 485–493.

Boles, J. S., Wood, J. A., & Johnson, J. (2003). Interrelationships of role conflict, role ambiguity, and work-family conflict with different facets of job satisfaction and the moderating effects of gender. *Journal of Personal Selling & Sales Management, 23*(2), 99–113.

Budig, M. J. (2006). Intersections on the Road to self-employment: Gender, family and occupational class. *Social Forces, 84*(4), 2223–2239.

Buttner, E. H. (1992). Entrepreneurial stress: Is it hazardous to your health? *Journal of Managerial, 4*(2), 223–240.

Chin, Y. F., Ismail, A., Ahmad, R. H., & Kuek, T. Y. (2012). The impacts of job stress characteristics on the workforce—Organisational social support as the moderator. *South Asian Journal of Marketing & Management Research, 2*(3), 1–20.

Fornell, C., & Larcker, D. F. (1981). Evaluating structural equation models with unobservable variables and measurement error. *Journal of Marketing Research, 18*(1), 39–50.

Garrity, E. J., O'Donnell, J. B., Kim, Y. J., & Sanders, G. L. (2009), An extrinsic and intrinsic motivation-based model for measuring consumer shopping oriented web site success. In S. Bandyopadhyay (Ed.), *Contemporary research in e-branding* (pp. 233–251). IGI Global.

Gefen, D., Straub, D. W., & Boudreau, M. C. (2000). Structural equation modelling and regression: Guidelines for research practice. *Communications of the Association for Information Systems, 4*(7), 1–70.

Gholami, R., Sulaiman, A., Ramayah, T., & Molla, A. (2013). Managers' perception on green information systems (IS) adoption and business value: Results from a field survey. *Information & Management, 50*(7), 431–438.

Grandey, A. A., & Cropanzano, R. (1999). The conservation of resources model applied to work-family conflict and strain. *Journal of Vocational Behaviour, 54*, 350–370.

Gudmunson, C. G., Danes, S. M., Werbel, J. D., & Loy, J. T. (2009). Spousal support and work–family balance in launching a family business. *Journal of Family Issues, 30*, 1098–1121.

Hair, J., Hollingsworth, C. L., Randolph, A. B., & Chong, A. Y. L. (2017a). An updated and expanded assessment of PLS-SEM in information systems research. *Industrial Management and Data Systems, 117*(3), 442–458.

Hair, J. F., Hult, G. T. M., Ringle, C. M., & Sarstedt, M. (2014). *A primer on partial least squares structural equation modelling (PLS-SEM)*. Sage.

Hair, J. F., Hult, G. T. M., Ringle, C. M., & Sarstedt, M. (2017). *A primer on partial least squares structural equation modelling (PLS-SEM)* (2nd ed.). Sage.

Hair, J. F., Ringle, C. M., & Sarstedt, M. (2011). PLS-SEM: Indeed a silver bullet. *Journal of Marketing Theory and Practice, 19*(2), 139–151.

Hallsten, L. (2005). Burnout and wornout: Concepts and data from a national survey. In A. S. G. Antoniou & C. L. Cooper (Eds.), *Research companion to organisational health psychology* (pp. 516–536). Elgar Publication.

Hallsten, L., Josephson, M., & Torgén, M. (2005). *Performance-based Self-esteem. A driving force in burnout process and its assessment* (Report No.: 2005:4). National Institute for Working Life.

Harter, S. (1990). Causes, correlates, and the functional role of global self-worth: A life span perspective. In R. J. Sternberg & J. Kolligan Jr. (Eds.), *Competence considered* (pp. 67–97). Yale University Press.

Hennessy, K. D., & Lent, R. W. (2008). Self-efficacy for managing work-family conflict: Validating the English language version of a hebrew scale. *Journal of Career Assessment, 16*(3), 370–383.

Henseler, J., & Sardtedt, M. (2013). Goodness-of-fit indices for partial least squares path modeling. *Computational Statistics, 28*(2), 565–580.

Hobfoll, S. E. (1989). Conservation of resources: A new attempt at conceptualizing stress. *American Psychologist, 44*(3), 513–524.

Hobfoll, S. E. (2001). The influence of culture, community, and the nested-self in the stress process: Advancing conservation of resources theory. *Applied Psychology, 50,* 337–370.

Hock, C., Ringle, C. M., & Sarstedt, M. (2010). Management of multi-purpose stadiums: Importance and performance measurement of service interfaces. *International Journal of Services, Technology and Management, 14*(2/3), 188–207.

Ionescu, D. (2004). *Women entrepreneurship: A second best solution?* [online]. Available at: file:///C:/Users/User/Desktop/FBC_020_0079.pdf. Accessed 12 April 2018.

Judge, T. A. (2009). Core self-evaluations and work success. *Current Directions in Psychological Science, 18,* 58–62.

Judge, T. A., Erez, A., Bono, J. E., & Thoresen, T. J. (2003). The core self-evaluations scale: Development of a measure. *Personnel Psychology, 5*(2), 303–331.

Judge, T. A., Locke, E. A., and Durham, C. C. (1997). The dispositional causes of job satisfaction: A core evaluations approach. In L. L. Cummings & B. Staw (Eds.), *Research in organisational behaviour* (Vol. 19, pp. 151–188). JAI Press.

Judge, T. A., Piccolo, R. F., Podsakoff, N. P., Shaw, J. C., & Rich, B. L. (2010). The relationship between pay and job satisfaction: A meta-analysis of the literature. *Journal of Vocational Behaviour, 77*(2), 157–167.

Kahn, R., Wolfe, D., Quinn, R., Snoek, J., & Rosentbal, R. (1964). *Organisational stress: Studies in role conflict and ambiguity*. Wiley.

Khairuddin, S. M. H. H. S. (2015). Occupational stress among entrepreneurs in Malaysian SMEs: A conceptual framework. *Review of Integrative Business and Economics Research, 4*(2), 53–60.

Khan, S. (2016). Social support for women entrepreneurs: A case of Pakistan. *Journal of Applied Environmental and Biological Sciences, 6*(2S), 9–16.

Kirkwood, J., & Tootell, B. (2008). Is entrepreneurship the answer to achieving work–family balance? *Journal of Management and Organisation, 14*(3), 285–302.

König, S., & Cesinger, B. (2015). Gendered work-family conflict in Germany: Do self-employment and flexibility matter? *Work, Employment & Society, 29*(4), 531–549.

Kossek, E. E., Lautsch, B. A., & Eaton, S. C. (2006). Telecommuting, control and boundary management: Correlates of policy use and practice, job control, and work–family effectiveness. *Journal of Vocational Behaviour, 68*, 347–367.

Kossek, E. E., & Michel, J. (2011). Flexible work schedules. *Handbook of Industrial-Organisational Psychology, 1*, 535–572.

Kossek, E. E., & Ozeki, C. (1998). Work–family conflict, policies, and the job–life satisfaction relationship: A review and directions for organisational behaviour–human resources research. *Journal of Applied Psychology, 83*(2), 139–149.

Lapierre, L. M., & Allen, T. D. (2006). Work-supportive family, family-supportive supervision, use of organisational benefits, and problem-focused coping: Implications for work-family conflict and employee well-being. *Journal of Occupational Health Psychology, 11*, 169–181.

Lee, J. S. K., & Choo, S. L. (2001). Work-family conflict of women entrepreneurs in Singapore. *Women in Management Review, 16*(5), 204–221.

Locke, E. A., McClear, K., & Knight, D. (1996). Self-esteem and work. *International Review of Industrial Organizational Psychology, 11,* 1–32.

Lombard, K. V. (2001). Female self-employment and demand for flexible, nonstandard work schedules. *Economic Inquiry, 39*(2), 214–237.

Malaysian Labour Force Survey Report. (2011). *Mean and median hours worked by sex and status in employment, Malaysia* [online]. Available at: www.statistics.gov.my/portal/download_Labour/files/labour_force/Laporan_Penyiasatan_Tenaga_Buruh_Malaysia2011.pdf. Accessed 22 April 2013.

Martilla, J. A., & James, J. C. (1977). Importance-performance analyses. *Journal of Marketing, 41*(1), 77–79.

Michel, J. S., & Clark, M. A. (2012). Investigating the relative importance of individual differences on the work-family interface and the moderating role of boundary preference for segmentation. *Stress and Health, 29*(4), 324–336.

Mohamad, M., & Bakar, M. S. (2017). Does work-family conflict affect women entrepreneurial success? *International Journal of Academic Research in Business and Social Sciences, 7*(3), 566–571.

Nasurdin, A. M., Ahmad, N. H., & Mohamed Zainal, S. R. (2013). Comparing work-family conflict and facilitation among male and female entrepreneurs in Malaysia. *International Journal of Business and Society, 14*(1), 149–162.

Palomino, M. N., & Frezatti, F. (2016). Role conflict, role ambiguity and job satisfaction: Perceptions of the Brazilian controllers. *Revista de Adminisração, 51*(2), 165–181.

Parasuraman, S., Purohit, Y. S., Godshalk, V. M., & Beutell, N. J. (1996). Work and family variables, entrepreneurial career success, and psychological well-being. *Journal of Vocational Behaviour, 48,* 275–300.

Preacher, K. J., & Hayes, A. F. (2004). SPSS and SAS procedures for estimating indirect effects in simple mediation models. *Behaviour Research Methods, Instruments, & Computers, 36,* 717–731.

Preacher, K. J. and Hayes, A. F. (2008). Contemporary approaches to assessing mediation in communication research. In A. F. Hayes, M. D. Slater, & L. B. Snyder (Eds.), *The Sage sourcebook of advanced data analysis methods for communication research* (pp. 13–54). Sage.

Rehman, S., & Roomi, M. A. (2012). Gender and work-life balance: A phenomenological study of women entrepreneurs in Pakistan. *Journal of Small Business and Enterprise Development, 9*(2), 209–228.

Richter, A., Schrami, K., & Leineweber, C. (2014). Work-family conflict, emotional exhaustion and performance-based self-esteem: Reciprocal relationships. *International Archives of Occupational and Environmental Health, 88*, 103–112.

Ringle, C. M., & Sarstedt, M. (2016). Gain more insight from your PLS-SEM results: The importance-performance map analysis. *Industrial Management & Data, 16*(9), 34–78.

Rizzo, J. R., House, R. J., & Lirtzman, S. I. (1970). Role conflict and ambiguity in complex organisations. *Administrative Science Quarterly, 15*(2), 150–163.

Sekaran, U. (2000). *Research methods for business: A skill-building approach.* John Wiley.

Semerci, A. B. (2016). The effect of social support on job stress on entrepreneurs. *Academy of Entrepreneurship Journal, 22*(1), 41–50.

Simmons, M. (2013). *Is the 70-hour work week worth the sacrifice?* [online]. Available at: http://www.forbes.com/sites/michaelsimmons/2013/05/13/is-the-70-hour-work-week-worth-the-sacrifice/. Accessed 10 August 2015.

Slack, N. (1994). The importance-performance matrix as a determinant of improvement priority. *International Journal of Operations and Production Management, 14*(5), 59–75.

Srivastava, A., Locke, E. A., Judge, T. A., & Adams, J. W. (2010). Core self-evaluations as causes of satisfaction: The mediating role of seeking task complexity. *Journal of Vocational Behaviour, 77*(2), 255–265.

Teoh, W. M. Y., Chong, C. W., Chong, S. C., & Ismail, H. (2016). Managing work-family conflict among entrepreneurs: An empirical study. *International Journal of Business Management, 11*(9), 179–191.

Tremblay, M., & Roger, A. (2004). Career plateauing reactions: The moderating roles of job scope, role ambiguity and participating among canadian managers. *International Journal of Human Resource Management, 15*(6), 996–1017.

Vadnjal, J., & Vadnjal, M. (2013). The role of husbands: support or barrier to women's entrepreneurial start-ups? *African Journal of Business Management, 7*(36), 3730–3738.

Völckner, F., Sattler, H., Hennig-Thurau, T., & Ringle, C. M. (2010). The role of parent brand quality for service brand extension success. *Journal of Service Research, 13*(4), 359–361.

Wan Rashid, W. E., Nordin, M. S., Omar, A., & Ismail, I. (2012). Work/family conflict: The link between self-esteem and satisfaction outcomes. *Procedia—Social and Behavioural Sciences, 65*, 564–569.

Watson, D. (2000). *Mood and temperament*. Guilford.
Wayne, J. H., Musisca, N., & Fleeson, W. (2004). Considering the role of personality in the work-family experience: Relationships of the big five to work-family conflict and facilitation. *Journal of Vocational Behaviour, 64*(1), 108–130.
Wong, K. K. (2013). Partial least squares structural equation modelling (PLS-SEM) techniques using smart PLS. *Marketing Bulletin, 24*, 1–32.

9

Barriers and Facilitators in Applying Industry 4.0 in Small and Medium Enterprises (SMEs) Owned by Graduate Entrepreneurs in Malaysia

Md Asadul Islam, Claire Seaman, Amer Hamzah Jantan, Choo Wei Chong, and Abdul Rashid Abdullah

Introduction

The economic growth of a country mainly depends on the growth and success of the business organizations. However, many business organizations close due to different factors, especially the failure of entrepreneurs working within those organizations (Pretorius, 2008). According to US Small Business Administration data almost 50% of Small and Medium-sized Enterprise (SMEs) fail in the first year itself and 95% tend to fail by the five-year mark and this is also similar in the case of

M. A. Islam
Faculty of Business, Design and Arts, School of Business (AACSB Accredited), Swinburne University of Technology (Sarawak Campus), Kuching, Sarawak, Malaysia

C. Seaman (✉)
Enterprise and Family Business School, Queen Margaret University, Edinburgh, Scotland, UK
e-mail: CSeaman@qmu.ac.uk

© The Author(s), under exclusive license to Springer Nature Switzerland AG 2021
P. Jones et al. (eds.), *Entrepreneurial Activity in Malaysia*, https://doi.org/10.1007/978-3-030-77753-1_9

Malaysia (Ahmad & Seet, 2009a; Kannan, 2016; Malaysian Reserve, 2017). Various reasons for the failure of SMEs have been identified in the entrepreneurship literature, including poor business planning (Van Gelderen et al., 2006), lack of knowledge to run a business and a deficiency of entrepreneurial management skills (Omar & Azmi, 2015; Tunggak et al., 2011). McGrath (1999) highlighted difficulties in managing uncertainty and others have noted factors including a lack of competitor knowledge (Kirzner, 2015; Martin, & Javalgi, 2016), pride (Cardon et al., 2011), lack of use of technologies (Cardon et al., 2011; Sharma & Varma, 2016) overconfidence (Cardon et al., 2011; Ucbasaran et al., 2006) and a limited government support (Singh Sandhu et al., 2011). These issues are reflected in Malaysian SMEs, which made up 97% of the business establishments providing 50% of total employment in this country (Abdullah et al., 2016; Chong, 2012; Kannan, 2016; Malaysian Reserve, 2017). The contribution of SMEs to the Malaysian gross domestic product (GDP) grew by 38.3% to RM521.7 million in 2018 from RM491.2 million a year before (SMEBiz, 2019).

However, recently SMEs owners in Malaysia are wary and confused about the implications of industry 4.0, i.e., the fourth industrial revolution (Yapp, 2019). It has been suggested that industry 4.0 would allow businesses to leverage real-time business intelligence, empowering smarter decisions, and greater automated efficiency (Baldassari & Roux, 2017; Jackson, 2018; Rüßmann et al., 2015). This was also supported by Baldassari and Roux (2017), who dismissed the claim that Industry 4.0 will reduce jobs while offering assurances that different jobs will be

---

A. H. Jantan
Faculty of Economics and Management, Universiti Putra Malaysia (UPM), Seri Kembangan, Malaysia

C. W. Chong
Department of Management and Marketing, Universiti Putra Malaysia (UPM), Seri Kembangan, Malaysia

A. R. Abdullah
School of Business and Economics, Universiti Putra Malaysia (UPM), Seri Kembangan, Malaysia

created. However, the current literature is divided on whether Industry 4.0 will result in an increase or decrease of jobs (Müller, Kiel et al., 2018b).

Several authors believe that Industry 4.0 can contribute to the development business performance and accelerate overall production processes as well as on the educational industry, i.e., higher education has been acknowledged in many previous studies (Baygin et al., 2016; Roblek et al., 2016; Rüßmann et al., 2015). However, Sommer (2015)claimed smaller SMEs are at higher risk in that they will become victims instead of beneficiaries of this revolution because larger businesses' production and service processes will be improved with quicker adaptation ability. By contrast, Önday (2018) argued Industry 4.0 is a opportunity for SMEs because it will improve efficiency in term of suppliers, interoperability and it can also contribute to reduce the errors and increase/improve production/service using Combined Augmented Reality and Modeling and Simulation. Müller, Buliga et al. (2018a) argued that fortune favors the prepared, therefore, the SMEs should prepare themselves for the adoption of industry 4.0 elements or processes to be successful in the market. They further argued that the application of Industry 4.0 will increase in coming years, therefore, it is better to adapt rather than ignoring it.

To adapt and cope with the challenges of Industry 4.0, it is important to develop an understanding of the existing and potential entrepreneurs of SMEs about both barriers and facilitators in applying industry 4.0 in the SMEs. However, the term industry 4.0 is complicated and still confuses many Malaysians and it includes different aspects (Baygin et al., 2016; Yapp, 2019). Educated (graduates) people, i.e., educated entrepreneurs are generally better placed than uneducated or semi-educated people to adapt to technological and other changes in the business organizations (Mankiw, 2008). However, in Malaysia, the graduates have opened businesses but most of them have failed to run the business profitably in the long run (Ahmad and Seet, 2009b). The failures are likely to increase if the existing and potential graduate entrepreneurs of SMEs do not clearly understand how to apply industry 4.0. Therefore, if barriers and facilitators in adapting the industry 4.0 in the SMEs can be convinced to graduate entrepreneurs of SMEs theatrically/practically, the performance of SMEs and their survival in the competitive Malaysian business environment could be enhanced and lengthy, respectively. In addition, resilience among entrepreneurs could be improved that may facilitate to cope with competitive adversity in the market (Rahman & Mendy, 2019; Seligman, 2011).

However, there is a significant lack of literature relating to Industry 4.0, evaluating the barriers and facilitators in applying the processes, elements, and strategies or tools for SMEs. Literature regarding Malaysia and advanced technology adoption is also nascent. This chapter addresses the gap by exploring and presenting the barriers and facilitators in applying industry 4.0 relating to SMEs in Malaysia. The research questions explored are:

- What are the barriers in adapting/applying industry 4.0 in SMEs of graduate entrepreneurs in Malaysia?
- What are the facilitators to overcome barriers in adapting/applying industry 4.0 in SMEs of graduate entrepreneurs in Malaysia?

Literature Review

Industry 4.0

Humanity is in the middle of a dramatic transformation in the production process due to the digitalization of manufacturing and this transition is being called industry 4.0 to represent the fourth industrial revolution that has occurred in many countries (Marr, 2018) while others are in the process of adopting (Bodrow, 2017; Marr, 2018; Müller et al., 2018b). Industry 4.0 is not only dramatically changing the manufacturing processes but also the service providing processes in the service organizations (Bodrow, 2017; Lee et al., 2014). Thus, industry 4.0 is receiving significant attention since the first industrial revolution in 1760 (Abidin et al., 2018; Rüßmann et al., 2015). However, astonishingly some dismiss industry 4.0 as merely a marketing buzzword, shifts are occurring in manufacturing that deserves the attention of people (Marr, 2018). However, significance, benefits, or necessity of industry

4.0 is widely acknowledged in the recent literature (Thames & Schaefer, 2016). Therefore, it is topical for every business owner to understand what industry 4.0 means for their business organizations, which could be any size of SME (Abidin et al., 2018; Oesterreich & Teuteberg, 2016). Industry 4.0 includes a variety of technologies, which enables business organizations to create a digitalized and automated manufacturing environment and value chain (Lasi et al., 2014; Schmidt et al., 2015). As a result, it improves both production quality and decreases time to market for products as well as enterprise performance (Brettel et al., 2014). Thames and Schaefer (2016) defined industry 4.0 as an associated paradigm that includes the Industrial Internet of Things, cloud-based manufacturing, and social product development. However, in broad concept, Kagermann et al. (2013) suggested that industry 4.0 can transform both manufacturing and service processes globally. Kagermann et al. (2013) argued that industry 4.0 can transform by meeting individual customer requirements, creating flexibility, optimized decision making, resource productivity, and efficiency, creating value opportunities through new services, responding to demographic change in workplace, work-life balance and a high wage economic that is still competitive (Bartodziej, 2017). Bartodziej (2017, p. 37) suggested these transformations correlate strongly with cost-reduction potentials. Therefore, it is high time for organizations regardless of size to adapt industry 4.0, i.e., establishment of the technologies associated with the industry 4.0.

Barriers in Applying/Adapting Industry 4.0

The SMEs literature identifies several barriers in adopting technologies, therefore, it is viable to predict these organizations will face those barriers in adapting industry 4.0. Bhagwat and Sharma (2007) identify the lack of financial resources in SMEs has been one of the difficulties for them to adapt technologies. This is supported by Meath et al. (2016) who argued the economic constraints of SMEs is always a significant barrier. The limited financial capital/capabilities of the entrepreneur(s) and lack of support from banks (lack of loans, higher interest rate) are also significant barriers for SMEs to adapt technologies and even to grow (Eniola & Entebang, 2015; Shuying & Mei, 2014; Wolcott et al., 2008). Applying industry 4.0 technologies is not only expensive but also complex and costly to maintain and update over the periods (Müller et al., 2018b; Theorin et al., 2017). Thus, financial limitations among SMEs are significant barriers in adapting industry 4.0 (Nicoletti, 2018). The financial limitation is also similar in the case of Malaysia where SMEs struggle to adopt advanced technologies in business operations (Chan et al., 2015).

By contrast, the lack of technical capabilities in SMEs is also common (Bhagwat and Sharma, 2007). Therefore, creating digital strategies would be difficult because of the lack of a digital strategy alongside resource scarcity would create challenges in the implementation of industry 4.0 (Schröder, 2016). Thus, Schröder (2016) argued availability of consistent data is a significant condition on the way to industry 4.0. Lack of standards and poor data security in SMEs are also significant barriers to switching to new industry 4.0 technologies (Chen et al., 2017; Pereira et al., 2017; Schröder, 2016). In addition, the problem with coordination and collaboration of industry 4.0 technologies with other parties is also a barrier for industry 4.0 implementation in organizations (Duarte & Cruz-Machado, 2017; Lee et al., 2014). Furthermore, industry 4.0 requires the flexible interface to integrate various heterogeneous comments, cyber-physical networks, and so on but these need integration for the smoother data exchange and analysis in operational processes, thus, lack of integration of technologies is a barrier for industry 4.0 establishment (Zhou et al., 2015).

Furthermore, the current global business environment is extremely uncertain (Ahir et al., 2019). Therefore, owner/managers have to think efficiently and take management approaches for a longer time but with flexible processes (Shamim et al., 2016). In such an uncertain business environment, investors, as well as entrepreneurs, are confused regarding what technologies to adopt due to technological evolution and the risks involved in sustaining successful business performance (Ericson & Doyle, 2004; Lynch et al., 2012). Thus, technological evolution and innovation have been changing the business environment and operational systems and even customers demand/perception (Lin & Hsieh,

2006; Luftman et al., 2017; Melville et al., 2004). For example, several major business organizations, which have failed due to losing focus e.g., Baan, Blockbuster, Hitachi, IBM, JCPenney, Kodak, LG, Motorola, MySpace, Nokia, Philips, Xerox, and Yahoo (Aaslaid, 2019). However, behind the failure of these organizations, their lack of innovation and adaptation of technological changes has been partly responsible (Singhal, 2017; Van Rooij, 2015). Therefore, it is critical for companies to ensure they adopt to the technologies to overcome the changing business environment. In this regard, the application of industry 4.0 can be effective to cope with the uncertain business environment.

Alternatively, lack of managerial interest and knowledge regarding the effectiveness are also significant challenges to adapt industry 4.0 in SMEs (Müller et al., 2018b). Implementing only industry 4.0 in the organization cannot work until new strategic approaches for holistic human resource management is implemented and developed continuously (Hecklau et al.,). Industry 4.0 will create a high level of complexity that results in enhanced competencies to work within a changing environment where retention of employees should be ensured (Benešová & Tupa, 2017; Shamim et al., 2016). Therefore, Onar et al. (2018) recommended organizations must need to improve their capabilities in terms of workforce expertise, improved leadership, strategic organizational policies, and appropriate business culture to diffuse industry 4.0. However, many SME owners perceive Industry 4.0 as costly in the short-term, whereas its expected benefits require time to unfold (Müller et al., 2018b). Therefore, it is argued that lack of interest of the entrepreneurs in adapting the industry 4.0 in the organizations as well as in developing their employees to manage the industry 4.0 is a significant challenge.

Furthermore, the lack of government support and policies has also been identified as one of the barriers to apply/adapt industry 4.0 in the organizations (BRICS Business Council, 2017). In this regard, the lack of specific guidelines and directions on industry 4.0 have been identified as a significant barrier (BRICS Business Council, 2017; Islam et al., 2018). In addition, scholars also argued legal issues relating to industry 4.0 are also not clear from local and international perspectives (Kusmin, 2018; Luthra & Mangla, 2018; Schröder, 2016). Therefore, these issues are also barriers along with others in adapting industry 4.0 in the organizations.

Facilitators in Applying/Adapting Industry 4.0

Although there have been a significant literature regarding the barriers and challenges in applying/adapting industry 4.0 in organizations (Benešová & Tupa, 2017; Müller et al., 2018b; Shamim et al., 2016; Zhou et al., 2015), there have been insufficient academic research has undertaken on the facilitators in applying/adapting industry 4.0 in organizations. Within the limited academic literature, Anderl et al. (2015) argued that commitment of senior managers and cross-disciplinary teams for industry 4.0 could be essential facilitators (Mittal et al., 2018). According to Müller et al. (2018b) strategic, operational, as well as environmental and social opportunities are positive drivers of Industry 4.0 implementation. However, the results presented by Müller et al. (2018b) were unclear regarding how these could be drivers or facilitators for industry 4.0 SMEs implementation. Thus, the qualitative nature of this study explores with explanation different facilitators in implementing industry 4.0 in Malaysian SMEs that could be used for further studies in other country and industry sector contexts.

Ganji et al. (2018) suggest internet-based technologies (IoT) and knowledge on these are the main facilitators for the industry 4.0 implementation in the organizations. However, the focus of this research is what could be effective to motivate or facilitate applying or adapting or establishing the IoT technologies and other technologies to apply/adapt industry 4.0 in the SMEs. Therefore, this motivates researchers to explore from the SMEs owners and industry experts. Nguyen et al. (2015) reported customers are the main driving force for IT adoption in the organization because to attract and retain them, SMEs must adopt various technologies. This is supported by Geissbauer et al. (2016), who argued giving customers priority could be a facilitator or motivation for the organizations to source technologies because these allow a closer interaction with customers and the adaptation of business models to market requirements (Pereira & Romero, 2017). From this perspective, it is reasonable to argue that giving priority to customers could be a facilitator for SMEs in Malaysia to adopt Industry 4.0 as customers always look for lower-cost products/services with reasonable quality.

Dassisti et al. (2017) argued that linking between the knowledge of managers and technologies can be effective in deploying IR4.0 in the SMEs. In this respect, flexibility in SMEs is very important for organizations and owners to learn to adopt the technologies. Furthermore, training is another significant facilitator in applying industry 4.0 in SMEs (Moeuf et al., 2019). Thus, the government can be an effective facilitator in applying/the industry 4.0 in the respective country by creating supportive legislation (Rojko, 2017). In the case of Malaysia, Yusof (2017) reported that the government of the country is aggressively undertaking various efforts to assist industry players in embracing industry 4.0 through the adoption of automation and smart manufacturing. There is a gap in the literature in that most of the studies primarily focused on the motivations or drivers for the industry 4.0, however, the majority omitted to explain how industry 4.0 can be implemented in SMEs which are always limited by financial and other constraints. This gap is common in the literature relating to industry 4.0 from developing economies and SMEs' perspectives. Therefore, this study would be an effective platform to further understand facilitators in applying/adapting industry 4.0.

Methodology

The empirical basis for this study is drawn from qualitative research. We undertook interviews with eight participants, four of whom were entrepreneurs (graduates) and four were industry experts relating to industry 4.0 (Nguyen, 2013). Participants were selected based on convenience sampling as it allowed the flexibility to diversify participants to include from various aspects of the technical and other issues associated with industry 4.0. Moreover, the specialist nature of the field of the study and its novelty denoted that this sampling was the most suitable to reach target participants who meet our criteria of selection. Thus, the first criteria were to be an entrepreneur of an SME in Malaysia and the second criteria was to be an expert regarding SMEs and technologies, i.e., industry 4.0.

Manual analysis was undertaken given the small sample (Rahman et al., 2019). The analysis of the collected data was thematic and sought to make sense of participants' responses. Manual analysis has been selected because it would be more effective since the sample is smaller while time and the ability to investigate the transcripts would also be saved (Rahman et al., 2019). In this respect, firstly the interview notes were reviewed to identify possible threads for the axial coding process to generate the codes (Rahman et al., 2019). Subsequently, we developed categories, which were grouped into final themes that formed the foundation for the analysis and discussion (Islam et al., 2019). The discussion of the results has been presented in the next section.

Findings

This section of the chapter includes the presentation and analysis of the collected data from the participants. The findings have been divided into two major sections, which are the barriers and facilitators in applying the Industry 4.0 in SMEs owned by graduate entrepreneurs in Malaysia relating to the objective and questions of the study:

- What are the barriers in adapting/applying industry 4.0 in SMEs of graduate entrepreneurs in Malaysia?
- What are the facilitators to overcame barriers in adapting/applying industry 4.0 in SMEs of graduate entrepreneurs in Malaysia?

Barriers in Applying Industry 4.0 in the SMEs

Financial Limitations

Financial limitations have been identified as the most significant barrier in applying industry 4.0 in SMEs in Malaysia by all the participants unanimously. Respondents suggested that most of the SMEs owned by the graduates suffer from lack of capital as well as working capital.

Therefore, they have very limited capabilities to fund the technological investments in the organizations even if there is a need for the technologies. They have pointed out some interesting aspects regarding this:

Participant 1 from a transport organization stated:

> When I start the business, I not only used my money from parents but also took loans from banks as well as I borrow from friends. However, over the last 2 years, I have not made significant progress and I cannot yet settle with the loans and borrows. For this reason, I cannot use updated technologies now because I do not have money. I can see transportation business is growing fast and it needs sophisticated technologies and I have no problem to use them but I cannot buy now for lack of fund.

In addition, Participant 4 added a similar opinion but added that financial support from government is rare while bank loans are not easy to obtain and are not beneficial due to interest and return issues. The respondent stated that:

> Almost every SME in Malaysia has been now suffering from the lower sales and the profit margin has been reduced due to the increased online shops where buyers can buy and get products delivered to door from other countries. Therefore, if I take loans from banks but interest and return deadline and also return on investment of the loans is low due to the higher cost but lower sales. So, cash capital for the technologies, you say IR 4.0 technologies in my hand very limited. Well, government's support I would say very limited now but cannot tell you anything about future.

Participant 8, a professor of a local university added:

> There are some conventional SME loans that works as the working capital for the SMEs in the organisations (manufacturing, wholesale, retail or service) but not much enough for the development of the technological set up. Moreover, the cash capital of the fresh graduates is always small and limited while they are also not given big loans in an easy way for the investment that's' return is not clear. So, I would say, limited money

is a problem for the entrepreneurs to adopt the internet of things, or simulation technologies I mean IR 4.0 technologies.

All other participants in the study noted the issue of financial limitations among graduate entrepreneurs of SMEs in applying industry 4.0 technologies.

Lack of Knowledge and Interest

Lack of knowledge and interest regarding industry 4.0 and its benefits has been identified as the barrier by all the participants. Participant 2, owner of a local manufacturing organization suggested:

> I am graduated last year but I didn't know much about the IR4.0 while I was doing masters. It is because I do not see it is a trend in the universities. It could be familiar to the science and technology students but not much common to other faculty students still now. Moreover, how it can benefit us is not clear as well to me and not even to my friends, who are in jobs as well as owners of small businesses. I also like to add that the universities and colleges are saying now about IR4.0 but it is not much articulated among them. So lack of knowledge regarding IR4.0 is also very much significant barrier in applying it in the organisations, which are owned by graduates because most of them are not much known to it.

Similarly, other participants identified that there is a significant lack of knowledge regarding IR4.0 among people in Malaysia as well as SME owners and even educated people. In this regard, Participant 7, an associate professor noted:

> I would like to say when you do know something, how can you use it and get its benefits. Most of us do not have much knowledge regarding IR4.0 and its technologies such as internet of things (IoT) cloud computing, artificial intelligence (AI), cyber-physical systems (CPS) and so on for the automation and data exchange and their application to the productions in factories or operations in service organisations. Moreover, we (universities or colleges) are not giving any sort of extensive training and knowledge on it to the students in a mandatory way.

However, participant 3 added that entrepreneurs have a lack of interest in IR4.0 stating that:

> I would say government is slow because I do not see any promotion from government side for the adoption of the IR4.0 technologies in the SMEs. It might be for the bigger companies but not for SMEs because if you go to other small businesses you can see may people do not know about it. I think government should support with money also because we (graduate SMEs owners) do not have money to settle everything.

Lack of Government Supports

Government is the most important stakeholder in facilitating the technologies in a country and it is also agreed by participants in this study. However, six participants out of eight suggested that the Malaysian government lacks support to IR4.0 adoption in especially in the SMEs. In this respect, participant 2 stated:

> I would say government is slow because I do not see any promotion from government side for the adoption of the IR4.0 technologies in the SMEs. It might be for the bigger companies but not for SMEs because if you go to other small businesses you can see may people do not know about it. I think government should support with money also because we (graduate SMEs owners) do not have money to settle everything.

However, participant 3 and 7, the Professors have responded differently that the government has been trying to adapt IR4.0 very seriously because they appreciate the benefits of IR4.0. Therefore, respective ministry has been trying to help organizations. However, it might take more time although the government is supportive.

Expensive and Uncertainty

The establishment of the technologies and training process are expensive while the profit is also uncertain because technologies keep evolving. Five participants out of eight concerned the uncertainty of profits from the investment. In this regard, participant 8 noted:

> We are in Malaysia still have lack of understanding regarding the mature models, framework and also technologies of IR 4.0. Furthermore, we do not know much its profitability and future because industry 4.0 is not a technology it is the combination of technologies. So if an entrepreneur sets up some technologies relating to IR 4.0 today but if it does not compatible after few months, then he or she will have to face huge loss. Furthermore, the return of the investment I mean ROI is also not certain as Malaysian economy is not growing well. So, you cannot just force or take the IR4.0 technologies in the SMEs, which are owned by the entrepreneurs

Similar opinions were proposed by four other participants regarding the high expenditure and uncertainty. In this respect, an entrepreneur of a restaurant noted:

> We take the order using internet as well as third party apps such as Food Panda, GrabFood, Epic Fit Meals.co, Honestbee, QuickSent and so on. I think these are good but expensive for me because they keep a significant portion of profit I assume. So if better something comes is better but if I guess that would be expensive and I will also have to think about profitability. Therefore, I am concern about the expenditure and the future of the IR 4.0 in the future in Malaysia.

Apart from the above barriers, lack of infrastructure with technologies especially in rural areas in Malaysia and limited training on IR4.0 were also raised by some participants.

Facilitators in Applying Industry 4.0 in the SMEs

The study investigated what could be the facilitators to overcome the barriers identified in the study to the participants, who have suggested some significant areas, which have been presented as facilitators in applying Industry 4.0 in the SMEs.

Government

Government has been identified as the most important stakeholder to facilitate IR4.0 in Malaysia specially in SMEs. All participants expressed similar opinions regarding the governments role in applying IR4.0 in SMEs. Participant 1 mooted:

> I think if government provides financial support for example donation for the SMEs to buy the technologies to apply IR4.0 then we (SMEs owners) can easily adapt because these are very expensive.

Participant 3, a graduate entrepreneur also added:

> Government should discuss about it in most of the conferences and seminars or in any programs because many of us do know much about it. Government can also promote it as the mandatory aspect to know. It is because in most countries like Germany, Japan, Singapore, China and so on IR4.0 is common among their citizens but not in Malaysia.

Participant 8, a professor stated:

> Government has already allocated some budget for SMEs but not for many for example RM500,000 for 60 SMEs will be given as grant out of 500 SMEs which will be under assessment by government (MPI, 2019). I also can see that there is a growth in the next years but not much. We need much faster approach because we will not be able to compete other countries if we do not take it much more seriously.

Courses on Industry 4.0

The professors as well as the graduate entrepreneurs have identified that universities and colleges should have courses on industry 4.0 and it should be in every department or faculty because entrepreneurs can be anyone with any degrees. However, Participant 8 stated:

> Most of the universities in Malaysia are now trying to get the IR4.0 knowledge common among students but many students still do not know

about it and its mechanisms. So I believe more initiatives are required. We should not think IR4.0 is only for science students but also for others because it will contribute to every student. Therefore, to make them capable to embrace IR4.0 technologies, universities and colleges should take significant responsibility

Financial Support

Financial support was unanimously acknowledged by all respondents. They noted that graduate entrepreneurs will be more welcoming if they are given grants or donations to buy the technologies to apply IR4.0 in their organizations. In this regard, the reduction of the interest of loans as well as lengthy return process of loans and flexible installments can also be effective for those entrepreneurs and others in applying IR4.0 in Malaysia.

Infrastructure Development and Collaboration

Directly or indirectly, all participants noted the importance of infrastructure development. From their opinions, it can be summarized that development WIFI, smart logistics, buildings or factories or shops with all technological facilities, flexible systems, universal frameworks, and even smart homes should be developed to embrace IR4.0. They also urged that collaboration between larger and SMEs or multinational companies and SMEs can also be effective in applying IR4.0.

Ensuring Security

Five out of eight participants identified that developing the security of the confidential information as well the protection from hackers is also required to motivate graduate entrepreneurs and others to adopt IR4.0 in their organizations. This will improve the confidence and trust of entrepreneurs to collaborate with other organizations in applying

IR4.0. It is also identified from participants opinion that some respondents feel uneasy embracing technologies because of concerns regarding cybersecurity.

Discussion and Conclusion

A number of barriers and facilitates in applying IR4.0 in SMEs in this study confirm findings from the previous research on this area. In terms of the barriers, graduate entrepreneurs have been facing the common barriers identified in the literature. Financial limitations, lack of knowledge and interest as well as a lack of training and courses from universities on IR4.0, lack of government support, expense and uncertainty, lack of infrastructure and technologies. These results confirm the prior literature (Bhagwat & Sharma, 2007; Chan et al., 2015; Duarte & Cruz-Machado, 2017; Ericson & Doyle, 2004; Lee et al., 2014; Lynch et al., 2012; Nicoletti, 2018; Pereira et al., 2017; Schröder, 2016; Zhou et al., 2015). However, a lack of relevant courses in universities have been established in this study as a barrier in applying IR4.0 in the SMEs owned by graduate entrepreneurs. This is a significant outcome that might be due to the lack of sincerity and approach of universities and colleges on offering IR4.0 for their students. Surprisingly, even though SMEs did not seem to be innovative and adapting the changes in technologies, participants appeared to be satisfied with the current processes of operations of products/services regarding the situation in Malaysia. This finding is inconsistent with the results presented by Van Rooij (2015) and Singhal (2017) who argued absence of innovation and adaptation of the technologies and processes could be responsible for the organizational failure in the market. In this respect, SME owners could be satisfied with the status quo. This finding could be an indication that Malaysian entrepreneurs are slow in adapting technological changes in their organizations but the reason for it might be numerous.

However, as the facilitators in applying IR4.0 in SMEs owned by graduates in Malaysia identified in this study included government supports, training, financial supports, infrastructure development, and collaboration are common as facilitators in the current literature (Dassisti et al.,

2017; Ganji et al., 2018; Mittal et al., 2018; Moeuf et al., 2019; Rojko, 2017; Wang et al., 2018). However, the courses on industry 4.0 at every faculty or department at universities and colleges as facilitators in adapting IR4.0 can be effective have been identified in this study is an addition to the prior literature. It is found that most of universities and colleges in Malaysia are not offering sufficient courses or training and not organizing regular seminars or conferences on the IR4.0 to improve the ideas regarding it. As a result, graduates from those universities with an entrepreneurship mindset have a lack of understanding regarding IR4.0 and cannot apply it in their organizations and are deprived of the benefits. Surprisingly, customers' demand and requirements have a significant impact on the organizations to adopt technologies or take different actions to meet their demands or requirements, but no participants claimed that the customers can be a facilitator. Thus, this is not consistent with the study conducted by Geissbauer et al. (2016) and Nguyen et al. (2015).

Overall, the study contributes to the knowledge regarding the industry 4.0 and its adaptation in an emerging economic context, i.e., Malaysia. The study identified several practical implications. Firstly, the study can support the graduate entrepreneurs to understand about the barriers and the facilitators in adapting/applying the industry 4.0 in the SMEs. Secondly, the study can also be significant for the government and industry planners to ease the barriers in applying and adapting industry 4.0 not only in Malaysia but also other emerging countries. Moreover, universities in Malaysia as well in other countries would benefit from this study to develop the courses integrating different information on the industry 4.0. Although this research contributes to the literature by delineating the barriers and facilitators in applying IR4.0 in SMEs owned by graduate entrepreneurs in Malaysia, some limitations exist that should be addressed in future research. Firstly, data was collected from small groups of participants through the semi-structured interviews, therefore, the results cannot be generalized and should be used cautiously. Hence, future studies should include more participants in the interviews or use the outcomes as constructs in survey questionnaires in quantitative studies. Furthermore, future studies can be conducted on larger firms in different other industries in Malaysia and other similar countries such as Indonesia.

References

Aaslaid, K. (2019). *50 Examples of corporations that failed to innovate.* Retrieved from https://valuer.ai/blog/50-examples-of-corporations-that-failed-to-innovate-and-missed-their-chance/.

Abdullah, N. A. H., Ahmad, A. H., Zainudin, N., & Rus, R. M. (2016). Modelling small and medium-sized enterprises' failure in Malaysia. *International Journal of Entrepreneurship and Small Business, 28*(1), 101–116.

Abidin, N. F. N. Z., Hasbolah, H., Mohamed, N., Khadri, R. R. R. D., Sidek, S., & Wan, W. M. Y. (2018). Malaysian technopreneur issues and challenges in 4th Industrial Revolution (4IR) era. *Proceedings of the 6th international seminar on entrepreneurship and business.*

Ahir, H., Bloom, N., & Furceri, D. (2019). *The global economy is being hit by higher uncertainty.* Retrieved from https://www.weforum.org/agenda/2019/05/the-global-economy-hit-by-higher-uncertainty/.

Ahmad, N. H., & Seet, P. S. (2009a). Dissecting behaviours associated with business failure: A qualitative study of SME owners in Malaysia and Australia. *Asian Social Science, 5*(9), 98–104.

Ahmad, N. H., & Seet, P.-S. (2009b). Understanding business success through the lens of SME founder-owners in Australia and Malaysia. *International Journal of Entrepreneurial Venturing, 1*(1), 72–87.

Anderl, R., Picard, A., Wang, Y., Fleischer, J., Dosch, S., Klee, B., & Bauer, J. (2015). Guideline industrie 4.0- guiding principles for the implementation of industrie 4.0 in small and medium sized businesses. In *VDMA forum industrie*, Vol. 4. ISBN: 978–3–8163–0687–0.

Baldassari, P., & Roux, J. D. (2017). Industry 4.0: Preparing for the future of work. *People & Strategy, 40*(3), 20–23.

Bartodziej, C. J. (2017). *The concept Industry 4.0* (pp. 27–50). Springer Gabler.

Baygin, M., Yetis, H., Karakose, M., & Akin, E. (2016, September). An effect analysis of Industry 4.0 to higher education. In *2016 15th international conference on information technology based higher education and training* (pp. 1–4). IEEE.

Benešová, A., & Tupa, J. (2017). Requirements for education and qualification of people in Industry 4.0. *Procedia Manufacturing, 11*, 2195–2202.

Bhagwat, R., & Sharma, M. K. (2007). Performance measurement of supply chain management using the analytical hierarchy process. *Production Planning & Control, 18*(8), 666–680. https://doi.org/10.1080/09537280701614407.

Bodrow, W. (2017). Impact of Industry 4.0 in service oriented firm. *Advances in Manufacturing, 5*(4), 394–400.

Brettel, M., Friederichsen, N., Keller, M., & Rosenberg, M. (2014). How virtualization, decentralization and network building change the manufacturing landscape: An Industry 4.0 perspective. *International Journal of Mechanical, Industrial Science and Engineering, 8*(1), 37–44.

BRICS Business Council (2017). *Skill development for Industry 4.0. A white paper by BRICS skill development working group,* BRICS Business Council, India Group. Retrieved from http://www.globalskillsummit.com/Whitepaper-Summary.pdf.

Cardon, M. S., Stevens, C. E., & Potter, D. R. (2011). Misfortunes or mistakes? Cultural sensemaking of entrepreneurial failure. *Journal of Business Venturing, 26*(1), 79–92.

Chan, F., Yusuff, R. M., & Zulkifli, N. (2015, August). Barriers to advanced manufacturing technology in small-medium enterprises (SMEs) in Malaysia. In *2015 international symposium on technology management and emerging technologies (ISTMET)* (pp. 412–416). IEEE.

Chen, B., Wan, J., Shu, L., Li, P., Mukherjee, M., & Yin, B. (2017). Smart factory of Industry 4.0: Key technologies, application case, and challenges. *IEEE Access, 6*, 6505–6519.

Chong, W. Y. (2012). Critical success factors for small and medium enterprises: Perceptions of entrepreneurs in urban Malaysia. *Journal of Business and Policy Research, 7*(4), 204–215.

Dassisti, M., Panetto, H., Lezoche, M., Merla, P., Semeraro, C., Giovannini, A., & Chimienti, M. (2017, March). Industry 4.0 paradigm: The viewpoint of the small and medium enterprises. *7th international conference on information society and technology.*

Duarte, S., & Cruz-Machado, V. (2017, July). Exploring linkages between lean and green supply chain and the Industry 4.0. In *International conference on management science and engineering management* (pp. 1242–1252). Springer.

Eniola, A. A., & Entebang, H. (2015). SME firm performance-financial innovation and challenges. *Procedia-Social and Behavioral Sciences, 195*, 334–342.

Ericson, R. V., & Doyle, A. (2004). *Uncertain business: Risk, insurance and the limits of knowledge*. University of Toronto Press.
Ganji, E. N., Coutroubis, A., & Shah, S. (2018, June). DCM 4.0: integration of Industry 4.0 and demand chain in global manufacturing. In *2018 IEEE international conference on engineering, technology and innovation (ICE/ITMC)* (pp. 1–7). IEEE.
Geissbauer, R., Vedso, J., & Schrauf, S. (2016). A strategist's guide to Industry 4.0. *Strategy + Business, 83*, 148–163.
Hecklau, F., Galeitzke, M., Flachs, S., & Kohl, H. (2016). Holistic approach for human resource management in Industry 4.0. *Procedia Cirp, 54*, 1–6.
Islam, M. A., Hunt, A., Jantan, A. H., Hashim, H., & Chong, C. W. (2019). Exploring challenges and solutions in applying green human resource management practices for the sustainable workplace in the ready-made garment industry in Bangladesh. *Business Strategy & Development., 3*(1), 1–12.
Islam, M. A., Jantan, A. H., Hashim, H., Chong, C. W., & Abdullah, M. M. (2018). Fourth industrial revolution in developing countries: A Case on Bangladesh. *Journal of Management Information and Decision Sciences, 21*(1), 1–9.
Jackson, D., (2018). *How Industry 4.0 will affect entrepreneurs*. Retrieved from https://www.entrepreneur-resources.net/how-industry-4-0-will-affect-entrepreneurs.
Kagermann, H., Wahlster, W., & Helbig, J. (2013). Umsetzungsempfehlungen für das Zukunftsprojekt Industry 4.0. Abschlussbericht des Arbeitskreises Industry 4.0. Deutschlands Zukunft als Produktionsstandort sichern. In *Promotorengruppe Kommunikation der Forschungsunion Wirtschaft— Wissenschaft*. Berlin.
Kannan. (2016). *11 reasons why SMEs fail*. Retrieved from https://leaderonomics.com/business/why-smes-fail.
Kirzner, I. M. (2015). *Competition and entrepreneurship*. University of Chicago Press.
Kusmin, K. L. (2018). Industry 4.0. In *IFI8101-Information Society Approaches and ICT Processes*.
Lasi, H., Fettke, P., Kemper, H. G., Feld, T., & Hoffmann, M. (2014). Industry 4.0. *Business & Information Systems Engineering, 6*(4), 239–242.
Lee, J., Kao, H. A., & Yang, S. (2014). Service innovation and smart analytics for Industry 4.0 and big data environment. *Procedia Cirp, 16*, 3–8.

Lin, J. S. C., & Hsieh, P. L. (2006). The role of technology readiness in customers' perception and adoption of self-service technologies. *International Journal of Service Industry Management, 17*(5), 497–517.

Luftman, J., Lyytinen, K., & Zvi, T. B. (2017). Enhancing the measurement of information technology (IT) business alignment and its influence on company performance. *Journal of Information Technology, 32*(1), 26–46.

Luthra, S., & Mangla, S. K. (2018). Evaluating challenges to Industry 4.0 initiatives for supply chain sustainability in emerging economies. *Process Safety and Environmental Protection, 117*, 168–179.

Lynch, J., Mason, R. J., Beresford, A. K. C., & Found, P. A. (2012). An examination of the role for business orientation in an uncertain business environment. *International Journal of Production Economics, 137*(1), 145–156.

Malaysian Reserve (2017). *Poor planning main cause for SMEs to cease operation*. Retrieved from https://themalaysianreserve.com/2017/11/22/poor-planning-main-cause-smes-cease-operation/.

Mankiw, N. G. (2008). *Principles of economics (p/420)*. Cengage Learning.

Marr, B., (2018). *What is Industry 4.0? Here's a super easy explanation for anyone*. Retrieved from https://www.forbes.com/sites/bernardmarr/2018/09/02/what-is-industry-4-0-heres-a-super-easy-explanation-for-anyone/#28fba4399788.

Martin, S. L., & Javalgi, R. R. G. (2016). Entrepreneurial orientation, marketing capabilities and performance: The moderating role of competitive intensity on Latin American International new ventures. *Journal of Business Research, 69*(6), 2040–2051.

McGrath, R. G. (1999). Falling forward: Real options reasoning and entrepreneurial failure. *Academy of Management review, 24*(1), 13–30.

Meath, C., Linnenluecke, M., & Griffiths, A. (2016). Barriers and motivators to the adoption of energy savings measures for small-and medium-sized enterprises (SMEs): The case of the Climate Smart Business Cluster program. *Journal of Cleaner Production, 112*, 3597–3604.

Melville, N., Kraemer, K., & Gurbaxani, V. (2004). Information technology and organizational performance: An integrative model of IT business value. *MIS Quarterly, 28*(2), 283–322.

Mittal, S., Khan, M. A., Romero, D., & Wuest, T. (2018). A critical review of smart manufacturing & Industry 4.0 maturity models: Implications for small and medium-sized enterprises (SMEs). *Journal of Manufacturing Systems, 49*, 194–214.

Moeuf, A., Lamouri, S., Pellerin, R., Tamayo-Giraldo, S., Tobon-Valencia, E., & Eburdy, R. (2019). Identification of critical success factors, risks and opportunities of Industry 4.0 in SMEs. *International Journal of Production Research, 57*(12), 1–17.

MPI. (2019). *Budget: Budget 2020 speech*. Retrieved from https://www.mpi.gov.my/index.php/en/media-2/mpic-in-the-news/250-news-general-2019/6930-budget-budget-2020-speech.

Müller, J. M., Buliga, O., & Voigt, K. I. (2018a). Fortune favors the prepared: How SMEs approach business model innovations in Industry 4.0. *Technological Forecasting and Social Change, 132*, 2–17.

Müller, J. M., Kiel, D., & Voigt, K. I. (2018b). What drives the implementation of Industry 4.0? The role of opportunities and challenges in the context of sustainability. *Sustainability, 10*(1), 247–261.

Nguyen, T. L. H. (2013). Barriers to and facilitators of female Deans' career advancement in higher education: An exploratory study in Vietnam. *Higher Education, 66*(1), 123–138.

Nguyen, T. H., Newby, M., & Macaulay, M. J. (2015). Information technology adoption in small business: Confirmation of a proposed framework. *Journal of Small Business Management, 53*(1), 207–227.

Nicoletti, B. (2018). The future: Procurement 4.0. In *Agile procurement* (pp. 189–230). Palgrave Macmillan.

Oesterreich, T. D., & Teuteberg, F. (2016). Understanding the implications of digitisation and automation in the context of Industry 4.0: A triangulation approach and elements of a research agenda for the construction industry. *Computers in Industry, 83*, 121–139.

Omar, C. M. Z. C., & Azmi, N. M. N. (2015). Factors affecting the success of Bumiputera entrepreneurs in small and medium enterprises (SMEs) in Malaysia. *International Journal of Management Science and Business Administration, 1*(9), 40–45.

Onar, S. C., Ustundag, A., Kadaifci, Ç., & Oztaysi, B. (2018). The changing role of engineering education in Industry 4.0 era. In *Industry 4.0: Managing the digital transformation* (pp. 137–151). Springer.

Önday, Ö. (2018). What would be the impact of Industry 4.0 on SMEs: The case of Germany. *International Journal of Management, 7*(2), 11–19.

Pereira, A. C., & Romero, F. (2017). A review of the meanings and the implications of the Industry 4.0 concept. *Procedia Manufacturing, 13*, 1206–1214.

Pereira, T., Barreto, L., & Amaral, A. (2017). Network and information security challenges within Industry 4.0 paradigm. *Procedia Manufacturing, 13*, 1253–1260.

Pretorius, M. (2008). Critical variables of business failure: A review and classification framework. *South African Journal of Economic and Management Sciences, 11*(4), 408–430.

Rahman, M., & Mendy, J. (2019). Evaluating people-related resilience and non-resilience barriers of SMEs' internationalisation: A developing country perspective. *International Journal of Organizational Analysis, 27*(2), 225–240.

Rahman, M., Billah, M. M., & Hack-Polay, D. (2019). What is hindering change? Anticipating the barriers to the adoption of enzyme-based textile processing in a developing country. *Business Strategy & Development., 2*(2), 1–11.

Roblek, V., Meško, M., & Krapež, A. (2016). A complex view of Industry 4.0. *Sage Open, 6*(2), https://doi.org/10.1177/2158244016653987.

Rojko, A. (2017). Industry 4.0 concept: Background and overview. *International Journal of Interactive Mobile Technologies, 11*(5), 77–90.

Rüßmann, M., Lorenz, M., Gerbert, P., Waldner, M., Justus, J., Engel, P., & Harnisch, M. (2015). Industry 4.0: The future of productivity and growth in manufacturing industries. *Boston Consulting Group, 9*(1), 54–89.

Schmidt, R., Möhring, M., Härting, R. C., Reichstein, C., Neumaier, P., & Jozinović, P. (2015, June). Industry 4.0-potentials for creating smart products: Empirical research results. In *International conference on business information systems* (pp. 16–27). Springer.

Schröder, C. (2016). *The challenges of Industry 4.0 for small and medium-sized enterprises*. Friedrich-Ebert-Stiftung.

Seligman, M. (2011). Building resilience. *Harvard Business Review, 89*(4), 100–106.

Shamim, S., Cang, S., Yu, H., & Li, Y. (2016, July). Management approaches for Industry 4.0: A human resource management perspective. In *2016 IEEE congress on evolutionary computation (CEC)* (pp. 5309–5316). IEEE.

Sharma, P., & Varma, S. K. (2016). Women empowerment through entrepreneurial activities of Self Help Groups. *Indian Research Journal of Extension Education, 8*(1), 46–51.

Shuying, Z., & Mei, Z. (2014). Theory of SMEs financial risk prevention and control. In *International conference on education, management and computing technology (ICEMCT)*.

Singh Sandhu, M., Fahmi Sidique, S., & Riaz, S. (2011). Entrepreneurship barriers and entrepreneurial inclination among Malaysian postgraduate students. *International Journal of Entrepreneurial Behavior & Research, 17*(4), 428–449.

Singhal, A. (2017). Antecedents of service innovation: Its success or failure. *International Journal of Management, IT and Engineering, 7*(1), 246–259.

SMEBiz, (2019). *Higher SME contribution to GDP*. Retrieved from https://www.thestar.com.my/business/smebiz/2019/08/05/higher-sme-contribution-to-gdp

Sommer, L. (2015). Industrial revolution-Industry 4.0: Are German manufacturing SMEs the first victims of this revolution? *Journal of Industrial Engineering and Management, 8*(5), 1512–1532.

Thames, L., & Schaefer, D. (2016). Software-defined cloud manufacturing for Industry 4.0. *Procedia Cirp, 52*, 12–17.

Theorin, A., Bengtsson, K., Provost, J., Lieder, M., Johnsson, C., Lundholm, T., & Lennartson, B. (2017). An event driven manufacturing information system architecture for Industry 4.0. *International Journal of Production Research, 55*(5), 1297–1311.

Tunggak, B., Salamon, H., & Abu, B. (2011). Training and long life learning for Islamic entrepreneur. *Jurnal Teknologi Sains Sosial, 55*(1), 121–144.

Ucbasaran, D., Westhead, P., & Wright, M. (2006). Habitual entrepreneurs experiencing failure: Overconfidence and the motivation to try again. In *Entrepreneurship: Frameworks and empirical investigations from forthcoming leaders of European research* (pp. 9–28). Emerald Group Publishing Limited.

Van Gelderen, M., Thurik, R., & Bosma, N. (2006). Success and risk factors in the pre-startup phase. *Small Business Economics, 26*(4), 319–335.

Van Rooij, A. (2015). Sisyphus in business: Success, failure and the different types of failure. *Business History, 57*(2), 203–223.

Wang, X. V., Wang, L., & Gördes, R. (2018). Interoperability in cloud manufacturing: A case study on private cloud structure for SMEs. *International Journal of Computer Integrated Manufacturing, 31*(7), 653–663.

Wolcott, P., Kamal, M., & Qureshi, S. (2008). Meeting the challenges of ICT adoption by micro-enterprises. *Journal of Enterprise Information Management, 21*(6), 616–632.

Yapp, E. (2019). *SMEs wary about Industry 4.0, but they shouldn't be, say industry reps*. Retrieved from https://www.digitalnewsasia.com/digital-economy/smes-wary-about-industry-40-they-shouldnt-be-say-industry-reps.

Yusof, A. (2017). *Government assists industry players to embrace Industry 4.0*. Retrieved from https://www.nst.com.my/business/2017/12/311823/government-assists-industry-players-embrace-industry-40.

Zhou, K., Liu, T., & Zhou, L. (2015, August). Industry 4.0: Towards future industrial opportunities and challenges. In *12th IEEE international conference on fuzzy systems and knowledge discovery (FSKD)* (pp. 2147–2152).

Index

Symbols

19 th century 14

A

Absorptive capacity 40, 52
Agglomeration 39
Agriculture 3, 13, 14, 29, 46, 74, 77, 127, 128, 137, 138, 140, 141, 150
Amanah Ikhtiar Malaysia (AIM) 87, 93, 100
ARPANet 61
ASEAN region 3, 18
Asia 30, 31, 129, 136

B

Bangsa Malaysia 23
Barisan Nasional alliance 17
Barriers 48, 121, 138, 187–192, 194, 196, 198, 201, 202
Biji Biji 123–125, 127, 130
Bill of Guarantees (BoG) 47
Biotechnology 37, 43, 44, 47, 70
Borneo Island 142, 151
British colonial rule 16
British Council 120, 121, 128–131
Bumiputera 21, 23, 24, 27, 30
Bumiputera Commercial and Industrial Community (BCIC) 22, 23

C

China 2, 11, 14, 15, 74
Coalition 17, 18, 25
Cognitive 42, 53, 139, 140, 142, 161
Collaboration behaviour 148

Colonial government 14, 15
Community Service Centre for the Deaf (CSCD) 124, 127
Compensation of Employees (CE) 29
Conservation of resources (COR) 6, 158, 160, 162
Core self-evaluations (CSEs) 6, 160–163, 167–177
Covid-19 60
Curriculum 2, 3, 97, 105
Cyberjaya 43, 44, 47, 50, 53
Cybersecurity 76

D

Datuk Seri Dr Wan Azizah Wan Ismail 75
Datuk Yap Yun Fook 126, 127
Democratic Action Party (DAP) 17
Dewan Negara 26
Digital Darwinism 60
Digital entrepreneurship 59, 60, 75
Digital Malaysia 80

E

East Coast Economic Region (ECER) 46
East Malaysia 6, 11–13, 27
EcoKnights 123, 125, 126, 130
eCommerce 60, 76, 79
Economic growth 2, 3, 20, 25, 28, 29, 31, 46–48, 62, 65, 68, 69, 77, 78, 86, 185
Eco-systems 3, 5–7, 31–33, 63, 64, 75–77, 80, 91, 120–122, 126, 128, 129, 131–133
Eco Yap 123, 126, 128, 130, 132

Education policy 16
Eighth Malaysian Plan (8MP) 24
Electronics 2, 40, 79, 101, 124
Eleventh Malaysian Plan (11MP) 25, 30
ENACTUS 87, 98, 101–105, 108, 110
Entrepreneurial attitudes 2, 138
Entrepreneurial behaviour 2–4, 7
Entrepreneurial education 2, 7, 104, 105, 132
Entrepreneurial learning process 6, 135, 136, 142, 144
Entrepreneurial University 48
Entrepreneurship 2–7, 15, 19, 22, 25, 31, 33, 59, 62–64, 66–73, 75, 79, 80, 85, 88, 93, 94, 98, 99, 103–105, 108, 117, 121, 125, 132, 133, 136–140, 142, 145, 147, 150, 151, 162, 175, 176, 186, 202
Environmental protection 121
Evolutionary theory of economic change 69
Exporting 2, 16, 33

F

Facilitators 50, 61, 187, 188, 192–194, 198, 201, 202
Federation of Malaya 16
Female entrepreneurship 2, 8
First Outline Perspective Plan (OPP1) 20
Fishing 14
Fourth industrial revolution ($IR) 32, 186, 188

G
Germany 29
Global Competitive Index 33
Global Entrepreneurship Index 33
Government 4, 5, 7, 12, 13, 17, 18, 20–26, 28–33, 38–41, 43–51, 53, 71, 72, 75, 78–81, 86, 87, 90, 93–96, 99, 100, 109, 110, 118–121, 123, 125, 126, 129–133, 139, 145, 146, 151, 186, 191, 193, 195, 197, 199, 201, 202
Graduate unemployment 3
Grameen Bank 87, 93, 100
Greater Kuala Lumpur (Greater KL) 46
Gross Domestic Product (GDP) 28, 29, 31, 33, 93, 104, 186
Gross National Income (GNI) 80
Gross National Product (GNP) 25

H
Higher Education Institutions (HEIs) 94, 95, 98, 99, 102–105, 110

I
Impact-Driven Enterprise Accreditation (IDEA) 126
Incubators 3, 47
Independence 4, 15–21, 28
India 14, 15, 85
Indonesia 12, 13, 85, 122, 129, 133, 203
Industry 4.0 7, 186–194, 196, 198, 199, 202

Information communication technology (ICT) 37, 43, 44, 46, 47
Innovation 4, 5, 7, 33, 37–44, 47, 48, 50, 62–72, 74, 75, 77, 78, 80, 86–92, 95, 102, 105, 106, 109, 127, 139, 141, 190, 191, 201
Innovation systems 5, 37–43, 52, 62–64, 67, 71, 72
Institut Teknologi MARA (ITM) 19
Internet 60–62, 75, 76, 96, 189, 192

J
Japan 2, 73, 94, 99

K
Keningau 126
Klang Valley 6, 46, 123–125, 128
Knowledge based economy 77
Knowledge intensive business services (KIBS) 74, 75
Knowledge intensive entrepreneurship (KIE) 5, 62–64, 67, 75, 80
Knowledge spill-over 4, 37, 38, 41, 43, 51
Kota Kinabalu 126
Kuala Lumpur 3, 12, 46, 53, 120, 124, 125, 128, 133
Kuala Lumpur city centre (KLCC) 47, 53
Kuala Lumpur international airport (KLIA) 47

Index

L

Light manufacturing 2
Logging 2

M

Majlis Amanah Rakyat (MARA) 19
Malacca Sultanate 15, 16
Malay Peninsula 13, 14
Malay region 14
Malaysia 2–7, 11–18, 20–34, 38, 43–47, 52, 59, 74–76, 78, 79, 85–87, 93, 94, 97, 99–109, 117–120, 122–130, 132, 133, 150, 151, 158, 162, 175, 176, 186–188, 190, 192–194, 196, 198–203
Malaysia Digital Economy Corp (MDEC) 59
Malaysian Global Innovation and Creativity Center (MaGIC) 86, 93, 94, 106, 109, 119–123, 126, 128, 129, 132
Malaysian Social Enterprise Blueprint (MSEB) 5, 86, 93, 99, 106, 109, 118, 120
Malay society 14
Malay States 13, 14
Medical technology 2
Micro, Small and Medium Enterprises (MSMEs) 32, 33
Ministry of Entrepreneur and Cooperative Development (MeCD) 24
Ministry of Entrepreneur Development (MED) 31, 119–122, 126, 130
Ministry of Higher Education (MHE) 94–96, 99
Ministry of International Trade and Industry 94, 98
Multimedia Development Corporation (MDeC) 46
Multimedia Super Corridor (MSC) 37, 43–53, 78, 79

N

National Development Plan (NDP) 22–24
National Economic Advisory Council (NEAC) 25
National Entrepreneurship Framework (NEF) 119
National Entrepreneurship Institute 98
National Entrepreneurship Policy 2030 31, 121
National Key Economic Areas (NKEAs) 45
National level systems (NLS) 39
National Mission Policy (NMP) 24
National Operations Council (NOC) 18
National Social Entrepreneurship Guidelines and Accreditation programme 122, 126, 130
National Transformation Programme 80
National Vision Policy (NVP) 23, 24
New Economic Model (NEM) 25
New Economic Policy (NEP) 18–24, 27, 32, 33
Newton Mobility Fund 142
Ninth Malaysia Plan (NMP) 24, 45

Non-government organizations (NGOs) 87, 99, 102, 110, 120, 123–125, 127, 130
Northern Corridor Economic Region (NCER) 46

O

OECD SME Policy index 3
Oil and gas 2, 46
Organisation for Economic cooperation and Development (OECD) 2, 3, 64, 73

P

Pakatan Harapan (PH) 17, 25, 30, 31
Palm oil 2, 6, 46, 136, 139, 140, 142, 145, 147, 149–151
Pangkor Treaty 13, 14
Parti Amanah 18
Parti Keadilan Rakyat (PKR) 17
Parti Pribumi Bersatu Malaysia (PPBM) 17
Pemangkin Usahawan Social Hebat (PUSH) 119, 123, 130
Penang 6, 12, 13, 15
Petronas Twin Towers 46
Pharmaceuticals 2, 40
Pluralistic society 14, 16, 18, 21
Porter's Diamond Model 50, 54
Prime Minister of Malaysia 30, 78
Proximity 4, 38–44
Public sector 2, 40, 74, 77, 78
Putrajaya International Convention Centre (PICC) 30

R

Regional areas 3
Regional economic development 45
Regional innovation systems 39, 40, 43, 45, 72
Registrar of Companies 130
Relational 42, 53
Research and development (R&D) 64, 74, 77, 109
Rice growing 14
Role ambiguity (RA) 6, 159, 162, 163, 167–171, 173–176
Rubber 2, 15, 16
Rukunegara 20
Rural smallholders 135, 138

S

Sabah 11, 12, 14, 24, 27, 30, 97, 118, 123, 124, 126–128, 139
Sabah Development Corridor (SDC) 46
Sarawak 11, 12, 14, 24, 27, 30, 118, 119, 123, 124, 126, 128
Sarawak Corridor Renewable Energy (SCORE) 46
Schumpeterian 66–68, 70
Science and technology 77, 78
Second Outline Perspective Plan (OPP2) 22
Selangor 12, 27, 124, 125
Shared Prosperity Vision 2030 (SPV) 25, 29, 30
Silicon Valley 39, 42–44, 46, 47
Singapore 2, 12, 13, 15, 29, 73, 99, 129, 162
Small and medium sized enterprise/s (SMEs) 2, 3, 7, 59, 60, 79,

120, 123, 130, 131, 175, 185–194, 196–202
Small and medium sized enterprises growth 2
Social capital 41, 42
Social enterprise 6, 7, 86–88, 93, 94, 97–102, 104, 107–110, 118–133
Social Enterprise Accreditation Guideline 5, 86, 92
Social Enterprise Blueprint 5, 86, 93, 99, 106, 109, 118, 120
Social entrepreneurship (SE) 4–6, 85–89, 93–100, 102, 104–110, 117–123, 125–133
Social infrastructure 4, 37, 42, 50–53
Social interaction 41–43, 51, 52, 146
Southeast Asia 8, 11
Spousal support (SS) 6, 160, 162, 163, 167–176
State of Johor 14
Structural 42, 53, 168–170
Students in Free Enterprise (SIFE) 98, 103, 108
Subsistence/informal entrepreneurship 3
Sultans 17
Sustainability 24, 25, 86, 88, 95, 98, 103, 105, 120, 121, 130, 147, 151
Sustainable Development Goals (SDGs) 118
System actors 38, 39, 41, 43, 44, 47, 52

T
Tanah Melayu 13, 17
Tanoti Crafts 123, 126, 128
Technology Park Malaysia 47
Tenth Malaysia Plan (10MP) 45
Thailand 2, 12, 85, 129, 133
Timber processing 2
Tin 13–16
Tin mining and smelting 2
Treaty of London 13
Triple helix 41, 47, 49, 50, 54
Trust based relationships 40

U
Unemployment 3, 29
United Kingdom (UK) 4, 12, 29, 44, 93, 118
United Nations Economic and Social Commission for Asia and the Pacific (UN ESCAP) 120
United Nations (UN) 104, 118, 119
United States of America (USA) 18, 29, 44, 103
Universities 3, 4, 7, 19, 39–44, 47–53, 63, 71, 72, 89, 90, 93, 94, 97, 99, 103, 105, 109, 145, 195, 199, 201, 202
Usahawan 121, 145

W
West Malaysia 11–13
Women entrepreneurs 6, 7, 96, 157–164, 172–177
Women in Social Enterprise (WISE) 95, 98
Work-family conflict (WFC) 6, 157–163, 167–177

Work schedule flexibility (WSF) 6, 158, 159, 162, 163, 168–175
World Wide Web (WWW) 62

Y
Yang Di Pertuan Agong 17, 26
Yayasan Hasanah 120
Youth unemployment 3